Praise for
The Condor's Shadow

The Condor's Shadow, well conceived and very well written, is an exceptionally useful book, and all the more so in a time of wildlife crisis. Among other things, it should serve to clarify hard decisions that our nation must face in regard to habitat preservation for the future.

—PETER MATTHIESSEN, author of *Wildlife in America*

The Condor's Shadow is written with clarity, eloquence, and even wit, and is every bit as wise as it is readable. For a general reader, it is an unalloyed delight; for a conservationist, it is nothing less than essential.

—T. H. WATKINS, former editor of *Wilderness* magazine,
Wallace Stegner Distinguished Professor of Western American Studies
at Montana State University

Much has been lost, but *The Condor's Shadow* reminds us how much survives, and shows how we can learn from the past to save and restore even more of America's natural heritage. David Wilcove has written a book that is both instructive and inspirational.

—ROGER F. PASQUIER, chairman,
RARE Center for Tropical Conservation

The Condor's Shadow

The Condor's Shadow

The Loss and Recovery of Wildlife in America

David S. Wilcove

FOREWORD BY EDWARD O. WILSON

W. H. Freeman and Company
New York

Cover and Text Design: Victoria Tomaselli

All photographs are © 1994 by Susan Middleton and David Liittschwager.

Portions of Chapter 1 originally appeared in the September 1989 issue of *Audubon*.

Library of Congress Cataloging-in-Publication Data

Wilcove, David Samuel.
The condor's shadow: the loss and recovery of wildlife in
America/David S. Wilcove.
p.   cm.
Includes bibliographical references (p.   ) and index.
ISBN 0-7167-3115-0
1. Endangered species—United States.   2. Wildlife
conservation—United States.   I. Title.
QL84.2.W53   1999
333.95'42'0973—dc21   99-12269
CIP

Printed in the United States of America

First printing, 1999

W. H. Freeman and Company
41 Madison Avenue, New York, NY 10010
Houndmills, Basingstoke   RG21 6XS, England

for my parents,
Beth Yellen Wilcove and Ralph Wilcove

Contents

Photographs

foreword

Edward O. Wilson

I t has been said, often, that God is in the details. Or is the Devil? Either way, whether we apply the metaphor to the glory of evolution's productions or to their ongoing destruction, the future of resource management and conservation lies in the attention we pay to the details, ecosystem by ecosystem and species by species. Global patterns mathematically described are important, but we are in at least equal need of case histories that disclose what is happening locally, on the ground, so to speak, where ecosystems and species are going extinct. We need rich, detailed information to avoid the stupid mistakes of the past.

That is what David S. Wilcove has provided here in his case-study analysis of the killing fields of America. The United States offers special advantages for such a study. It has undergone more environmental destruction during the past two centuries, especially through deforestation and the damming of streams and rivers, than has Europe. In addition, the decline of its natural habitats and species has been better monitored than in other parts of the world where similar rapid change is occurring. This combination of contemporaneity and a relatively good database makes the United States a favorable laboratory for the study of endangerment and extinction.

In developing his story, Wilcove shows that the fate of each species, even when tied closely to that of other species in the same ecosystem, has unique properties that must be understood thoroughly in order to save and restore the species. For example, the Carolina parakeet was hunted to oblivion. In contrast, the ivory-billed woodpecker was a victim of the destruction of the southern old-growth forests on which it depended. The bald eagle disappeared from much of the United States because of yet another change, DDT in the environment. Case studies of each species and ecosystem in turn, founded on data from extensive fieldwork and evaluated by the principles of ecological theory, are the heart of conservation biology. They are the best science has to offer to secure the survival of our fauna and flora. For the time being, as Wilcove demonstrates, they defy easy generalization.

Not just the United States, but the world at large desperately needs the kind of study this book reflects. It is ever useful to keep the big picture of population and environment in mind when making this extrapolation. In the world as a whole, as many as 10 million species, or 99 percent of wild global biodiversity (as opposed to cultivated and weedy species) are in precarious condition. Humanity has taken the rest of life with it into a historical bottleneck consisting of the interaction between a still-expanding human population and diminishing per capita resources. It is true that on a worldwide basis, per capita production is rising, but at a cost: the consumption of Earth's resource capital. We are like a family who lives at a higher level of consumption by using up its savings and selling its house.

As I write, the world population is approaching 6 billion. It will very likely reach 8 billion within 20 to 30 years, then peak and slowly subside. Natural resource experts generally agree that two of the necessities of life are growing short enough to put a severe strain on a population of even the present size. The first is per capita arable land, which has been declining worldwide for over 30 years. The second is water, which is also growing shorter on a per capita basis, and with particular detriment to a large number of inherently water-scarce countries. Both land and water resources have absolute limits that are now in sight. Humanity, for example, already consumes 40 percent of the runoff water available. Total crop productivity has kept pace with population growth through the use of fertilizers, the spread of Green Revolution crop strains, and the expansion of croplands, but the improvement rate is declining, and here, too, the limits are in sight.

Meanwhile, the developing nations, which are home to 80 percent of the world's population and almost all of its growth, are striving to improve their quality of life to the level of the developed countries. They will not succeed. The reasons are best clarified by the concept of the ecological footprint: the amount of productive land needed to sustain the existing quality of life for an average person in a given country or region. The ecological footprint is the land consumed for food and water production, waste management, habitation, and other necessities. Pieces of the footprint come not just from land around the personal home but from all around the world: a bit of Costa Rica for coffee, a piece of Kuwait for petroleum, some of California and a half-dozen other states for a personal computer, and so forth. The ecological footprint of an average person in developing countries is about an acre. In the United States it is 12 acres. For the entire world population to achieve the standard of living of the United States would require two more planet Earths.

Humanity is not going to acquire two more planet Earths. Instead, pressure will continue to increase—in fact, accelerate—to use up the last remaining forests, savannas, and other natural environments, especially in the tropical developing countries, where more than half the world's species of plants and animals live.

Such is the great drama of crisis and opportunity that has formed in the living world. It deserves far more of our attention. The United States, which has already lost about 1 percent of its own species and reduced another third to threatened or endangered status, has a special responsibility to set an example for the rest of the world with its own conservation policy and to provide leadership in science and technology. Wilcove's fine contribution gives important support to the argument for such a new and enlightened American ethic.

Acknowledgments

Many readers will notice that this book is modeled after Peter Matthiessen's classic *Wildlife in America*, surely one of the most insightful and eloquent books ever written about wildlife. Since its original publication in 1959, it has been a source of inspiration for countless aspiring naturalists and conservationists, including me.

There are, however, a number of important differences between my book and Matthiessen's. Matthiessen wrote from the point of view of a historian as he chronicled the long and often grim history of human interactions with wildlife. My perspective is that of an ecologist. I am fascinated by the ways in which changes in the landscape, additions and subtractions of species, and all the other consequences of human activities have affected the ecosystems of America. The science of ecology has blossomed since the late 1950s, providing a wealth of information and insights that were not available to Matthiessen when he wrote the first edition of his book. Whole fields of study, such as island biogeography and conservation biology, have sprung up in the intervening decades. And issues that were not even blips on the radar screen of the conservation movement in the late 1950s (for example, logging of the old-growth forests inhabited by the northern spotted owl) have become titanic battles. My hope is that the two books will complement each other.

I began writing this book during a sabbatical at Stanford University's Center for Conservation Biology. I am grateful to Paul Ehrlich and Dennis Murphy for allowing me to work there. Funding for that sabbatical was made possible by a Pew Scholarship in Conservation and the Environment. I thank the Pew Charitable Trusts for its support of my work, and my previous employer, The Wilderness Society, for nominating me for that award. Wes Jackson graciously took me on a tour of the Kansas prairies when I needed to learn more about that ecosystem. I completed my research and writing in Washington, D.C., drawing upon the incomparable resources of the Smithsonian Institution and the Library of Congress. I thank Gary Graves from the Division of Birds at the National Museum of Natural History for granting me access to the Smithsonian as a researcher.

I am very fortunate that so many friends and colleagues were willing to take time from their busy schedules to review portions of the manuscript. Foremost among them are Malcolm Hunter, Michael Bean, Roger Pasquier, Barksdale Maynard, Robert Bonnie, and Margaret McMillan, who took on the task of reading the entire manuscript. Individual chapters were reviewed by David Allan, Tim Brush, Joanna Burger, Andrew Cohen, Fritz Knopf, Jaan Lepson, Dan Luecke, Carole Mandryk, Tom Marshall, Larry Master, Mark Robertson, Scott Robinson, Fred Samson, Mike Scott, Tim Searchinger, Stan Senner, Jack Ward Thomas, and Fred Wagner. My collective debt to all these people is enormous. They have steered me away from embarrassing errors, freely shared their insights and ideas, pointed me in the direction of neglected references, and repaired my prose. I am equally indebted to the hundreds of scientists whose work forms the heart of this book. Their publications are listed in the bibliography, but it seems only fitting to mention them here, too.

David Liittschwager and Susan Middleton kindly contributed the photographs of endangered species that appear in this book. No amount of verbiage could capture the beauty of these animals as well as they have done.

Margaret McMillan provided invaluable assistance in researching many of the topics discussed in this book. Additional research assistance was provided by Linus Chen. I also thank Diana Niskern at the Library of Congress for patiently tracking down dozens of obscure references, and Neel Scott for preparing the bibliography. For legal advice, I am grateful to Gary Greenstein.

At W. H. Freeman and Company, I have had the pleasure of working with two fine editors. Jonathan Cobb guided me through the early and middle stages of this project. Without his wise counsel, this book would never have seen the light of day.

Erika Goldman then guided me through the final stages of editing and production. Norma Roche skillfully copyedited the manuscript. I thank Mercedes Foster for introducing me to the staff of W. H. Freeman.

Throughout this time, I have had the good fortune to be employed by the Environmental Defense Fund. A more rewarding place to work is difficult to imagine. I thank Fred Krupp, Melinda Taylor, and Michael Bean for allowing me time to work on this book. I owe a special debt of gratitude to Michael Bean, Robert Bonnie, and Margaret McMillan for their willingness to put up with a book-obsessed colleague for so long.

Finally, an endeavor of this sort inevitably brings to mind those people whose indirect assistance has been invaluable. In my case there are four. For over a decade, T. H. Watkins has been my literary mentor. I thank him for his encouragement and advice. When I was a graduate student at Princeton University, I was privileged to work with three extraordinary professors: John Terborgh, Robert May, and Henry Horn. They taught me to see the world in a different light, and for that I will always be grateful.

David S. Wilcove
Arlington, Virginia
November 4, 1998

I take infinite pains to know all the phenomena of the spring, for instance, thinking that I have here the entire poem, and then, to my chagrin, I hear that it is but an imperfect copy that I possess and have read, that my ancestors have torn out many of the first leaves and grandest passages, and mutilated it in many places. I should not like to think that some demigod had come before me and picked out some of the best of the stars. I wish to know an entire heaven and an entire earth.

Henry David Thoreau
Journals, March 23, 1856

The Arrival

from the shores of Alaska's Saint Lawrence Island, one can look across the Bering Sea and see the mountains of Siberia looming in the distance. Flocks of seabirds— puffins, auklets, and eiders—skitter across the choppy, gray waters, crisscrossing the gap that separates two nations and two continents. From this vantage point in such a remote and desolate part of the world, it is difficult to believe that much has changed in and around the Bering Straits.

Yet for most of the past 60,000 years, the Bering Straits did not even exist. The world was in the midst of the Ice Age, and vast ice fields covered much of North America. With so much of the earth's water bound up in snow and ice, sea levels were at least 300 feet lower than they are today, and many areas now covered by shallow seas were dry land. Where the Bering Straits now are, a vast plain called Beringia connected the Chukchi Peninsula of Siberia to the Alaskan mainland, linking the two continents. During occasional warm spells, the ice fields would shrink, and meltwater would raise the level of the oceans, recreating the Bering Straits. In this way, a tenuous land connection between North America and Asia flickered into and out of existence. Because the climate in this region was too dry for sustained snowfall, most of Beringia (when it appeared) was ice-free and passable to man or beast. If we accept the prevailing view among anthropologists, it was here that humans first crossed from the Old World into the New.

The precise timing of this event remains a topic of considerable debate among anthropologists. The oldest archaeological sites in present-day Alaska are less than 12,000 years old, but most scientists believe people actually reached the New World (eastern Beringia) well before then, perhaps as far back as 20,000 years ago.

According to the conventional hypothesis, after colonizing Beringia, humans were blocked from advancing into the heart of the North American continent by two immense, intersecting ice fields: the Laurentide ice field, which stretched across the eastern half of the continent almost to the Rockies, and the Cordilleran ice field, which originated in the mountains of Northwestern Canada and extended south along the Pacific coast to the vicinity of Seattle, Washington. Then, approximately 12,000 years ago, a warming climate caused a corridor to open between the two ice fields, paralleling the Rocky Mountains. Through this corridor traveled the descendants of the Beringians, bringing humans into contact with North American wildlife for the first time.

What these first Americans or Paleoindians encountered was an abundance and diversity of large animals that rivaled, perhaps even surpassed, today's Serengeti. Camels, horses, mastodons, mammoths, bison, and giant ground sloths ranged over the tundra, grasslands, and forests. Stalking them was a formidable array of predators, including saber-toothed cats, cheetahs, lions, wolves, and giant bears. Circling overhead, awaiting the opportunity to pick apart the carcasses, were eagles, vultures, and condors. Yet by about 8,000 years ago, virtually all of these species were gone. Most vanished within a thousand years or so of the opening of the ice-free corridor in an extinction spasm of breathtaking speed and magnitude.

The disappearance of these animals remains one of the great scientific mysteries of our time. Was it purely coincidental that the loss of these species, many of which had thrived for millions of years, followed on the heels of the arrival of the first humans? We know from the discovery of several kill sites (places where the butchered remains of mammoths, bison, and other species have been found commingled with spearheads and other human artifacts) that the earliest Americans preyed upon the great mammals. Could they have actually eradicated them? Many scientists believe so, pointing out that the species that vanished at the close of the Ice Age tended to be large and edible; most of the smaller species, such as voles and shrews, did not disappear. Scientists have also constructed models of the population growth rates and hunting abilities of the Paleoindians to demonstrate how these Stone Age hunters could have eradicated so many mammals in such a short period of time. Moreover, similar extinction spasms affecting large mammals have occurred at other times on other continents, linked in each case to the arrival of humans. And, if one assumes that Paleoindians extirpated the mammoths, horses, ground sloths, and other grazers and browsers, then the other extinctions fall into place: The saber-toothed cats, American cheetahs, lions, and other large predators were doomed when humans eradicated their prey species. So too were most of the scavenging vultures and condors.

But, as noted previously, the human invasion of North America occurred at a time when the climate was changing rapidly. Could climate change, then, be primarily responsible for the extinction of these animals? Indirectly, perhaps. By studying fossil pollen grains, scientists have deduced that the warming trend at the end of the Pleistocene caused massive changes in vegetation across much of the continent. In the East, spruce forests that had dominated much of the land were suddenly replaced by forests consisting of pines, firs, and a variety of hardwoods. In the Pacific Northwest, Douglas-firs and red alders replaced lodgepole pines. If these new ecosystems proved unsuitable as habitats for the large grazers and browsers, then extinction might follow.

Other factors weighing against human culpability for the disappearance of the Ice Age mammals include the relatively small number of kill sites that have been discovered to date, and some evidence that humans settled the New World long before the opening of the Cordilleran-Laurentide corridor. For example, many anthropologists now believe that a prehistoric settlement discovered in southern Chile is at least 12,500 years old. To have reached Chile that long ago, humans would have had to settle in Beringia and then head south at least 14,000 years ago, well before many of the big mammals disappeared. Although the Cordilleran-Laurentide corridor was not open that long ago, the northwestern coastline may well have been passable then, especially with the aid of watercraft, and it could have provided an early route for human exploration and expansion. Should additional studies confirm that Paleoindians settled most of North America more than 12,000 years ago, the overhunting hypothesis would need to be revised or abandoned because the extinction of the mammals would no longer coincide with the arrival of humans.

On the other hand, it is entirely possible—even probable— that a combination of climate change and overhunting doomed the great mammals. Neither explanation excludes the other. If a changing climate reduced the habitats of many Ice Age mammals to small, isolated patches, then the arriving humans may have quickly wiped out the remnant populations of mammals in those patches. What is certain is that the arrival of humans marked the beginning of a transformation of the North American landscape that is second to only the Ice Age itself in its impact on wildlife. At some point after their arrival in the New World, the earliest Americans ceased being nomadic hunters (if, indeed, they ever were truly nomadic) and began modifying the land to suit their needs—using fire to create new growth for deer and quail, clearing patches of forest to grow crops, damming and diverting small streams for irrigation, and building settlements. Actions such as these, replicated through the centuries and magnified by human ingenuity and ambition, would eventually produce the contemporary American landscape, one in which every square mile has been altered by humans. How these changes, from past to present, have affected the wildlife of the United States is a topic that has long fascinated ecologists and conservationists. It is the subject of this book.

There can be little doubt that humans have essentially reconfigured the American landscape. Today, more than 85 percent of the virgin forests of the United States have been logged, 90 percent of the tallgrass prairies have been plowed or paved, and 98 percent of the rivers and streams have been dammed, diverted, or developed. In the process, hundreds of species have vanished completely, many others have declined to the point of endangerment, and still others are drastically reduced in number.

Yet, despite all these changes, the United States is far from a biological wasteland. There are more acres of forest in the East today than there were at the beginning of the twentieth century, and many of our lakes and rivers are cleaner now than they were just 25 years ago. Some species that teetered on the brink of extinction less than a century ago have rebounded spectacularly. Indeed, the vast majority of species that graced this nation 100, even 1,000, years ago are still with us, and new species arrive almost daily. A few of these newcomers are natural colonists, flying, swimming, or crawling to this continent on their own. Most, however, are transported and released by people, either intentionally for economic or aesthetic reasons or accidentally, as stowaways aboard ships, planes, and trucks.

Thus, avid readers of natural history are understandably confused when they read first one article lamenting the growing roster of endangered species and then another extolling the miraculous recovery of the bald eagle or California sea otter. For every story describing the "recovery" or "rebirth" of a particular lake or forest, there is one announcing the loss or degradation of some other ecosystem. At times it seems as though we inhabit two worlds. In one, the native plants and animals constitute a fragile, interconnected community of life, easily and irreparably damaged by our actions. In the other, the flora and fauna are a collection of resilient survivors, capable of persisting, even flourishing, in our backyards and cities and in the scraps of habitat we leave for them.

The key to making sense of this confusion lies in the realization that species and ecosystems differ in their resilience to change. Some ecosystems are more easily damaged than others, in large part because some species are better able to tolerate the activities of people. Virtually all of the forests that now exist in New England were at one time or another cut down by loggers or turned into farmland. The woods we see today tend to be much younger than those encountered by the Pilgrims, and in most cases they lack the complexity and diversity of the virgin forests. But they are forests nonetheless, doing most of the things we expect forests to do: cleansing the air, producing timber, sustaining wildlife. Their presence is a testament to the ability of some species and ecosystems to rebound from intensive exploitation by people. But in Hawaii, where thousands of acres of rainforest have been cleared for farming and ranching as well, the land shows little evidence of recovery. The forests that have regenerated there consist almost entirely of alien trees and shrubs, and they retain virtually none of the native wildlife.

If there is an overall pattern to the postcolonial changes in America's wildlife, it is one of diminishing returns, in which ecosystems and species respond to and recover from the abuses leveled at them, but with predictable and irreversible losses. Passenger pigeons and green-blossom pearly mussels are gone forever; forest songbirds return each spring to the eastern woodlands, but in diminishing numbers, as the forests are gnawed away by suburban sprawl; and the once great salmon runs of the Columbia River have been reduced to a trickle by dams, overfishing, and excessive logging. On the other hand, here and there, one sees signs of hope and recovery, from the reappearance of birdwing pearly mussels in a Tennessee river when the vegetation along its banks is restored to the sighting of a jaguar in the mountains of New Mexico after a 90-year absence. These cycles of recovery and loss will be a recurring theme in this book.

No single book can do justice to the full diversity of wildlife in this country, and I have had to make some difficult choices. I have given birds and mammals a disproportionate share of attention in the chapters that follow—disproportionate, that is, to their relative abundance compared with other types of animals, such as insects and mollusks. In doing so, however, I am adhering to a long (albeit unfortunate) tradition in ecology. Birds and mammals are simply much better known and better studied than most other groups of animals. Not being a botanist, I have chosen not to emphasize plants, although they are as worthy of attention as animals. Aficionados of the south-western deserts and Alaskan tundra will find that these magnificent ecosystems are essentially ignored too. My decision to omit them in no way reflects a belief that they have been unaltered by humans or are unworthy of protection. Rather, I chose examples that I felt could best develop the central themes of this book, which required my taking a selective rather than an all-inclusive view of American ecosystems. Before delving into particular ecosystems, however, let us begin with a brief overview of the current status of America's wildlife, which will provide a backdrop for the more detailed discussions that follow.

Somewhat in excess of 100,000 native species (terrestrial and freshwater) have been identified in the United States, including over 16,000 ferns, conifers, and flowering plants, 2,500 vertebrates (mammals, birds, reptiles, amphibians, and fishes), and roughly 75,000 insects. These 100,000 or more species represent an unknown fraction of the nation's total flora and fauna—unknown because scientists have no idea how many insects, mites, fungi, and other little creatures remain undiscovered and undescribed in wildlands and backyards across the country. The actual number of species in the United States is probably several times the known number.

Only for a few well-studied groups, such as flowering plants, vertebrates, and butterflies, do scientists have enough information to assess how well they are faring. Based on its studies of these better-known groups, The Nature Conservancy estimates that approximately 1 percent of America's plant and animal species have vanished over the past two to three centuries. An additional 16 percent are in immediate danger of extinction, and another 15 percent are considered vulnerable. Thus, about a third of America's species are "of conservation concern," according to the Conservancy. The remaining two-thirds "appear to be relatively secure at present."

What, then, distinguishes the species at risk from the secure ones? Biologists have debated this issue for years, examining traits such as body size, diet, population density, and habitat preferences to determine which of these factors correlate with vulnerability to extinction. On a more fundamental level, the key factor is tolerance: Some species thrive in human-altered environments, others do not, and the ones that do not, tend to become endangered. Since the end of the Ice Age, virtually every species that has vanished from the United States has done so with a push (either intentional or accidental) from people.

"From prehistory to the present time," writes Harvard biologist Edward O. Wilson, "the mindless horsemen of the environmental apocalypse have been overkill, habitat destruction, introduction of animals such as rats and goats, and diseases carried by these exotic animals." To these we may add a fifth horseman, air and water pollution, although some might consider it a form of habitat destruction. Of the five, habitat destruction is by far the most significant. It has been implicated in the decline of 85 percent of the endangered plants and animals in the United States. The spread of non-native or alien species is the next biggest threat, harming 49 percent of our vanishing species, followed by pollution (affecting 24 percent), overkill (17 percent), and diseases (3 percent).

These five horsemen are the central characters in this book. We shall explore how they have affected the wildlife in different regions of the country, how each has waxed or waned over time, and how they have interacted with one another to produce the contemporary American fauna. Viewed in this light, none of these threats is as simple as it seems. For example, the conversion of a forest to a shopping center or a prairie to a cornfield is as close to an example of absolute habitat loss as one can imagine. Yet the shopping center will harbor its share of starlings and house sparrows (both are non-native species brought to this country in the nineteenth century), and the cornfield will become a mecca in the fall and winter for crows and blackbirds seeking the waste grain.

This is not to suggest that no harm is done when natural areas are paved or plowed—far from it. Starlings and crows are poor substitutes for the scarlet tanagers and prairie chickens that preceded them, and there is little else to enjoy in the way of wildlife in such mutilated landscapes. But this extreme example does serve to highlight the flip side of habitat destruction: Whenever the habitat of one species is destroyed, habitat for another is created. In this way, habitat alteration creates winners and losers. Unfortunately, the winners are all too often the very species least in need of protection or least welcome in our midst—from starlings to Norway rats to carp—while the losers may vanish forever.

Deciding whether a particular change represents habitat destruction is not always easy. A forest fire can alter the landscape for centuries and drive away certain plants and animals, but it also creates opportunities for other species. The Kirtland's warbler, one of America's rarest birds, nests exclusively in stands of 6- to 20-year-old jack pines in central Michigan. Once the trees age beyond 20 years, the warblers abandon them. Under natural conditions, these birds depend upon periodic forest fires to kill the old trees and regenerate the young stands they require (the seeds of the jack pine are encased in cones that open only upon exposure to intense heat, such as that generated by a fire). In that respect, the Kirtland's warbler has plenty of company: Across the country, hundreds, perhaps thousands, of species depend upon wildfires to create the particular habitats they require. And fires, unlike shopping centers, are reversible: With time, the ecosystem returns to something approximating its original condition. All of these factors argue against equating forest fires with habitat destruction. On the contrary, the seemingly benign act of fire suppression, until recently practiced with zeal across the nation, has proved to be a much more serious threat to wildlife.

But if we accept the ecological value of forest fires, should we then also favor timber cutting, which, superficially at least, mirrors the effects of fire by producing young vegetation? In fact, there are important differences between the two. In the case of a fire, the organic matter that does not go up in smoke is returned to the soil as the charred remains of trees and shrubs, whereas in the case of a timber harvest, most of the organic matter is removed from the site to become two-by-fours, paper, or other wood products. Forest fires also have a capricious quality; they will often consume one stand of trees, lightly singe an adjacent stand, and bypass a third one altogether. The resulting mosaic of habitats sustains a wide array of species. Timber cutting, on the other hand, tends to be far more uniform, at least the way it is practiced across much of the country today. Great swaths of forest are cleared of their older trees and replaced with seedlings, and the time between cuttings may be as little as 15 to 40 years, thereby preventing the forest from ever reaching old age again. For species that inhabit only the older forests—the northern spotted owl being the most famous example—logging can be a serious threat. Yet in Michigan, foresters have successfully used logging as a substitute for fire to create young pine stands for the Kirtland's warbler. Logging, like grazing, is neither all good nor all bad. It must be evaluated in the context of the ecosystem where it takes place and the manner in which it is practiced.

Context, in fact, is everything when thinking about habitat destruction. How seriously a particular action will affect wildlife is usually related to the extent to which the ecosystem has already been altered or destroyed. A generation of ecological research has demonstrated that when natural areas are chopped apart by commercial development or agriculture, species will vanish from the remaining patches of habitat, especially if those patches are very small or very isolated from one another. A crude rule of thumb holds that each tenfold reduction in the amount of habitat results in a 50 percent loss in the numbers of species within it. Thus, one might expect a 1,000-acre patch of forest to hold twice as many species of forest-dwelling songbirds as a 100-acre patch, all things being equal. Moreover, that 1,000-acre tract provides a very different (and generally safer) environment for those forest songbirds than do twenty patches of 50 acres each. It's not simply the total amount of habitat that determines which species thrive and which decline; it's how that habitat is distributed across the landscape. This concept is a key insight of contemporary ecology, and I shall return to it when I consider the history of the eastern forests and Midwestern grasslands.

All of Wilson's "mindless horsemen"—indeed, all of the forces that drive species to extinction—represent surprisingly complex issues. Most anglers casting for brown trout in Pennsylvania or striped bass in California are unaware that they are matching wits with alien species, brought to their new homes from Europe and the eastern United States, respectively, in the nineteenth century. Although complaints against the striped bass are few, the brown trout has been implicated in the decline of a variety of native fishes, both as a predator and as a competitor. Why some alien species become pests and others do not remains a mystery, but part of the answer lies in the nature of the ecosystems to which they are introduced. Isolated, species-poor regions, such as the Hawaiian Islands or the rivers and springs of the arid West, seem especially vulnerable to damage by non-native plants and animals. In later chapters, we shall explore why this is so.

The linkages between species, whether between a plant and its pollinator or a predator and its prey, drive the cycles of loss and recovery. To some people, these linkages are evidence of a delicate and intricate machinery of nature. Remove one part—even a seemingly insignificant one—and the entire machinery may grind to a halt. It is a compelling image, but not a very accurate one. Were it so, the eastern forests would be a biological wasteland, given that over the course of two centuries, we have managed to exterminate most of the large mammals that once lived there, including bison, elk, mountain lions, and wolves, not to mention the most abundant bird on earth, the passenger pigeon. Yet, as noted earlier, today's forests retain the vast majority of plants and animals that were present prior to European settlement.

What is undeniably true, however, is that the removal of one part—one species—from an ecosystem can lead to the demise of other species, and there is no way of knowing ahead of time where the chain reaction will end. Sometimes the losses seem small and constrained: when the Carolina parakeet disappeared at the beginning of the twentieth century, so too did the little mites that lived among its feathers, mites that occurred on no other species of bird. At other times, the losses are part of a cascade of events with unanticipated, even improbable, consequences. The settlers who eradicated wolves, mountain lions, and other large predators across much of this nation in the nineteenth and twentieth centuries could not have imagined that by doing so they would cause the disappearance decades later of wildflowers in Maryland and beavers in Yellowstone National Park, yet according to some ecologists, that is precisely what has happened.

No amount of wishful thinking on our part is going to resuscitate the Carolina parakeet, much less its feather mites. But if the pieces remain—if the species have not vanished completely—can we reconstruct the natural landscapes that once supported them? This is the process of ecosystem restoration, a kind of biotic healing that sometimes occurs without human intervention, but more often requires application of even more determination and energy than we used to destroy the ecosystem in the first place. Across the country, restoration efforts are under way, from the Everglades to the tallgrass prairies to the forests of the Sierra Nevada. The results are decidedly mixed. In some places, a reasonable facsimile of the precolonial flora and fauna has been reassembled, but elsewhere, misuse of the land has thrown the ecosystem into a new "steady state," one in which a very different assemblage of species has taken hold of the land and cannot be dislodged. This phenomenon is especially evident in parts of the Southwest and Hawaii, where alien grasses have invaded abused forests and rangelands and altered environmental conditions in ways that facilitate their own growth at the expense of native species. In such cases, there seems to be no practical way to reassemble what we have disassembled.

Perhaps it's just as well that we fail from time to time. We need a few conspicuous failures to remind us how poor we are at predicting—much less undoing—the consequences of our own actions. As children or young adults, we develop a mental image of what the natural world looks like, and it becomes the template by which we assess the magnitude of change in the wildlife and wildlands around us. But because each generation independently undergoes this type of "imprinting," the cumulative, long-term changes in our fauna are difficult to comprehend.

When I began watching birds in Buffalo, New York, I remember how the old-timers were always complaining that the spring migration just wasn't what it used to be. The birds, they groused, were scarcer, a fraction of the numbers that once filled the woods. And I, a brash young kid at the time, attributed their concerns to the infirmities of old age: weaker eyesight, poorer hearing, that sort of thing. Now, 30 years later, I find myself complaining, too, and I must either admit that I'm getting older or concede that the old-timers were right. Or both. I will never really know how numerous the songbirds were 50 or 60 years ago, and the boys and girls who are starting their birdwatching adventures today will never know what it was like to be in the woods of upstate New York some 30 years ago. This generational amnesia may be the greatest impediment to a lasting conservation ethic in America. Only when we take the time to assemble the bits and pieces of information from past generations and present them in an ordered way can the cycles of change, the losses and gains, in our wildlife populations be appreciated. And only then are we likely to cherish those species and wildlands that might otherwise pass unnoticed from this country and this world.

CHAPTER ONE

The forest Primeval

I live on the outskirts of Washington, D.C. From time to time, a business meeting or ballgame requires me to travel to Baltimore, a distance of approximately 40 miles as the crow flies. My route takes me through the center of Washington and then in an easterly direction along the Baltimore-Washington Parkway. Sealed inside my automobile, I have plenty of time to ponder how the landscape around me has changed since the arrival of European settlers.

Let us imagine this same journey taken in three different years in May: in 1498, 1898, and 1998. What we see and hear will be typical of what is happening in much of the eastern United States, although the particular species and the timing of events may differ.

Traveling between the two nonexistent cities in 1498 amounts to a major expedition, for we must proceed on foot, taking advantage of whatever game trails or Indian pathways we find. For most of the journey we travel within a magnificent old-growth forest. Oaks, chestnuts, and beeches tower above us. Beneath them are two or three layers of smaller trees, while jack-in-the-pulpits, mayapples, and other wildflowers cover large portions of the forest floor. The songs of red-eyed vireos, black-and-white warblers, scarlet tanagers, and other songbirds fill the morning air, but the birds themselves are surprisingly difficult to spot in the tall trees. In wet mud along the Patuxent River floodplain (marking roughly the halfway point in our journey), we find the tracks of a mountain lion, as close as we shall come to spotting the elusive cat. Proceeding farther, we startle a herd of elk, glimpsing a dozen tawny rumps as they disappear within the forest. Had we begun our trip in January instead of May, we might well have encountered bison, but they have since moved north, where they will remain until the snow once again brings them back to our area.

It is now 1898, and our trip will require the better part of a day with horse and carriage. In downtown Washington (a city of approximately 278,000 people), we spot flocks of house sparrows and pigeons searching for food in the muddy streets. The sparrows are the descendants of birds that were brought from Europe and released in the city in 1871. The pigeons date back to the colonial era, when they were carried across the Atlantic to serve as food and pets. Because we are proceeding at a leisurely pace, we are able to spot robins, blue jays, and cardinals in backyards and tree-lined streets; unlike the sparrows and pigeons, these birds are native to this region. Exiting the city, we pass through miles and miles of farm fields and hedges. Meadowlarks are stationed every few hundred yards along the fence posts, staking out their territories with loud, sweet whistles. Bobolinks hover above, singing their ecstatic trills and buzzes, while bobwhite quail call from the edge of a nearby woodlot. With more time we might explore the woodlots scattered among the fields; if we did, we would surely encounter some vireos, warblers, and tanagers, much as we did in 1498. But by and large we are in farmland, not forest, and the land belongs to the meadowlarks, not the tanagers.

The most recent trip is, of course, the easiest one, just an hour's drive if the traffic is light. As we pass through Washington (now a city of over half a million people), pigeons peer down at us from monuments, rooftops, and overpasses. House sparrows and starlings squabble over scraps of food around a garbage can. The starlings, which were not around at the turn of the century, are descendants of a flock of sixty brought from Europe in 1890 and released in New York City's Central Park; their progeny subsequently spread across the entire continent. Upon entering the Baltimore-Washington Parkway, we begin to tally the dead mammals along the roadside (the live ones being far too elusive to spot from a car). We record raccoons, opossums, skunks, and the occasional dog or cat. Approaching the forests lining the Patuxent River, we pull over, exit the car, and begin walking into the woods until the din of the highway has largely vanished. All around us red-eyed vireos are singing, and we quickly pick out the songs of a black-and-white warbler and a scarlet tanager—precisely the species that greeted us at this very spot half a millennium earlier. Wanting to see the brilliant red and black hues of the tanager, we hike farther, but succeed instead in spooking a white-tailed deer and a gray squirrel. With time running out, we return to the car and continue the drive, arriving in Baltimore in time for breakfast. Stopping at a fast food restaurant, we are greeted by another contingent of starlings and house sparrows, fighting over scraps.

Our time travels have highlighted a cycle of profound ecological importance: the destruction and subsequent regeneration of the forests of eastern North America. So thorough were the settlers and timber companies that, over the course of about two centuries, almost every acre of virgin forest from Maine south to Florida and west to the Great Plains fell to the ax or saw. The cutting began along the eastern seaboard, spread to the Ohio Valley and the Midwest around the time of the Civil War, and moved north to the upper Great Lakes at the close of the nineteenth century. "The pattern of the spread of lumbering . . . was one of a continuously expanding wave of exploitation, which, despite local pauses and advances, moved with generally gathering momentum westward across the continent, with an important projection that swept down through the South." Today, less than 2 percent of the virgin forest of the eastern United States still stands, a bleak tribute to the insatiable hunger for farmland and timber that characterized the settling of the East.

The cutting of the virgin forests coincided with an era of unregulated hunting and trapping that reached its peak in the latter half of the nineteenth century. The breadth and magnitude of this overexploitation are difficult to overstate, especially in comparison with today's stringent bag limits and seasonal restrictions on hunting. Overexploitation equaled or exceeded deforestation as a factor in the disappearance of mammals and birds from the eastern forests. Together, the one-two punch of deforestation and overhunting eliminated virtually all of the large predators and hoofed mammals in the East. Well over a century later, the ecological consequences of their elimination are still unfolding before our eyes, as populations of other plants and animals increase or decrease in response.

In only a handful of places, such as Minnesota's Boundary Waters and the southern Appalachians, do sizable tracts of virgin forest remain, places where a person can hike among the big trees for several hours and feel as though he has stepped into the boots of pioneer naturalists Mark Catesby or John James Audubon. Elsewhere, ecologists search diligently for every remaining acre of primary forest, and the discovery of even the tiniest scrap is deemed worthy of celebration. None of these primeval forests, not even the largest tracts, contains the full array of species that greeted the first European settlers.

What were these original forests like? It is tempting to portray the precolonial landscape of the eastern United States as an unbroken blanket of primeval forest, a green wilderness where a squirrel could scamper from the Atlantic Ocean to the Mississippi River without ever touching the ground. However appealing this image might be, it is also inaccurate. Natural disturbances such as fires, windstorms, and insect outbreaks, combined with fires and clearings perpetuated by American Indians, assured that the "blanket" was, in fact, something of a patchwork quilt, consisting of forest patches of different ages and sizes. From Massachusetts southward, most tribes had strong agricultural traditions, clearing the forests around their settlements to plant maize, potatoes, squash, sunflowers, beans, tobacco, and other crops. As the fertility of the soil diminished and crop yields fell, as the supply of fuelwood surrounding their villages was exhausted, as populations of game animals declined, or as the volume of refuse reached intolerable proportions, the tribes would abandon their fields, allowing the forests to regenerate. This "slash-and-burn" method of farming would be replaced with more efficient but less sustainable modes of exploitation when the European settlers arrived. In addition, many tribes burned the forests in the spring and fall to create better habitat for deer, quail, and other game animals and to maintain grasslands and clearings.

Estimates of the precolonial population of the United States and Canada range over an order of magnitude, from one to twelve million. By any estimate it was a substantial number, capable of altering the vegetation over much of the East. The accounts of early European settlers describe large areas devoid of trees and forests so open that one could gallop horses through them. Describing the landscape around Salem, Massachusetts, in 1630, one colonist wrote: "[T]here is much ground cleared by the Indians . . . and I am told that about three miles from us a man may stand on a little hilly place and see diverse thousands of acres of ground as good as need to be, and not a Tree on the same." Adding to the mosaic-like quality of landscape was the natural diversity of the plants themselves. Historian William Cronon relates the experience of explorer James Rosier, who, while ascending a river in Maine in 1605, encountered great, old oaks growing in open fields, dense thickets of shrubs and saplings, and conifers so tall they were fit to serve as "masts for ships of 400 tun," all in the space of 4 miles.

Although the virgin forests were never as vast as sometimes imagined, and while the Indians altered the face of the land more extensively than previously thought, there seems little doubt that on the whole the precolonial forests were grander and more extensive than anything we enjoy today. Colonist after colonist wrote home to England to gloat about the magnificent trees that were so abundant in the new land. Today, we live surrounded by woods that bear little resemblance to the forests that greeted those first settlers. "Our whole concept of a healthy and mature forest now applies to something that once would have been considered inferior and scraggly." We will never know the full impact of the deforestation of eastern North America on its wildlife. The effects of deforestation are difficult to disentangle from the effects of overhunting, the accounts of early naturalists are woefully inadequate for unraveling such a complex puzzle, and many of the clues disappeared with the great trees. But we can be certain that the impact was enormous.

While it is now difficult even to imagine a bison, gray wolf, or mountain lion roaming the forests of New Jersey, Delaware, or Maryland, at one time these species were an integral part of the fauna of eastern North America. In the Northeast, they were joined by caribou and moose. Exactly how common these species once were will never be known, but one can gain some appreciation for their former numbers by examining old hunting records. In 1760, for example, north of Harrisburg, Pennsylvania, two hundred settlers encircled an area of approximately 700 square miles and slowly marched inward, shooting any animal they saw. Their goal was to rid the area of the mountain lions and wolves that "had been troubling the more timid of the settlers," but their blood lust extended well beyond those two species. By the end of the hunt, the settlers had killed "41 panthers [mountain lions], 109 wolves, 112 foxes, 114 mountain cats [bobcats], 17 black bears, 1 white bear, 2 elk, 198 deer, 111 buffaloes, 3 fishers, 1 otter, 12 gluttons [wolverines], 3 beavers and upwards of 500 smaller animals." The numbers of wolves and mountain lions in particular are surprisingly high even for an area of that size, casting some doubt on the accuracy of the count. But the fact that there were significant numbers of large predators and ungulates (hoofed mammals) in the eastern forests in the colonial era seems indisputable.

A population that values domestic livestock, avidly consumes wild game, and has little knowledge of ecology is likely to show little tolerance for wild predators. The settling of the East, therefore, was marked by a concerted effort to eliminate its wolves and mountain lions. By the mid-1600s, New England colonists were already complaining about livestock depredation by gray wolves, and they employed bounties, poisons, and special hunters to get rid of them. Wolves were extirpated from New England by the 1860s, and from New York and Pennsylvania by the start of the twentieth century. Farther south, they held on a little longer in the Appalachian Mountains, but vanished in the beginning decades of the twentieth century. Today, in the eastern United States, gray wolves survive only in the northern Great Lakes region.

A second species of wolf, intermediate in size between the gray wolf and coyote, once occurred in the swamps and forests of the southeastern United States, from North Carolina south to Florida and west to Texas, Oklahoma, Arkansas, and Missouri. The red wolf does not hunt in big packs or kill large livestock (although poultry and newborn calves are occasionally taken). Indeed, this timid animal hardly posed an economic or physical threat to the farmers who killed it. Although the red wolf managed to persist in the East far longer than the gray wolf, by the late 1960s it had been reduced to a single population living in eastern Texas, a population that was in imminent danger of genetic disintegration because the wolves were hybridizing with coyotes. In the mid-1970s, the U.S. Fish and Wildlife Service staged a Dunkirk-like rescue of the red wolf, bringing as many of the wild animals as possible into captivity. Of the four hundred canines captured by the Service, only forty were judged to be "pure" enough red wolves to use in a captive breeding program. The program worked well, enabling the Service to move on to a much tougher challenge: reintroducing red wolves into the wild. In 1987, the Service began releasing animals in the Alligator River National Wildlife Refuge and nearby Pocosin Lakes National Wildlife Refuge in coastal North Carolina. This effort has, predictably enough, encountered pockets of local resistance, but far less opposition than one might have expected, given the troubled history of people and wolves.

The mountain lion, too, was eradicated from virtually its entire range in the East, but due to its extraordinarily elusive nature, the precise dates of its demise are impossible to determine. The last bounty in Connecticut was paid in 1769, while in Vermont and New Hampshire lions persisted for about a century longer. In New York, they survived in the Adirondack Mountains until the very beginning of the twentieth century. The southern Appalachians became one of the last refuges for eastern mountain lions, where they were reliably recorded until the 1930s. In the more remote and mountainous regions of Virginia, Tennessee, and North Carolina, sightings of mountain lions are still reported from time to time, but one should probably assume they represent either escaped "pets" or misidentifications, rather than miraculous survivors of centuries of persecution. Occasional sightings in New England may represent escaped captives or possibly wandering individuals from the wilder parts of Canada. Remarkably, a tiny population of about thirty to fifty mountain lions still survives in the Everglades, but it seems only a matter of time until a combination of natural mortality and pressure from Florida's ever-growing human population snuffs out this ember of eastern wildness.

The elimination of big predators from nearly all of the eastern United States was an ecological experiment of enormous proportions, an experiment conducted long before there were ecologists to deduce its results. To guess at the consequences, therefore, one must turn to recent ecological studies from a variety of locales. A growing number of biologists believe that top predators play a critical role in maintaining the diversity of species within natural communities. In tropical forests, for example, jaguars, mountain lions, and ocelots are thought to depress populations of their prey species, which include various seed-eating rodents and omnivorous mammals such as the coatimundi, a tropical relative of the raccoon. In places where the cats have been shot out, which means almost any forest accessible to people with guns, these prey species are an order of magnitude more abundant. If populations of seed-eating mammals increase in numbers because they have fewer predators, they can suppress the regeneration of various trees by consuming large numbers of seeds. Tree species diversity can thus be reduced, causing the loss of additional species that depend upon certain types of trees. Furthermore, omnivorous mammals such as coatimundis consume the eggs and young of ground-nesting birds. As their numbers increase in the absence of big cats, they can drive ground-nesting birds to extinction.

As we shall see, both these phenomena—a reduction in plant diversity and the disappearance of ground-nesting birds— are occurring today in the eastern United States, and the historic loss of top predators is a principal cause. However, I suspect few such effects would have been apparent in the nineteenth or early twentieth centuries. The settlers were hell-bent on killing both predators and prey. Populations of bison, elk, caribou, deer, and even raccoons could not have responded to the absence of predators at that time because they too were being ruthlessly exploited.

The bison were the first to go. Although most people today think of them as animals of the Great Plains, at one time bison ranged as far east as Pennsylvania, New York, and perhaps New England, and south to Florida. The last bison east of the Appalachians was killed at the appropriately named Buffalo Cross Roads, near Lewisburg, Pennsylvania, in 1801, and the last individuals east of the Mississippi were a cow and her calf taken in West Virginia in 1825. Elk persisted somewhat longer, retreating as did the bison and mountain lions into the Appalachian wilderness. The last native elk in Virginia and Pennsylvania were shot in 1855 and 1867, respectively. Caribou, now usually regarded as denizens of the tundra, once occurred as far south as the northern Great Lakes and Maine. Gone from Maine by 1908, they held on in the Great Lakes region until the 1940s.

Even the white-tailed deer, so common today, was once nearly extirpated from the East due to unregulated hunting. Like the other large ungulates of the East, they experienced a tremendous population decline in the first two centuries of European settlement, when predation by a rapidly growing human population more than compensated for the absence of wolves and mountain lions. By the end of the eighteenth century they had vanished from large portions of New England, and they were so scarce in Maryland at the turn of the twentieth century that some naturalists thought them locally extinct. As late as 1950, one Maryland naturalist would write:

> In a number of other ways this large mammal has difficulty adjusting itself to ever-expanding civilization. They are gradually being restricted to such a limited range of freedom that their future as abundant big game does not appear to be rosy.

In contrast to the bison, elk, and caribou, whose demise appeared to evoke little concern, the disappearance of deer clearly alarmed the settlers. A deer reserve was set up in Cecil County, Maryland, as early as 1661, and Massachusetts declared a closed season on deer hunting in 1694. The imposition of strict hunting laws, coupled with reintroduction efforts and forest regrowth, would eventually enable the white-tailed deer to stage a spectacular comeback. To the suburban homeowners whose ornamental shrubs are now being browsed into oblivion, the ability of the white-tailed deer to adjust to "ever-expanding civilization" is no longer in doubt.

Another group of mammals avidly sought by the settlers was the furbearers. Ermine, otter, mink, marten, fisher, wolverine, bear, wolf, lynx, raccoon, beaver, fox, and other mammals were trapped and traded with zeal wherever they were found. The Great North Woods, "that wilderness of forest lakes, of loons and geese, moose and bear" extending from the northeastern United States west to the Great Lakes and north to Hudson Bay, became the epicenter of the fur trade, yielding spectacular numbers of pelts. A sale by the famous Hudson Bay Company in November 1743 disposed of the skins of 26,750 beavers, 14,730 martens, and 1,267 wolves. Although none of these animals was driven to complete extinction by the fur trade, some were obliterated from parts of their range. The marten and fisher vanished from the Appalachian Mountains, the wolverine from northern New England and the Adirondacks.

The premier furbearer, the one whose pelt drove more people to trap in more places than any other, was the beaver. Relentlessly pursued over the course of two centuries, it was almost eliminated east of the Mississippi River by the mid-nineteenth century. Its disappearance surely had profound ecological consequences, although we are once again forced to guess at them in the absence of substantive data. The beaver is a "keystone species," an animal upon which a large number of other species depend for their survival. The ponds beavers create provide important habitats for waterfowl, herons, turtles, frogs, and fish; the trees killed by rising water levels serve as nesting and foraging sites for woodpeckers and chickadees, and as convenient perches from which hawks, flycatchers, and bluebirds watch for their prey (and for each other). None of these species is found only near beaver ponds, but all would be less common in their absence—and presumably were a century ago. Historian William Cronon suggests another, more important way in which the beaver's disappearance may have affected natural diversity in New England. When the old beaver dams finally collapsed for lack of maintenance, soils rich in the organic debris that had accumulated behind the dams were exposed. Dense grass quickly grew on the sites, providing abundant forage for domestic livestock. The exposed pond bottoms also became prime cropland for enterprising farmers. "The death of the beaver in fact paved the way for the non-Indian communities that would soon arrive."

Despite the trapping pressure, scattered populations of beavers must have persisted in the wilder corners of the Northeast, the Appalachians, and the South, for the animals have made a wonderful comeback, aided in some places by reintroduction programs. Today, watching one of the big rodents swimming along a polluted creek in the middle of Washington, D.C., it is hard to imagine that such an animal could ever be coveted, much less extirpated, for its skin.

As noted in the introduction, there is a well-established relationship between the size of an ecosystem and the number of species it sustains. This species-area relationship, which holds that a tenfold reduction in the amount of habitat results in the loss of approximately half of the species within that habitat, might lead us to expect hundreds, if not thousands, of species of plants and animals to have vanished due to deforestation in the East. But, in fact, there is no evidence of such a cataclysmic loss of wildlife. A few authors have even used the absence of a long roster of eastern extinctions as evidence that contemporary concerns about the loss of species (both in this country and elsewhere) are unwarranted. In fact, the relatively small number of forest-dwelling species that are known to have become extinct in the East does not necessarily invalidate either the species-area relationship or the angst of environmentalists. To see why this is so, we shall focus on the best-known and most intensively studied group of American animals, birds. Of the approximately 160 species of birds known to have nested in the eastern forests, only 4 are now extinct: the Carolina parakeet, passenger pigeon, ivory-billed woodpecker, and Bachman's warbler.

It comes as a surprise to most people to learn that, until the beginning of the twentieth century, a native parrot flourished in the eastern United States, ranging as far north as New York and Wisconsin and as far west as eastern Colorado. Loud and gregarious like most parakeets, it fed on the seeds of cockleburs, cypress trees, maples, elms, and other native plants, but also developed a fondness for the fruit and grain grown by settlers. Flocks of two or three hundred would descend upon orchards, where the emerald green and yellow parakeets would clamber over the branches, biting into the apples, pears, or peaches and pulling the unripe fruit off the trees. Often they were met with a volley of gunfire. Here their sociability became their undoing, for instead of fleeing, the surviving birds would circle around and screech at their fallen flockmates, permitting the shooter to kill more birds. As early as 1831, Audubon would comment upon the decline of the Carolina parakeet: "Our parakeets are very rapidly diminishing in number; and in some districts, where twenty-five years ago they were plentiful, scarcely any are now to be seen." By the end of the nineteenth century only a few birds remained, animated fugitives eagerly pursued by collectors. To Frank Chapman, preeminent ornithologist of his time, fell the dubious honor of recording the last wild flock of parakeets: thirteen birds sighted on the northeastern side of Lake Okeechobee, Florida, in April 1904. A handful of individuals survived in captivity for about a decade longer, with the last individual dying in 1918.

It is difficult to imagine that wanton shooting alone could have driven the Carolina parakeet to extinction; the species occurred over much of the Southeast, and it lived in some of our most impenetrable forests. The eventual clearing of those forests must have been an additional factor, although most ornithologists probably would rank shooting as the primary cause of its demise.

If the Carolina parakeet's disappearance is somewhat perplexing, the extinction of the passenger pigeon is, on first inspection, unbelievable. Once the most abundant bird on earth, with flocks so vast they literally darkened the midday sky, it was gone by the start of the twentieth century. Observers who witnessed the great flocks were convinced the species was all but indestructible, and the two answers put forth to explain most extinction events during this era—hunting and deforestation—are less than satisfying in this case. True, millions of pigeons were slaughtered, but the number taken was a small fraction of the wild population, and the birds disappeared much faster than the forests they inhabited. The key to understanding why the passenger pigeon disappeared is understanding how it lived and, in particular, its unique relationship with the beeches, oaks, and hickories that dominated upland forests in the eastern half of the continent.

All of these trees produce abundant, nutritious nuts, the mainstay of the passenger pigeon's diet. Both the trees and the pigeons shared a common survival strategy, one founded on the old adage of safety in numbers. Beeches, oaks, and hickories do not produce a steady crop of nuts each year. Instead, all of the trees of a given type in a locality will produce an enormous crop only once every few years, a phenomenon known as masting. Ecologists believe this habit arose as a defensive strategy: by flooding the area with nuts, the trees are able to overwhelm the hungry squirrels, turkeys, bears, blue jays, and other seed predators, thereby increasing the probability that at least a few seeds will survive to sprout and grow to maturity.

The passenger pigeon responded to this trick by adopting a nomadic lifestyle. During the fall and winter, flocks wandered through the eastern forests in search of masting trees, sometimes covering hundreds of miles in a day. As spring approached, they formed immense breeding colonies in areas where large crops of nuts from the previous autumn remained on the forest floor. The nests were flimsy stick platforms, and the adult birds lacked any effective means of defending them. Instead, the pigeons followed a strategy of overwhelming abundance—grouping together in colonies so vast that no predators could consume all of the eggs and nestlings. One such nesting aggregation in Wisconsin was estimated to cover more than 750 square miles and contain over 136 million birds.

Against hawks, foxes, and raccoons, the strategy was a resounding success—witness the incredible abundance of pigeons—but against *Homo sapiens* it proved fatal. People besieged the nesting colonies, cutting down or burning trees filled with nests, suffocating incubating birds with sulfur, knocking young birds from their nests with poles, and luring adult birds to the ground where they could be netted. Much of this slaughter was undertaken by professional market hunters who supplied cities with pigeon meat. From a single nesting colony near Grand Rapids, Michigan, hunters shipped 588 barrels—more than 100,000 pounds—of pigeons to market.

As early as the late 1600s, natural historians along the eastern seaboard were remarking that the wild pigeons seemed much less common than in previous years, an observation they made with increasing frequency as time passed. "Some years past they have not been in such plenty as they used to be," wrote one naturalist in 1770. "This spring I saw them fly one morning, as I thought in great abundance; but everybody was amazed how few there were; and wondered at the reason." The last major nesting in New England occurred near Lunenburg, Massachusetts, in 1851. A decade later the big flocks were gone from New York and Pennsylvania. A few states passed laws to protect nesting colonies, but they were rarely enforced. More typical was the reaction of the Ohio state senate to a proposal to control the harvest in that state: "The passenger pigeon needs no protection. Wonderfully prolific, having the vast forests of the North as its breeding grounds, traveling hundreds of miles in search of food, it is here to-day and elsewhere to-morrow, and no ordinary destruction can lessen them or be missed from the myriads that are yearly produced." In fact, the passenger pigeon was far from prolific—most pairs produced only a single offspring each year—and the destruction under way was far from ordinary. The vast majority of pigeons nested in a handful of enormous colonies scattered across the East, and it was precisely those colonies that were being targeted by hunters.

By the latter half of the nineteenth century, the northern Great Lakes states had become the passenger pigeon's last stronghold. Here the birds fell victim to two seemingly unrelated advances in technology: the expansion of the railroad and the invention of the telegraph. The railroads enabled commercial hunters to reach even the most distant colonies and ship birds back to eastern markets; the telegraph ensured that hunters quickly learned about the locations of any new colonies. The end came with remarkable speed. The total population of passenger pigeons in 1878 was estimated at 50 million birds; by the 1890s, only scattered individuals could be found. Less than one hundred days into the new century, on March 24, 1900, the last wild passenger pigeon was killed in Pike County, Ohio. The last captive individual, an aged female named Martha, died on September 1, 1914, at the Cincinnati Zoo. One would like to think that in her final months Martha invoked some measure of pity from the curious onlookers who came to see her huddled on the floor of her outdoor cage, alone and dying, immobile and inert save for the blinking of her beady eyes. Instead, the keepers had to rope off the area around the cage to keep people from throwing sand at her to make her move.

Why the pigeons disappeared so rapidly, dropping from tens of millions in 1878 to virtually none 20 years later, has long puzzled ornithologists. Recently, ornithologists David Blockstein and Harrison Tordoff have proposed a compelling explanation for that final demise. During this critical 20-year period, they suggest, hunters managed to disturb every major breeding colony for a period of time exceeding several pigeon generations. The species collapsed as entire cohorts died without replacing themselves.

Although the overwhelming majority of pigeons nested in the big colonies, a small number consistently nested in small groups or as lone pairs. Blockstein and Tordoff believe that without the safety in numbers conferred by the large colonies, these smaller groups could not produce sufficient numbers of offspring to sustain the species. Their flimsy nests and defenseless young were easy targets for predatory birds, mammals, and snakes.

The loss of the passenger pigeon must have had profound ramifications for forest ecosystems, altering the lives of predators and prey, shifting and changing the pathways of nutrients and energy in ways we will never know. One wonders what happened to the tons of mast that in years past were consumed by the pigeon flocks. Did they go into the making of more squirrels, bears, turkeys, and blue jays, animals that may have prospered from the pigeon's demise? Did oaks, hickories, or beeches increase in abundance in forest stands because more seeds were able to germinate? The questions are numerous and, for lack of evidence, timeless. Hiking through a forest today, I find it difficult to believe that the phenomenon of the passenger pigeon ever existed. Only a nation wilder and bigger than anything I am capable of imagining could have sustained the clouds of pigeons that once swept across its skies.

That wilder nation was also home to the ivory-billed woodpecker. A magnificent black bird with big white patches on its wings and neck, the ivorybill inhabited the bottomland forests of the Southeast. It was an extreme dietary specialist, feeding almost exclusively on beetle larvae that it extracted from the bark of recently deceased trees. One surmises that only the oldest forests provided sufficient food, for the woodpeckers avoided younger forests, including those that regenerated after logging. Not only did the ivorybill require old forests, it required large amounts of them. In the only scientific study of the species, completed on the eve of its extinction, biologist James Tanner calculated that its maximum density was one pair per 6.25 square miles. Even as far back as the days of Audubon, prescient observers were noting its decline. By the beginning of the twentieth century, it was a very rare bird; the last confirmed breeding records in the United States are from the early 1940s. Although it remains the Holy Grail of American birdwatchers, with persistent rumors of its presence in remote forests, most ornithologists now concede that it vanished from the United States sometime in the past 40 years. A separate population occurs in Cuba, but it too is critically endangered, if not extinct. The ivorybill belongs to a different era. Its presence today in the sterile, industrial forestlands of the South, however wonderful a thought, would be as out of place as a buckskin-clad settler with a musket in the streets of modern-day Atlanta.

The fourth bird to vanish from the eastern forests is in many ways the most mysterious. The Bachman's warbler, a 4.25-inch yellow and black songbird, nested in the bottomland hardwood forests of the southeastern United States and wintered exclusively in Cuba. First described by Audubon in 1833, it was not seen again (except for a Cuban record) for over 50 years. There followed a flurry of sightings across the Southeast, but by the 1930s the species had again become exceedingly rare. A few were seen as recently as the 1960s, but the lack of any certain reports since that time, despite growing numbers of birdwatchers, suggests that Audubon's enigmatic warbler has vanished forever. Ornithologists continue to debate the cause of its demise, with most theories focusing on the destruction of its breeding habitat, wintering habitat, or both. According to one theory, Bachman's warbler was a habitat specialist on its breeding grounds, choosing the extensive stands of wild cane (bamboo) that grew in the understory of bottomland forests in the Southeast. Much of the warbler's breeding range has been cleared to grow soybeans, rice, and other crops, and most of its wintering habitat has been converted to sugarcane. Perhaps this combination of summer and winter deforestation was sufficient to drive the species to extinction. Given that this tiny, innocuous bird was never hunted for its flesh or its plumes, it seems reasonable to presume that deforestation was the primary culprit behind its disappearance.

Thus, we have identified two birds, the ivory-billed woodpecker and Bachman's warbler, whose extinction was probably caused by the deforestation of the East, and two others, the Carolina parakeet and passenger pigeon, for which deforestation was a contributory factor. Even if we attributed the extinction of these last two species entirely to deforestation, ignoring for the moment the obvious role that overhunting played in their demise, we would still be left with a remarkably small list of birds that perished as a result of the clearing of the eastern forests. Yet by some estimates, nearly a quarter of the eastern deciduous forest was cleared between 1850 and 1909, and by the time of World War I, virtually all of it had been logged at least once. With this magnitude of forest loss, why didn't more birds (and, by extension, other types of animals) become extinct?

The answer may lie in the fact that the cutting of the eastern forests, while extremely thorough, took place over the course of two centuries. At no point during that time was the East ever completely deforested. Cutover forest lands were able to regenerate when settlers moved on to new frontiers. Even at the height of deforestation, forests still covered approximately half of their presettlement area. Thus, there were refuges for forest-dwelling species. If most of the animals living in the eastern forests had had very small ranges or could survive only in virgin forests, then the number of extinctions would surely have been much greater. Fortunately, at least with respect to birds and mammals, most of the species found in eastern forests have relatively large ranges, and they are able to persist in younger, second-growth stands. The ivory-billed woodpecker, with its requirement for old-growth forests, perished.

However, lest one become complacent about the seemingly low number of species that have perished over the past two centuries, it is worth remembering that our knowledge of the biodiversity of the United States is shamefully incomplete, especially with respect to plants and small organisms such as insects. Many species may have disappeared before we knew they existed. For example, a scientist with an eye for little things has recently discovered six species of feather mites in the plumage of museum specimens of the Carolina parakeet. Given that feather mites tend to be very specific in their choice of hosts, these six species in all likelihood vanished along with the parakeet. On October 1, 1765, the father-and-son naturalists John and William Bartram discovered a stand of small trees with showy white flowers growing along the banks of the Altamaha River in eastern Georgia. The trees proved to be an undescribed species in the tea family, subsequently named

Franklinia alatamaha in honor of both a great statesman and a fine river. For unknown reasons, *Franklinia* disappeared from the Altamaha River, where it was last recorded in 1803. Despite numerous searches, no one has found another wild specimen of the species, although it survives in cultivation. It is hard to believe that the world's only population of *Franklinia* was the tiny one the Bartrams happened to stumble upon in their wanderings. Perhaps other populations existed but were destroyed before botanists could find them. How many other obscure but irreplaceable species disappeared as European settlers took control of the land is anyone's guess.

The conversion of forests to farmland during the eighteenth and nineteenth centuries was a disaster for some species and a bonanza for others. Open-country birds like the eastern meadowlark, bobolink, dickcissel, vesper sparrow, and grasshopper sparrow moved into places that once were suitable habitats for forest-dwelling species like the pileated woodpecker, broad-winged hawk, and worm-eating warbler. The chestnut-sided warbler, for example, is a colorful songbird that nests in brushy areas but avoids mature forests. It was so rare in Audubon's time that the great naturalist encountered it only once in all his travels. Today, birdwatchers throughout the eastern United States know it as a common migrant and breeding species. Perhaps some subtle, undetected change in the environment enabled the chestnut-sided warbler population to explode over the past 150 years, but a simpler explanation is that the clearing of forests created a wealth of new habitat for this species.

Subsequently, however, as cities grew and settlers spread westward to subdue the central plains and Rocky Mountains, marginal cropland in the East was abandoned, permitting forests to regrow. From the beginning of the twentieth century until quite recently, the amount of forest in the Northeast, central Atlantic region, and South was increasing. By the late 1970s, the East had recovered approximately 60 percent of its original forest area. In parts of New England, this percentage is considerably higher.

The regeneration of the eastern forests had two effects on wildlife. First, species associated with fields and pastures declined. The best evidence for these declines comes from data gathered by the U.S. Fish and Wildlife Service for its national Breeding Bird Survey. Among the birds that declined significantly in the East between 1966 (the year the survey began) and 1991 are bobwhite, loggerhead shrike, eastern meadowlark, grasshopper sparrow, vesper sparrow, Henslow's sparrow, and savannah sparrow. All are species that inhabit fields, hedgerows, and other early successional habitats; they probably reached their maximum abundance in the East a century ago and declined as forests and, to a growing extent, concrete replaced farm fields. In recent decades, the regal fritillary, a stunning black and orange butterfly, has disappeared from almost all of the places where it once occurred in the eastern United States. A grassland insect from the Midwest, it may have spread eastward with the clearing of the forests and may now be retreating to its historical haunts.

A second consequence of the regrowth of eastern forests was an increase in the numbers and distribution of forest-dwelling animals. At the beginning of the twentieth century, the white-tailed deer, beaver, black bear, and wild turkey were gone from much of the East. All have staged spectacular comebacks, regaining most or all of their original ranges. Their recovery is part of the folklore of American wildlife management — conspicuous, undeniable successes in a field that has traditionally seen more losses than wins. The extent to which one may attribute their rebounding numbers to forest regeneration versus imposition of stricter hunting laws is debatable; the latter probably had as much or more to do with it than reforestation. All four species also benefited from intensive, hands-on reintroduction efforts. Far more remarkable than these recoveries is the fact that one can hike into a forest in Massachusetts, Maryland, Georgia, or Kentucky and see nearly all of the animals — large and small — that would have occurred there at the time of Columbus. No government agency or private organization returned black-and-white warblers, pygmy shrews, or spotted salamanders to the regenerating forests. They reappeared on their own, reclaiming the land with alacrity when their habitats returned.

In some parts of the country, however, the forests now occupying the land bear little resemblance to the original vegetation. Nowhere is this more apparent than in the southeastern United States, where one of the largest and most distinctive forest ecosystems in North America, the longleaf pine ecosystem, has been all but obliterated, even though millions of acres of trees remain. The virtual disappearance of this ecosystem illustrates the difference between reforestation and restoration.

When the Spanish began their explorations of North America in the sixteenth century, longleaf pine forests covered approximately 74 million acres in the southern United States, from Virginia south to Florida and west to Texas. These forests consisted of nearly pure stands of tall, columnar longleaf pines growing atop a carpet of wiregrass and herbs. Frequent wildfires, spawned by summer thunderstorms and set by Indians, kept the understory clear of competing oaks and other hardwoods, producing a remarkably open, parklike setting. (The longleafs, with their thick, fire-resistant bark, were able to withstand these fires and continue growing.) On an additional 18 million acres subjected to less frequent fires, longleaf pines grew in association with other pines and hardwoods, producing mixed stands with a less open structure. In total, then, longleaf pines once occurred across 92 million acres (equal to nearly 144,000 square miles) in the Southeast.

Today, less than 3 percent of this land still has longleaf pines. Loggers made small but constant inroads on the longleaf forests from the 1700s until the mid-1800s, at which point the advent of steam power, including steam locomotives and steam-powered sawmills, enabled them to attack the forests with a vengeance. An equally important factor in the demise of the longleaf forests was the growth of the naval stores industry. In the centuries before the development of petroleum-based substitutes, southeastern settlers used tar, pitch, rosin, and turpentine extracted from pines to lubricate the axles of their wagons. Sailors used these same products, collectively called naval stores, to waterproof sails, caulk leaks, and protect hulls against shipworms. Without these products, the economy would have ground to a halt. Because the longleaf pine was the premier source of naval stores, it was preferentially sought out by the manufacturers. As demand for these products grew both domestically and internationally, millions of acres of longleaf pines were quite literally bled to death.

In its youth, the longleaf pine is a slow-growing tree, so once the land had been cleared of them, other types of trees began to fill in the gaps. Moreover, during much of the nineteenth century, the Southeast was overrun with feral hogs, which fed extensively on longleaf pine seedlings. Beginning in the 1870s, many of the southeastern states passed laws requiring livestock owners to fence in their animals, but not before considerable damage had been done. Fires, too, were becoming rarer events, as a result of both active suppression by concerned landowners and communities and the passive suppression that occurs when farm fields act as firebreaks. Without fire, the young longleafs could not compete against other, faster-growing pines and hardwoods.

The demise of the longleaf forests has been a disaster for a diverse collection of plants and animals that once thrived within that ecosystem. Arguably the best known of these is the red-cockaded woodpecker, a small black-and-white bird that lives in the pine forests of the Southeast, especially those containing longleaf. The red-cockaded woodpecker prefers to nest in pine trees suffering from a fungal infection that softens the heart-wood, enabling the woodpeckers to drill their nest cavities. Because the fungus typically strikes older trees, the birds cannot persist in young stands. In this respect, the red-cockaded wood-pecker is reminiscent of the ivorybill, which also required old forests. The typical age of a red-cockaded woodpecker cavity tree is anywhere from 60 to 180 years old, depending upon the nature of the forest. Because the birds expend considerable amounts of time and energy excavating each cavity, families of woodpeckers jealously guard their cavity trees and use them for generations. When the woodpeckers finally abandon a cavity, it is usually taken over by a titmouse, chickadee, flying squirrel, or other cavity-loving animal. Although the woodpeckers are loath to abandon their cavities, they will do so if the hardwoods in the understory grow too tall. Thus, the woodpeckers also require frequent wildfires to keep the hardwoods in check.

Being a habitat specialist like the red-cockaded woodpecker has advantages and disadvantages. In the vast primeval longleaf pine forests, the little birds must have prospered and been exceptionally common. But as the longleaf pine ecosystem came under attack by settlers, loggers, turpentiners, and livestock, the woodpeckers suffered. The red-cockaded woodpecker was added to the federal endangered species list in 1970. In 1990, the American Ornithologists' Union estimated that fewer than 10,000 of them were left. More ominous was the finding that the woodpeckers had declined by over 20 percent just since the early 1980s. The ornithologists concluded that forestlands in the Southeast were not being managed in ways conducive to the survival of the woodpecker: slash and loblolly pines were being planted in place of longleaf pines; cutting cycles were too short to supply the older trees needed by the birds, and the lack of fire was enabling hardwoods to grow up among the pines. Not surprisingly, the red-cockaded woodpecker is hardly alone in its march toward extinction. At least twenty-seven other plants and animals associated with the longleaf—wiregrass ecosystem have been added to the federal endangered species list, with dozens more under consideration for listing.

It should be emphasized that the issue here is not the amount of forest per se. There are still millions of acres of pine forest in the Southeast. But, by and large, they contain slash and loblolly pine instead of longleaf, the trees are not allowed to grow very old, and they lack the open, parklike structure and wiregrass understory that characterized the original ecosystem. The land has been reforested; it has not been restored.

What has happened to the longleaf pine forests is an extreme example of a more widespread phenomenon. All of today's second-growth forests differ in various ways from the precolonial forests. As a consequence of both natural succession and human interference, some tree species are more common now than they were a century or two ago, and others are much rarer. The age profile of the forests has also changed, with most of the old growth having been replaced with much younger stands in which all of the trees are roughly the same age. Nonetheless, among the better-studied organisms at least, the vast majority of forest-dwelling species have managed to re-establish themselves in these second-growth forests. Their ability to recover from over two centuries of exploitation might inspire some confidence in the tenacity of nature—were it not for some disturbing recent trends.

In some of the more densely populated eastern states, forest cover has begun to decline again for the first time in almost a century as cities and suburbs spread into undeveloped areas. Maryland, for example, is currently losing forests at a rate of approximately 10,000 acres per year. The Maryland Office of Planning recently predicted that the state would lose 330,000 acres of forest between 1988 and 2020. And unlike the conversions of forests to farm fields in the past, these losses are destined to be permanent. Pennsylvania has fared somewhat better, with modest increases in forest cover posted through the 1960s and 1970s. But the increase has not been uniform; net losses in the lower Susquehanna River basin have been balanced by increases in less populated areas elsewhere.

We are already witnessing one unfortunate consequence of this newest round of deforestation: In a number of localities throughout the eastern United States, forest-dwelling songbirds are disappearing, even from protected parks and woodlots. Nowhere has this phenomenon been better documented than in the forested parks in and around Washington, D.C. In Cabin John Island, a protected floodplain forest located in Glen Echo, Maryland, just outside the District border, naturalists have been conducting censuses of breeding birds since the late 1940s. During this time, the density of nesting birds has declined by about 50 percent. This decline has not been uniform among all species, however. One group in particular, the Neotropical migrants, has suffered disproportionate losses. These are the birds that breed in the United States and Canada, but winter principally in Latin America and the Caribbean. Several Neotropical migrants, including Kentucky warblers, wood thrushes, scarlet tanagers, yellow-throated vireos, hooded warblers, and Louisiana waterthrushes, have disappeared completely as breeding species. Others, such as red-eyed vireos and northern parula warblers, have suffered major population declines. In contrast, populations of most resident species in Cabin John Island—birds such as the Carolina chickadee and downy woodpecker that do not undertake long migrations— have remained stable or even increased.

A few miles away in Washington's Rock Creek Park, breeding populations of Neotropical migrants have declined by 70 percent over the past four decades. There, too, a variety of migratory thrushes, warblers, and vireos (largely Neotropical migrants) that once bred in the park have vanished, while populations of most residents and short-distance migrants have increased or remained stable. Neither the forests of Rock Creek Park nor those of Cabin John Island have changed dramatically since the 1940s. The trees may have grown larger, and winter storms may have buffeted the woods from time to time, but both places remain largely undisturbed and undeveloped. The surrounding lands, however, have become increasingly developed, a point painfully obvious to longtime residents of the area.

Similar declines in songbird populations have been noted in other woodlands in New Jersey, Connecticut, and Illinois, pointing to a widespread problem. Further evidence is provided by annual surveys conducted under the auspices of the U.S. Fish and Wildlife Service. For the past decade, these surveys have recorded declines in populations of Neotropical migrants, although the statistical significance of those trends is, not surprisingly, the subject of some debate among ornithologists.

Ornithologists have also discovered that some Neotropical migrants are invariably absent from small woodlots and can be found only in large tracts of forest. The worm-eating warbler, for example, is a small olive songbird that inhabits oak woodlands, where its dry little rattle of a song complements the dry oak leaves that crackle and crunch underfoot as one tries to sneak up on the bird. Although the normal territory or home range of a pair of worm-eating warblers is only a few acres, the species is rarely encountered in forests smaller than several hundred acres. The aptly named black-and-white warbler is another example of an "area-sensitive" species, also shying away from forests that are smaller than several hundred acres.

These sorts of discoveries lead to two conclusions. First, many of our parks and woodlots, especially those in urban and suburban areas, are failing to save the songbirds that breed within them. Second, some species will survive only within large, unbroken expanses of forest, a discomfiting notion in an age when woodlands are regularly chopped into ever smaller pieces for the sake of more highways, shopping malls, and houses.

Forest fragmentation—as this process is termed by ecologists—harms songbirds primarily by reducing their output of offspring. Rates of nest predation are dramatically higher in small woodlots than in large forest tracts—by one estimate as much as fifty times higher—and they are especially high in woodlots in suburban neighborhoods compared with woodlots in rural areas. Three factors account for this rise in nest predation rates.

First, smaller woodlots have a higher proportion of forest edge to forest interior. Because some nest predators are more common around edges than in the forest interior, small or irregularly shaped forest fragments can be expected to have higher densities of predators than large, continuous ones. Second, urban and suburban neighborhoods offer a bonanza of food and hiding places for animals adaptable enough to use them. Unfortunately, many of the animals that thrive in these areas are opportunistic nest predators, such as raccoons and opossums. According to one estimate, at least 17,000 raccoons reside in the District of Columbia, one for every 35 human residents. Add to these native species the dogs and cats we keep as pets, and pressures on forest songbirds seem overwhelming, as indeed they are.

While studying this problem in the early 1980s, I attempted to identify likely nest predators by hiding artificial nests containing fresh quail eggs in suburban woodlots in Maryland. Next to each nest I placed a small piece of cardboard lightly coated with a dark masonry powder. A nest-robbing animal, in theory, would leave a telltale footprint on the track board. The method turned out to be far less successful than I had hoped, but it permitted me to identify six predators: opossum, raccoon, striped skunk, dog, cat, and blue jay. All are animals that benefit mightily from their association with people, some because they are kept as pets, others because they raid our garbage cans, and still others because we intentionally attract them to our homes by supplying food. Neotropical migrants are particularly vulnerable to nest predators because many species construct open, cuplike nests, which they place on or near the ground. Titmice, chickadees, and woodpeckers—all nonmigratory species—nest in the relative security of tree cavities and are less likely to be harmed by these predators.

Finally, urban and rural woodlots no longer harbor the top predators such as wolves, bobcats, or mountain lions that at one time might have kept populations of opossums, raccoons, and skunks in check. The disappearance of songbirds today is partly a consequence of the extermination of the big predators well over a century ago.

In addition to nest predators, forest songbirds must also contend with the brown-headed cowbird, a parasitic blackbird that lays its eggs in the nests of other birds. The female cowbird usually removes an egg from the host's nest and substitutes one of her own. The cowbird nestling tends to hatch sooner and grow faster than the host's own offspring, often starving them to death or crowding them out of the nest. Prior to the arrival of white settlers, cowbirds were most common in the midcontinent, where they followed the herds of bison and ate the insects stirred up by the big mammals. As eastern forests were converted to farm fields and pasturelands, cowbirds increased in numbers and spread eastward. Today, they seem as content perched on the back of a cow in Maine as they do atop a bison in Montana. The waste grain that remains in farm fields after harvesting has proved to be a valuable winter food source for cowbirds, enabling more of them to survive this traditionally lean period of the year. Still other cowbirds find sustenance at the bird feeders maintained by kind-hearted homeowners throughout the country. The world, in short, has become a bigger and richer place for cowbirds.

Many of the bird species traditionally parasitized by cowbirds have developed their own defensive strategies, the result of eons of cat-and-mouse games between the two camps. These potential hosts can recognize a foreign egg in their nests and will either toss it out or abandon the nest altogether. But most of the forest-dwelling songbirds of the East are not so clever. They have had little evolutionary exposure to cowbirds and seem unable to recognize cowbird eggs or nestlings as different from their own offspring; consequently, they are easy targets. The Kirtland's warbler, the handsome black, gray, and yellow songbird that nests exclusively in a small area of jack pine forest in central Michigan, was nearly extirpated by cowbirds. During the 1960s, cowbirds were parasitizing 70 percent of the nests, far more than would allow the warbler to sustain itself. A cowbird control program was implemented, sharply reducing the incidence of parasitism and saving the species from almost certain extinction. But the price we must pay to keep the Kirtland's warbler with us is eternal vigilance: If the control programs are ever stopped, the warbler will surely vanish.

Is the Kirtland's warbler an extreme case, or does it represent a sign of things to come? In portions of Illinois, ornithologists have recorded parasitism rates of 75 to 100 percent in populations of wood thrushes, hooded warblers, red-eyed vireos, summer tanagers, and other forest songbirds. Such rates are vastly above the levels that would permit these songbirds to sustain themselves—so high, in fact, that one wonders how any birds at all survive in Illinois. Perhaps Illinois's songbird populations are sustained by emigrants from larger populations in the Ozarks, where forest cover is more extensive and rates of cowbird parasitism are correspondingly lower. Or perhaps we are missing some crucial insight into the dynamics of cowbirds and their hosts, some quirk of population biology that enables the hosts to persist despite intense parasitism. Optimists cling to the latter hope, while realists bet on the former and predict that, should the Ozark forests become as fragmented as those of Illinois, songbird numbers throughout the Midwest would plummet. As odd as it seems, only our largest forest pre-serves—those precious few national parks and national forests containing thousands or tens of thousands of acres of protected forests each—may be up to the task of safeguarding our forest songbirds.

Songbirds are not the only creatures to suffer because the big predators of the East have been eradicated. The absence of these predators may be contributing to an overabundance of white-tailed deer, turning growing numbers of farmers, home-owners, and biologists against an animal that has long symbol-ized all that is gentle and graceful in nature. With wolves and mountain lions long gone, hunting is now the principal check on deer numbers. Hunters annually kill 2 to 3 million whitetails in the United States, and automobile collisions claim at least another half million. Yet these losses have not stifled the growth of the nation's whitetail population. From city parks to national parks, deer are everywhere. Farmers report increasing crop losses due to deer depredation; homeowners have seen their azaleas, yews, and backyard vegetable gardens disappear nibble by nibble; and foresters complain bitterly that deer are prevent-ing forest regeneration by consuming young trees. Deer seem to do especially well in suburban neighborhoods, where browse is plentiful and hunters nonexistent. They have rebounded from less than half a million individuals in the United States at the end of the nineteenth century to between 18 and 25 million today. During the 1980s, Maryland's deer population virtually tripled. New York's deer population has doubled over the past 20 years. In Indiana, kills by hunters—an index of overall population size—jumped 400 percent during the 1980s.

Unfortunately, the small pockets of wilderness that we have set aside as nature preserves are sometimes unable to sustain high numbers of deer without considerable ecological damage. Biologists in many parts of the East have reported declines in native plant species due to deer. In Maryland's Catoctin Mountain Park, for example, browsing by deer has nearly eliminated the purple-fringed orchids; park officials now place fences around individual plants to protect them from the deer herds. Botanists working in Wisconsin's Chequamegon National Forest have asserted that an overabundance of deer is preventing certain plants, including hemlocks and yews, from regenerating, while in the Great Smoky Mountains, areas with large deer populations have lost over a quarter of their herbaceous (non-woody) plant species. Some state game departments have increased the number of deer a hunter can legally kill and are encouraging the harvest of more does, but whether these steps will actually reduce deer densities remains to be seen. In the meantime, we would do well to ponder what we mean by an overabundance of deer. By most accounts, the number of white-tails in the country today is equal to or less than the number that existed at the time of the Pilgrims. The problem is that open space has been dramatically reduced. Squeezing an equivalent number of deer into a smaller amount of predator-free habitat has produced a host of ecological imbalances.

One can be at least mildly optimistic that a solution to the deer problem will be found, perhaps through expanded hunting seasons, the development of a new contraceptive, or—dare one hope?—the reintroduction of wolves and mountain lions into the wildest areas. But another, more serious threat to the integrity of our forests is less likely to be foiled: the systematic elimination of trees, one species at a time, by introduced diseases and pests. The most famous example is the American chestnut. Until the beginning of the twentieth century, the American chestnut was one of the most important trees of the eastern forest, numerically, economically, and ecologically. In parts of the Appalachians, over 30 percent of the canopy trees were chestnuts. It was a massive tree, reaching nearly 100 feet in height and 4 feet in diameter, and produced prodigious amounts of meaty nuts. It was prized for its wood, used to make furniture, musical instruments, and caskets; its tannin; and its nuts, which were eaten by humans and livestock alike. Chestnuts were also consumed by a variety of wild animals, including black bears, white-tailed deer, and turkeys.

A fungus, accidentally brought to the United States in 1904 in a shipment of Asian chestnut trees destined for a nursery, caused the ecological extinction of the American chestnut. The blight swept across the country, turning hundreds of millions of chestnuts into leafless corpses and eliminating the species as a canopy tree. It was a loss comparable to the extinction of the passenger pigeon, and like that horrific event, one whose consequences are still poorly understood. This much we know: Like a Roman legion closing ranks, oak and hickory seedlings grew to fill in the canopy gaps created by the death of the chestnuts; an important food source for wildlife was eliminated; and six or more species of native moths that laid their eggs in the foliage of chestnut trees are now presumed extinct (other species dependent upon the American chestnut have surely vanished, too, but we have no record of them).

American chestnuts possess the remarkable ability to sprout from their stumps, and throughout the eastern forests, one still finds an abundance of small, spindly chestnut sprouts. Before the sprouts have much of a chance to grow, however, they are inevitably attacked and killed by the fungus. The stump then sends up another batch of sprouts, which suffer the same fate. The cycle repeats over and over again until the root stock eventually dies. To some ecologists, the sprouts are a curiosity, a living example of how brutally an introduced pathogen can destroy a naive host. To my eyes, they are a pathetic lot, each cluster marking the spot where less than a century ago, something grander and more beautiful stood.

One might be tempted to dismiss the whole matter of the chestnut blight as an ugly historical accident—a cautionary tale about the importance of inspecting imported plants and animals—were it not for the fact that the same story is repeating itself over and over again. Dutch elm disease, caused by a fungus accidentally imported from Europe around 1930, has eliminated American elms from many forests and residential areas. The hemlock woolly adelgid, a tiny Asian insect, was first spotted on the East Coast in 1951 and is now killing eastern hemlocks from New England to the southern Appalachians. The related balsam woolly adelgid, brought over from Europe in 1908 (again, accidentally), is responsible for destroying an entire ecosystem: the forests of Fraser firs and red spruces that once occurred exclusively atop a few mountains in the southern Appalachians. The adelgids target the Fraser firs, but many of the spruce trees die as well, perhaps because with the firs gone, they are more vulnerable to airborne pollutants and high winds. The results, as visitors to the Great Smoky Mountains see all too clearly, are mountaintops covered with dead and dying trees. The demise of the Fraser firs has meant significant declines in populations of nesting birds and the near-extinction of the spruce-fir moss-loving spider, a tiny relative of the tarantulas that lives within the tangles of moss on living trees. Elsewhere, the butternut fell victim to an alien fungus introduced about 1967, and is now a candidate for protection as an endangered species. Finally, a fungus of unknown origin began attacking American dogwoods in the 1970s, and now threatens to eradicate them from forests throughout the East. With them will go one of the earliest and most elegant signs of spring: a burst of whiteness, like a snowfall suspended at eye level, in a forest that is just beginning to turn green.

In all, the U.S. Forest Service estimates that over three hundred alien pests, insects, and diseases are attacking America's forests, affecting oaks, pines, firs, larches, maples, willows, beeches, hemlocks, and many other species. For each of these pests, we might be able to find a control, but an endless stream of invaders will not be met with an endless stream of money. In an age of global commerce and fast transport, the spread of more pests and pathogens seems inevitable and, like the hapless victims in an Agatha Christie novel, the trees will disappear, one species at a time.

CHAPTER TWO

A Wilderness to the West

By the close of the nineteenth century, the eastern wilderness was nearly gone. The tidal wave of timber cutting that began in New England in the 1600s had swept through the central Atlantic states in the mid-1800s, moved across the Great Lakes states during the 1880s, and reached the Deep South by the end of the century. The timber companies began to gaze longingly toward the conifer forests of the Pacific coast, Cascades, Sierra Nevada, and Rockies. A thriving timber industry had been in existence since the mid-1800s along parts of the Pacific coast, servicing cities such as San Francisco and Seattle and providing wood to fuel the Gold Rush. But without a transportation infrastructure, access to most of the West's forests had been limited, sparing much of the land from the deforestation that had befallen the East. Now, at the start of a new century, an expanding railroad network and a growing West Coast population made it possible for the timber companies to target the western forests.

Ranchers, of course, had long since discovered the vast emptiness of the West—an emptiness just waiting to be filled with livestock. Starting with the Spanish colonization of the seventeenth century and reaching a zenith at the close of the nineteenth, most of the West became a giant rangeland, harboring millions upon millions of cattle and sheep. Along with their livestock, the ranchers brought their customary hatred of big predators, a hatred that would blossom into a government-sponsored campaign to extirpate grizzlies, wolves, coyotes, and other species from the region.

Federal, state, and territorial authorities saw the exploitation of the West's natural resources as a necessary means to settling and developing the frontier; the country's nascent conservation movement feared this development would devastate the region's forests and wildlands. Thus, the lines were drawn for a battle that has lasted well over a century, a battle between competing visions and traditions, between those who would break the wilderness and use its resources for the betterment of society versus those who argue that there is no better use of the land than wilderness itself. Every year the actual battlefield shrinks in size, diminished by each clearcut and each mile of road punched into the remaining wilderness; consequently, the stakes get higher and the disputes become more rancorous.

Complicating the search for any simple resolution to such conflicts is the complexity of the land itself. The Rocky Mountains, Cascades, and Sierra Nevada run like parallel spines down the continent, creating gradients in elevation and rainfall that foster a diverse array of ecosystems. Different ecosystems, in turn, respond in different ways to natural disturbances such as fires, ice storms, floods, and landslides. To understand the recent ecological history of the western forests and rangelands, then, one must first understand how the human imprint on the land, typically manifested in the form of logging and ranching, interacts with the natural disturbances that have always been a part of the scene.

We shall begin by focusing on two regions of the West where the interplay of natural and human disturbances has altered the richness and abundance of wildlife in markedly different ways. One is the Greater Yellowstone region, encompassing 18 million acres of some of the wildest, most scenic land in the coterminous United States, including our oldest and most famous national park. The other is a giant band of forest, consisting largely of ponderosa pines, that stretches across northern and central Arizona. Here the same activities that have changed the face of Yellowstone—logging, grazing, predator control, and fire suppression—have been pursued with equal vigor, but the consequences have been very different. Finally, we shall briefly consider the magnificent forests of the Sierra Nevada and the Pacific Northwest.

Yellowstone National Park captured the nation's attention in the summer of 1988 when extensive wildfires ripped through it and the surrounding national forests. Millions of Americans watched in disbelief as images of the fires dominated the evening news. Against a backdrop of charred stumps, reporters solemnly announced that the nation's oldest national park had been destroyed. Frightened residents of the small towns dotting the perimeter of the park anxiously waited to see if the flames would engulf their homes and businesses, and wondered who was to blame.

Over the course of the summer, 25,000 men and women tried to contain the fires by digging 665 miles of fire lines, bulldozing 137 miles of firebreaks, and dumping 1.2 million gallons of fire retardant and 8.4 million gallons of water on the flames, at a cost of about $120 million. It was the largest effort at fire control in the nation's history, and it was essentially futile. Autumn rains and cooler temperatures, not firefighters, put an end

to the fires of 1988. By the time the smoke cleared, approximately 1.4 million acres in the Greater Yellowstone region
had burned, including 990,000 acres within the park itself.
There were calls for the resignations of the director
of the National Park Service and the superintendent of
Yellowstone, as well as strident accusations that none of this
would have happened had the Park Service somehow acted
more responsibly. The main problem, critics asserted, was the
Park Service's new fire policy.

In the late 1800s and early 1900s, a series of fierce wildfires,
many caused by sloppy logging practices, had swept across millions of acres in the northern Great Lakes region and the Northwest, burning forests, destroying towns, and killing hundreds of
people. This destruction, coupled with growing fears of a timber
shortage, prompted a national effort to prevent and suppress
wildfires. Almost from the time of the park's establishment in
1872, the custodians of Yellowstone had been willing participants
in this endeavor, working hard to put out all fires within its borders, regardless of whether they were started by humans or lightning. But it was not until after World War II that Yellowstone
had enough resources at its command to do so effectively.

By the late 1950s, however, a growing number of scientists
had begun to question the wisdom of routinely suppressing all
fires within national parks, given that wildfires are a natural part
of many ecosystems. For proof that fires "belonged" in national
parks, they argued, one had only to look at the trees. The cones
of most lodgepole pines, the dominant tree species in Yellowstone, will not open and release their seeds unless they are
heated by flames, a clear indication they have adapted to fiery
environments. Also, meadows and rangelands, which constitute
important habitats for a variety of animals, become choked with
brush if they do not burn on occasion.

Faced with mounting evidence of the ecological importance
of fire, in 1972 Yellowstone changed its fire management policy
from one of immediate suppression to one that is frequently but
inaccurately termed a "let-burn" approach. Under the revised
guidelines, lightning-caused fires in the park were allowed to
burn, provided they did not threaten human life, property,

cultural sites, or natural features of special value, such as the habitats of endangered species. Natural fires that did not meet these conditions, as well as all those caused by humans, were immediately suppressed. Each and every fire had to be evaluated in light of these criteria, with the result that many apparently natural fires were quickly suppressed.

Even in the calamitous summer of 1988, only 31 of the 248 fires in the Greater Yellowstone area were allowed to burn for any length of time; firefighters fought to extinguish the others as quickly as possible (with little success, however, due largely to the weather). Seven fires that summer were responsible for 95 percent of the area burned, and 5 of these originated *outside* the park's boundaries. Although it may have been politically expedient to blame the Park Service for the events of 1988, doing so was pointless. The real culprit was the forest itself. Its combustible nature, combined with hot, dry, windy weather, made the fires of 1988 inevitable and unstoppable. But that forest, made to burn, was also blessed with the phoenix-like ability to rise from its own ashes.

There is, in fact, historical precedent for the seemingly unprecedented events of 1988. Studies of tree rings and burn patterns reveal that comparable fires swept through the Yellowstone region between 1690 and 1710 and again between 1730 and 1750. That fires of this magnitude did not occur again for almost three centuries may simply reflect the fact that for most of that time the trees were younger and less flammable. Fire suppression after World War II may have delayed the onset of the fires—even made them more extensive by allowing more dead wood to accumulate in the forests—but it could not change what was destined to happen in 1988: another major conflagration in a place that has burned in the past and will burn again in the future.

The immediate effect of the fires on Yellowstone's wildlife was surprisingly minor. Approximately 1 percent of the 31,000 elk summering in the park perished, along with an even smaller percentage of the park's bison, moose, and mule deer. The following winter, biologists recorded exceptionally high rates of mortality within the park's elk herds, which they attributed to a heavy snowpack coupled with fire damage to important wintering areas. Between one-half and one percent of the park's grizzlies were thought to have died, along with vast numbers of smaller creatures such as reptiles and rodents, but apparently not a single animal species was extirpated from the park by the fires.

What has changed—and changed profoundly—is the age profile and structure of the forests. Hundreds of thousands of acres of older forest have been replaced by regenerating stands. Animals that thrive in recently burned areas, such as black-backed woodpeckers, olive-sided flycatchers, and mountain bluebirds, have prospered, while those associated with older stands, such as pine martens and great gray owls, have presumably declined. Such ebbs and flows are a natural feature of Yellowstone, as much a part of its character as Old Faithful, and ordinarily nothing to worry about. Only when the ecosystem itself has been greatly diminished in size, when asphalt, condominiums, and clearcuts have whittled away at the wildlands, do natural events such as fires threaten the survival of species. Under such circumstances, populations of some animals may become too small to rebound from natural disturbances. For the moment, that does not appear to be a problem in the Greater Yellowstone region.

A visitor traveling to Yellowstone today gawks in amazement at the acres of skeleton trees and the incongruous patches of green where the flames inexplicably skipped around a patch of forest. But there are also verdant hillsides untouched by fire. From a biological perspective, everything and nothing has changed. As a panel of scientists convened to study the effects of the fires concluded, "We can state with confidence that events similar to those of 1988 have altered [Greater Yellowstone Area] ecosystems in the past. Still, the Yellowstone of 2072 will not be the same as that of 1872, just as the landscape of 1872 was unique compared with previous times. . . . Big changes occurred in 1988, and it is safe to assume that such changes will occur again in the future. Indeed, such change is the *sine que non* of wilderness." Contrary to the news reports from the summer of 1988, fire is not, and never has been, a threat to Yellowstone. The true dangers lie elsewhere—in the overabundance of certain species and the underabundance of others, and most importantly, in the exploitation of the surrounding national forests.

Today, the biggest issue bedeviling Yellowstone's administrators may be the question of what, if anything, to do about the park's thriving elk population. Elk are far and away the most numerous large mammals in Yellowstone, where they are a ubiquitous sight in the park's meadows, grasslands, and forest edges. On crisp autumn days, when the aspens have turned to gold and the skies seem impossibly blue, the bulls utter a peculiar bugling call that echoes across the valleys. Then, as snow begins to fall in the higher elevations, the elk march down to their winter range. Yellowstone's largest herd, now numbering close to 20,000 individuals, winters in the northern section of the park, along the Lamar, Yellowstone, and Gardner river drainages.

Over the course of the past century, the park's approach to managing its elk herds has gone from pampering the animals to culling them to leaving them alone. The one truly consistent feature has been controversy. For a decade or so after Yellowstone was established in 1872, hunting went unchecked, until control of the land was turned over to the U.S. Cavalry and eventually the National Park Service (which was created in 1916). For years, the Army and then the Park Service zealously protected the elk, eradicating their predators and supplying the herds with additional food during the winter. In response to pleas from western ranchers, the U.S. Biological Survey, predecessor of today's Fish and Wildlife Service, had recommended a national campaign to exterminate wolves at the beginning of the century. In 1914, Congress made the Biological Survey the nation's chief predator control agency, a responsibility it carried out with ruthless efficiency. Within 12 years, rangers had killed at least 136 wolves in Yellowstone. Eventually, the wolves were completely eliminated from the park and surrounding lands. So successful, in fact, was the extermination program that the Rocky Mountain wolf was added to the federal endangered species list in 1974. Yellowstone's mountain lions and wolverines were also shot, trapped, and poisoned almost to oblivion.

One might have predicted that the park's elk, now finding themselves in a well-guarded, predator-free home, would
explode in numbers. Unfortunately, historical records of
Yellowstone's elk population are confusing and fraught with
errors, making it impossible to reconstruct population trends
with great confidence. The data suggest the northern herd
may have numbered around 1,500 individuals in the late
1870s, when hunting was widespread, increasing to 20,000–
30,000 by 1919, after a period of protection (although some
scientists doubt the number was that high). Regardless of
what the actual population was, by the 1920s wildlife managers were convinced that Yellowstone's northern elk herd
was exceeding the capacity of its winter range. Thousands
were removed from Yellowstone by park officials. Some animals were captured alive and released elsewhere; others were
killed and butchered, and the meat donated to charity.
Culling kept the winter herd at around 8,000–10,000 individuals from the 1930s through the 1950s, and as low as
3,172 in 1968.

In the 1960s, however, the elk reduction program became
increasingly unpopular for two reasons. First, as Yellowstone's
herds dwindled, fewer animals strayed outside the park where
hunters could take them. Hunters, outfitters, and guides began to see the reductions as harmful to their interests, and
they brought the issue to the attention of their congressional
representatives. Second, the Park Service itself was moving
away from a policy of intensive wildlife management toward
one that favored natural processes. In 1963, a National Parks
Advisory Committee, appointed by the Secretary of the
Interior and chaired by wildlife biologist A. Starker Leopold,
concluded that the goal of the national parks should be to
maintain the land "as nearly as possible in the condition that
prevailed when the area was first visited by the white man.
A national park should represent a vignette of primitive
America. . . . [O]bservable artificiality in any form must
be minimized and obscured in every possible way." Although
the Leopold committee did not oppose Yellowstone's elk

reduction program, its report has been wrongly interpreted as a condemnation of hands-on management of wildlife populations.

In 1969, the Park Service ended the removal program, citing a new understanding of the dynamics of elk populations. Yellowstone's elk, park scientists concluded, would be held in check by the process of "natural regulation." In the absence of human interference, elk numbers would be controlled by a combination of density-dependent factors and severe winter storms. If the population grew too large, the resulting competition for food would reduce numbers to a more sustainable level. If an unusually harsh winter dropped the population below the capacity of the range, the elk would rebound. Thus, while the number of elk might fluctuate over the course of time, it should stay within more or less stable bounds. Similarly, barring any change in climate, these principles should apply to the plants eaten by the elk as well—roughly the same amount of aspen and willow should be present in the park each year. If this paradigm of natural regulation is correct, visitors to Yellowstone today should see an ecosystem that is similar to the one that awed explorers in the mid- to late 1800s.

Or should they? The Indians who lived in the region for millennia, setting fires and hunting wild game, are gone. Predators such as grizzly bears and wolverines are reduced in numbers. And some of the areas outside the park where Yellowstone's elk traditionally spent the winter have been destroyed by development, perhaps causing the animals to remain inside the park. Have these changes significantly altered the Yellowstone ecosystem?

Comparisons of photographs taken inside the park in the late 1800s, early 1900s, and 1980s reveal major changes in the vegetation. In the oldest photographs, the stands of aspen contain trees of many different sizes and ages, including short, young plants. Their trunks are white and unscarred down to the ground, and numerous shrubs and forbs are growing beneath the trees. In later photographs, the young trees are gone, and only the tall, old ones remain, indicative of extensive browsing by elk. The lower portions of the trunks are blackish, a sign of scar tissue that develops when browsing animals have stripped off the bark. And grasses have replaced shrubs and forbs in the understory, another indication of extensive browsing. Tall willows, a favorite food of elk, have also declined inside Yellowstone. In 41 of 44 photographic comparisons, the tall willow stands had totally disappeared. In the other three photo sets, only about 10 percent of the original willows remained.

Factors other than elk have been proposed to explain the changes in Yellowstone's vegetation, including fire suppression, climate change, and natural succession. But in places where elk cannot browse the vegetation, including some fenced areas in the park, aspen and willows are growing vigorously, suggesting these other factors alone cannot account for the observed vegetation changes. At the very least, if climate change is stressing the park's aspen and willow stands, then browsing by elk is making it that much harder for these plants to survive. The case against the elk appears to be strong, and it is certainly consistent with what we have seen in other parts of the country where deer populations have increased in the absence of predators.

In the opinion of some ecologists, the decrease in aspen and willow has had ripple effects elsewhere within the Yellowstone ecosystem. Beavers, which use both aspen and willow for food and dam building, appear to have declined precipitately within the park. Reported to be common from the 1830s through the early 1900s, they are now "for all practical purposes . . . ecologically absent from the northern range." Their disappearance is particularly significant because they are a keystone species within the Yellowstone ecosystem. According to one study, a beaverless creek in the northern Rockies contains only about 4 to 8 acres of riverbank ("riparian") or wetland habitat per stream mile; beavers expand the riparian zone to nearly 40 acres per mile.

The loss of riparian habitat stemming from the decline in beavers has been cited as the cause of a decline in the park's small population of white-tailed deer. Other animals, ranging from songbirds to trout to grizzlies, are alleged to have suffered as well, although the evidence in these cases is at best weak and circumstantial. Nonetheless, few scientists would dispute the notion that beavers are a critical component of the Yellowstone ecosystem. If their demise (or that of other species) can be linked to the presence of too many elk, then the Park Service faces a difficult dilemma: Should it correct the situation, and if so, how?

First of all, it is far from clear what a "healthy" Yellowstone should look like. Most scientists have assumed that this part of the country always sustained a healthy, diverse population of ungulates, including elk, bison, bighorn sheep, mule deer, white-tailed deer, and pronghorn. But after reviewing the journals from twenty separate expeditions conducted in the Greater Yellowstone region from 1835 to 1876, ecologist Charles Kay reached a surprising (and controversial) conclusion: Big game was scarce in the park and surrounding areas during this period. Out of a total of 765 days spent in the Yellowstone region by these explorers, elk were recorded on only forty-two occasions, for an average of one elk observation every 18 days. Bison were even scarcer, with only three sightings logged during the entire time. Because the habitat is obviously capable of supporting much bigger game populations than these observations indicate, Kay attributes the historical scarcity of large mammals to hunting by Indian tribes living in the area. (The Park Service, it should be noted, does not accept Kay's hypothesis; its historians point out that some of the early explorers reported an abundance of big game. The relevant question then becomes one of frequency: How often were large numbers of elk and bison sighted? Kay's calculations would suggest not often.)

If the Park Service were to take literally the Leopold Committee's recommendation that "the biotic associations within each park be maintained . . . as nearly as possible in the condition that prevailed when the area was first visited by the white man," and if Kay's overhunting hypothesis is correct (a big "if"), then the Park Service would be forced to reduce ungulate numbers to a level plainly unacceptable to most people. An alternative might be to foster conditions similar to those that existed at the close of the nineteenth century, after the Indians had been driven from the park but before the intensive manipulation of predators and prey by the Park Service.

Recreating those conditions requires restoration of the park's missing predators, a step the federal government has finally taken. Starting in the 1960s, environmentalists lobbied the Department of the Interior to reintroduce gray wolves into the park, but until recently all such plans were uncompromisingly squelched by ranchers and their obedient representatives in Congress. In the late 1980s, however, congressional resistance began to weaken in the face of strong public support for wolf reintroduction—according to a 1989 Park Service poll, visitors to Yellowstone supported it by a 6–1 margin—and a mandate under the Endangered Species Act that federal agencies use their authority to recover endangered species. In January 1995, 14 wolves were trapped in Canada and transported to Yellowstone National Park in the first of several planned reintroductions. They spent their first few weeks confined to large outdoor pens, guarded around the clock by employees of the same federal agencies that were responsible for eradicating their ancestors. In March, with a delegation of reporters and government potentates looking on, the animals were released from their pens, marking a new and uneasy détente between people and predators in the American West.

Freed from their cages, the wolves have thrived beyond all expectations, forming packs, reproducing, and preying upon the park's abundant ungulates. By the beginning of 1998, Yellowstone's wolf population had increased to 84, and ecologists were already beginning to detect significant changes in the ecosystem. In some areas, 50 percent or more of the coyotes have been killed or displaced by wolves, as the latter reclaim their position of dominance in Yellowstone. Because coyotes are voracious consumers of voles, ground squirrels, and pocket gophers, biologists are predicting that a diminished coyote population will translate into more food for the park's owls, hawks, badgers, foxes, and pine martens; anecdotal observations suggest these other predators are, in fact, on the increase. The wolves themselves have exhibited an overwhelming preference for elk. In the northern range, where elk are most abundant, each wolf pack has killed an average of 150 to 175 elk per year.

Moose, bison, and deer have also been taken, but at a much lower rate. The resulting carcasses have provided additional food for the park's many scavengers, including its grizzly bears, eagles, ravens, foxes, and even coyotes.

It is still too early to judge how great an effect the wolves will have on Yellowstone's elk. The U.S. Fish and Wildlife Service estimates that a fully restored wolf population in Yellowstone could reduce populations of elk by 5–30 percent (the 30 percent value applying only to some small herds), deer by 3–19 percent, moose by 7–13 percent, and bison by up to 15 percent. Other models predict no significant reduction in elk numbers. Even if wolves do not significantly reduce the number of elk, their presence may force the herds to move around more, thereby decreasing the amount of time they spend in the aspen and willow stands.

But what if the wolves have little effect on the elk? What next? The federal government could attempt to purchase additional land to serve as winter range for the northern herd, but in an era of tight budgets and anti-federal sentiment, the prospects of doing so are slim. Moreover, there is little evidence that purchasing more winter range would solve the problem. Should the park then go back to shooting or capturing elk to reduce the herd? Many people (myself included) are reluctant to condone a policy of intensive management of wildlife populations in national parks, but if Charles Kay and other critics of Yellowstone's "natural regulation" philosophy are correct, what other options remain? One ecologist, who is convinced that the large elk population is devastating the park, has framed the decision facing the public as follows:

> If people want a drive-through game park with large numbers of animals standing around to provide car-window photo ops, such as prevails today, then so be it. But they need to know that the consequences of eliminating biodiversity are the ultimate conversion of the northern range into an elk pasture. The latter will be mostly exotic grasses, largely devoid of woody vegetation and its associated animal life, and with bare, sloughing stream banks.

If, on the other hand, the public wants its national park to contain a diverse, healthy, intact ecosystem in a sea of human-altered landscapes, then it will take active management. . . . This will include reduction and control of the elk herd by one or more of the several means available, and quite possibly reduction of bison as well.

The debate over Yellowstone's elk is essentially a debate over what it means to protect a piece of nature. At a time when the wilderness is steadily shrinking, when human influences, past and present, are ubiquitous, the option of laissez-faire management is no longer available. The Park Service understands this, and so do its critics. The question is how intensively we should manipulate those few precious places we had the foresight to set aside in order to escape an overmanipulated world of our own making.

In the long term, however, the greatest threats to Yellowstone lie outside its borders, not inside. When Congress established the park in 1872, its primary motivation was to protect the geysers, mudpots, and other geothermal features of the region. The boundaries were drawn more or less as a giant rectangle, measuring approximately 63 by 54 miles and containing over 2.2 million acres of wildlands. An enormous park by anyone's standards, Yellowstone is nonetheless too small to sustain a viable population of grizzlies within its borders, or even to encompass all of the wintering ranges of its elk and bison herds. Crucial to the well-being of these and other species are the 11 million acres of federally owned national forests surrounding the park: the Gallatin and Custer National Forests to the north, the Bridger-Teton to the south, the Shoshone to the east, and the Beaverhead, Targhee, and Caribou to the west. An additional 3.2 million acres of privately owned land also can be considered part of this "Greater Yellowstone Ecosystem."

Unlike national parks, national forests are managed under a multiple-use mandate, according to which logging, grazing, mining, and oil and gas extraction are considered legitimate uses of the land. To the U.S. Forest Service falls the unenviable task of balancing these activities against its obligation to protect wildlife. Yet neither the Forest Service nor the legislators who oversee this agency have historically shown much inclination toward "balance"; instead, they have permitted—even encouraged—resource development at the expense of the region's wildlands and wildlife. To fully appreciate this point, one need only take an airplane flight across the boundary between Yellowstone National Park and the Targhee National Forest. A clean, straight line, as sharply delineated as the lines on a map, separates the park from the national forest. To the west are clearcuts—miles and miles of clearcuts, courtesy of the Forest Service—while to the east lie the untouched pine forests of the park.

After World War II, a booming housing industry and a growing economy raised the demand for wood. In response to political pressure, the Forest Service increased logging in the national forests, including those surrounding Yellowstone. Annual harvest levels in the seven forests climbed from 79 million board feet in 1961 to nearly 160 million in 1970 to over 200 million throughout most of the 1980s. In the process, the agency built over 6,600 miles of logging roads—enough to travel from New York to California and back again. Hundreds of thousands of acres of wildlands have been dissected by roads and clearcuts. In fairness to the Forest Service, it should be noted that no species has yet vanished from the Yellowstone ecosystem on account of logging. But the roads and attendant human activity have displaced grizzlies from large portions of the ecosystem and are widely considered to be the preeminent threat to this endangered population. The wolverine is another rare mammal that does not thrive in close proximity to people, and it too is at risk of disappearing from the region. A small number of other vertebrates, including the great gray owl and pine marten, prefer mature forests, and one may assume their numbers have declined commensurately with timber harvesting, although not to the point of endangerment. And outfitters who make their living conducting hunting expeditions complain that there are now too few elk in the forests outside the park.

Timber companies sometimes compare their handiwork with that of nature, arguing that if wildfires are a natural part of the ecology of Rocky Mountain forests, and if logging mimics wildfires, then shouldn't clearcuts be considered an acceptable substitute for the wildfires that are now so often suppressed? The flaw in this logic lies in the second assumption, that logging mimics wildfires. In particular, forest fires leave behind numerous standing dead trees, called snags, that provide important feeding, perching, and nesting sites for birds and other wildlife. Clearcuts do not. In the national forests, loggers leave behind a few dead trees when they remove the living ones from a site, but the density of snags left in a clearcut is typically much lower than that associated with a major forest fire.

Logging of the national forests surrounding Yellowstone might be easier to accept if it could be justified economically. But it can't. The government's costs for preparing sites for harvest, building logging roads, and reforestation routinely exceed the revenues collected from timber sales. According to economists at The Wilderness Society, in 1996 the Forest Service lost over $2,200,000 on its timber program in the Yellowstone region. The trees are simply too small, their rate of growth too slow, and the terrain too rough to make commercial logging a profitable enterprise.

The same can be said for grazing. More than 5 million acres of federal lands in the Yellowstone region are open to livestock grazing, providing forage for nearly 75,000 cattle and 120,000 sheep. While many ranchers are responsible users of public lands, mismanaged or overstocked herds have damaged wildlife habitat. A 1987 study decried the lack of accurate data on the condition of most federal rangelands in the Yellowstone region, but estimated that 37 percent of the rangelands within the seven national forests were in fair, poor, or very poor condition. Approximately 49 percent were judged to be in good condition, and 14 percent in excellent condition. For decades, the federal government has charged grazing fees that fall well below the rates charged on comparable private lands; not surprisingly, the grazing program in the Yellowstone region (and throughout the West) has been a money-losing proposition for the Treasury. The livestock industry has thus far blocked most efforts to bring the fees up to market rates by arguing that any significant jump would drive many ranchers out of business.

What is surprising to many people is how minor a role extractive industries such as logging and ranching play in the region's economy. The twenty counties encompassing Yellowstone and its national forests have enjoyed tremendous economic growth over the past quarter century. Between 1969 and 1989, for example, the workforce grew by 66,000 jobs, an increase of 68 percent. Personal income nearly doubled. But the source of this growth was the service industries, retail and wholesale trade, real estate, and construction, not the extractive industries. More than 94 percent of the new jobs were generated in sectors of the economy other than mining, logging, ranching, and farming. In 1969, extractive industries employed one in every three workers in the Yellowstone counties; within 20 years, that ratio had dropped to one in six. As one environmental organization noted,

> As long as public and private lands in the region continue to provide minerals, energy fuels, and timber, these industries will remain important to some communities. But extractive industries are fickle partners in economic growth. Over reliance on them has made communities highly susceptible to 'boom and bust' cycles—peaks of growth and prosperity followed by troughs of depression, unemployment, and low wages.

The Bozeman bars that once served bourbon to mining engineers now serve fine California wines to software designers, doctors, and vacationing couples. Old-timers may wince, and the whole scene is surely ripe for parody, but no one (least of all the bar owners) can ignore the fact that timber, grass, and minerals no longer fuel the economy of the northern Rockies.

This is not to say that the growing population tied to the "service sector" has no effect on wildlife. On the contrary, the conversion of large farms and ranches into countless subdivisions poses no less of a threat to the region's wildlife than the

clearcuts and mines on federal lands. The lands used for ranching and farming tended to be valley bottoms and other level
areas along watercourses—prime wintering range for large
mammals and habitat for over sixty sensitive species of plants
and animals. While ranching and farming are hardly benign
practices, they at least had the effect of keeping much of this
land in a relatively undeveloped state (a point that should not
be forgotten in the debate over grazing fees). That awkward
harmony is disappearing quickly. According to a 1991 survey,
more than a million acres in the Yellowstone region have been
subdivided into plots of 200 acres or less—evidence of a "huge
and accelerating conversion of farmland and open space to
residential use." Subdivisions mean roads, gas stations, stores,
septic tanks, lawns, golf courses, and all of the other accou-
trements people bring with them when they flee the big cities
in search of a quieter life closer to the wilderness. Consequently, the region's bighorn sheep, bald eagles, grizzlies, and
pronghorn find themselves squeezed out of yet another part of
the Yellowstone ecosystem.

One is tempted to portray Yellowstone as a symbol of what
is happening across the West, to extract from its history some
general lessons about the effects of European settlement and
extractive industries on the Western flora and fauna. Indeed,
parts of this history have been replicated throughout the
American West: the early ascendancy of the ranching and
logging industries, the jihads waged against both predators and
fire, the changing economic profile of the communities as
extractive industries give way to service-oriented ones. But, as
noted earlier, the West is a region of tremendous natural diversity, and the same ingredients mixed together in different places
can yield different results. To appreciate this fact, one need only
look some 600 miles to the south of Yellowstone, where an
almost unbroken band of ponderosa pine forest, 25 to 40 miles
wide and nearly 300 miles long, sprawls across northern and
central Arizona. Here the same activities that have changed the
face of Yellowstone—logging, grazing, predator control, and
fire suppression—have been pursued with equal vigor, but the
consequences have been quite different.

Lt. Edward Beale, commanding a band of camels that was supposed to revolutionize transportation in the Southwest, crossed northern Arizona in 1857 and again in the winter of 1858–1859. "We came to a glorious forest of lofty pines," he wrote, "through which we have travelled ten miles. The country was beautifully undulating, and although we usually associate the idea of barrenness with the pine regions, it was not so in this instance; every foot being covered with the finest grass, and beautiful broad grassy vales extending in every direction. The forest was perfectly open and unencumbered with brush wood, so that the travelling was excellent." Other travelers exploring this region in the latter half of the nineteenth century were similarly impressed with the widely spaced pines, open understory, and thick swales of bunchgrass. The annual forage production on a single acre could exceed 1600 pounds.

A visitor today encounters a very different forest. Dense thickets of young pines, firs, and oaks fill the understory, reducing visibility and hindering travel; the luxuriant bunchgrass is virtually gone; and pine trees much older than a century are few and far between. The transformation is so pervasive that a casual observer can be forgiven for thinking the forests have always looked this way. In fact, the changes occurred over a remarkably short period and were the result of two activities: livestock grazing and fire suppression.

Until the late 1800s, low-intensity fires burned through these ponderosa pine stands every 2 to 10 years. The fires rarely harmed the big pines, whose thick bark was impervious to the flames, but they killed most of the pine seedlings and shrubs growing in the understory and allowed the bunchgrasses to prosper. Most were ignited by summer lightning strikes; others were started by Indians to capture game, clear trails, and displace enemies. (In their general appearance and relationship with fire, these forests were reminiscent of the longleaf pine stands of the southeastern United States.)

The Indians living in this region managed to keep the white settlers at bay for over three hundred years—from the mid-sixteenth century to the late nineteenth. But with the defeat of the Apaches in the early 1870s, the land was ripe for settlement and exploitation. First in were the stockmen, and in less than a decade the ponderosa pine forests were overrun with sheep and cattle. A fierce two-year drought in 1892 and 1893 killed hundreds of thousands of livestock, but not before the beasts had devastated the rangelands. As the territorial governor of Arizona lamented in his annual report of 1893, "In nearly all districts, owing to overstocking, many weeds have taken the place of the best grasses. In other places where ten years ago the end of the wet season would find a rich growth of grass, now it is of inferior quality, or less quantity, or does not exist at all."

Next in were the loggers. Although Spanish settlers (and before them, Indians) had been cutting ponderosa pines for centuries, commercial logging of these forests did not begin in earnest until the end of the nineteenth century. The rate of cutting jumped sharply during the latter part of World War I and, with a few peaks and troughs along the way, continued to climb for most of the twentieth century. By the 1940s, every accessible ponderosa pine forest in Arizona and New Mexico had been heavily logged. Moreover, the growing importance of the timber industry in the Southwest strengthened the government's commitment to fighting the "scourge" of forest fires— even if those fires were responsible for creating the very forests the government was so keen to protect.

In fact, the sheep and cattle had already reduced the principal fuel for those fires by devouring the bunchgrass that once carpeted the forest floor. Whatever fires did arise as a result of summer thunderstorms were promptly suppressed by forest rangers and stockmen. Pine seedlings quickly took hold and filled in the understory, along with firs and oaks that were formerly excluded from the stands by fire. Contemporary ponderosa pine forests, therefore, consist of much denser stands of smaller, younger trees than was the case a century ago. By examining the old stumps in a regenerating ponderosa pine forest near Flagstaff, Arizona, one group of scientists concluded that the density of ponderosa pines had increased from 26 trees per acre in 1883 to 292 trees per acre in 1994; the average diameter of the trees had declined by 45 percent (largely because the big, old trees had been removed).

How all of these changes have affected the fauna of the ponderosa pine forests must remain something of a mystery, given the lack of data from a century ago. We can, however, make some educated guesses, based on knowledge of the habitat requirements of various species and the way they respond today to fire, grazing, and logging. As is so often the case, most of the relevant studies focus on birds, partly because there are so many scientists who study them and partly because birds are so easy to count. Species that nest or forage in shrubs and small trees in the understory have probably increased as a result of fire suppression, while those that forage on the ground have probably declined. Thus, we might expect to find more hermit thrushes and western tanagers and fewer chipping sparrows in today's forests than in those of a century ago. Birds that forage or nest in snags probably have declined as well, inasmuch as modern forestry, with its emphasis on short cutting cycles and fire suppression, is not conducive to snag formation. Such birds include purple martins, pygmy nuthatches, and most woodpeckers.

It should be noted, however, that no bird species associated with the ponderosa pine forests has vanished completely. (The only possible exception is the thick-billed parrot, discussed in a later chapter.) This lack of extinctions recalls the history of the eastern forests, which suffered the loss of only four birds despite extensive deforestation over the past three centuries. Like their eastern counterparts, most of the ponderosa pine birds appear capable of surviving in a wide range of forest types and stand ages. I can think of none that is restricted to virgin forests. Moreover, the amount of forest cover in the mountains of Arizona and New Mexico never dropped as precipitously as it did in the East because little of the forestland was converted to other uses, such as farms, pastures, and cities. Among mammals, the Mexican wolf and grizzly were both extirpated from this region, largely because they were considered threats to the livestock industry. Their demise had more to do with trapping, shooting, and poisoning than with habitat changes stemming from logging and fire suppression. The abundances of other mammals undoubtedly have changed as well, in much the same way bird populations have shifted, but little research has been done on this topic.

Faced with a highly unnatural forest, today's forest managers find themselves on the horns of a dilemma. There is now sufficient fuel in the form of accumulated needles, young trees, and dead trees to support a major conflagration, one large enough and hot enough to destroy even the biggest trees. That possibility appeals to no one, neither environmentalists, who want to preserve the remaining old forests, nor loggers, who depend upon them for their livelihoods. Consequently, ecologists and foresters have begun debating how to restore the magnificent open forests of a century and a half ago. Many believe the overgrown stands will need to be thinned by hand and then subjected to frequent, intentionally set and well-controlled fires—all at considerable expense. Because most of the remaining old-growth ponderosa pine forests are tucked away in wilderness areas, national parks, and other protected places, this course of action would involve intensively manipulating the vegetation in precisely those areas that have been set aside as sanctuaries. Shall we permit loggers and pyrotechnicians to cut trees and set controlled fires in such places as part of an ecological restoration project? If we do not, are we then prepared to see these forests go up in smoke when a wildfire strikes?

These questions resemble the ones asked about Yellowstone after the fires of 1988, but there are profound differences in the role fire plays in the two regions. In Yellowstone, the lodgepole pine forests are adapted to—and the product of—the great conflagrations that occur every few centuries. A few decades of fire suppression had relatively little impact on the behavior of the fires. In Arizona and New Mexico, however, the ponderosa pine forests were the product of frequent, low-intensity fires that killed the seedlings but spared the larger trees. A few decades of fire suppression, coupled with a long history of overgrazing, were enough to change the structure of the forests (by allowing the understory to develop) and hence the behavior of the fires.

Nor were such changes confined to the Southwest. Open, parklike forests once occurred in parts of Washington, Oregon, California, Idaho, Montana, Utah, and Colorado, primarily at low elevations on dry or south-facing slopes. Many of these forests were dominated by ponderosa pines; others contained a mixture of pines, firs, and Douglas-firs. All were a product of frequent, low-intensity fires, and all have been dramatically re-shaped by livestock grazing and fire suppression. In California's Sierra Nevada, for example, the stately ponderosa pine and Douglas-fir forests that inspired John Muir and countless others have changed radically over the past century. In a scenario uncannily similar to what transpired in Arizona, vast numbers of sheep released in the latter half of the nineteenth century quickly stripped the forest floor of most of its grass. Then, beginning in the early 1900s, forest managers adopted a policy of fire suppression. The result has been a buildup of needles and woody debris on the forest floor and the growth of dense stands of shade-tolerant, fire-sensitive trees (such as white firs) in the understory. Once again, land managers find they have changed the pattern of fire—from frequent, low-intensity burns that maintained open stands of widely spaced trees to sporadic, high-intensity burns capable of destroying even the largest trees.

On the west side of the Cascades and along the Pacific coast, a moister, milder climate gives rise to some of the world's tallest and most diverse evergreen forests. These are the "spotted-owl forests," the stands of ancient, towering Douglas-firs, hemlocks, cedars, and spruces that constitute the last primeval forests in America and are the subject of some of today's most divisive environmental battles. Although they share many plants and animals with the drier interior forests, the westside forests bear little resemblance to those open, park-like stands. Numerous trees of different sizes and shapes crowd the understory, creating what foresters refer to as a multilayered canopy. Fallen trees in various stages of decay are strewn across the forest floor, and snags, some of them hundreds of years old, are interspersed among the living trees. The result is a forest of tremendous structural complexity, capable of sustaining a rich array of plants and animals.

In Washington and Oregon, the most impressive stands tend to be those dominated by Douglas-firs, which can exceed 300 feet in height. Because their seedlings do not grow well under shade, Douglas-fir stands cannot replace themselves—the offspring literally are overshadowed by their parents. Western hemlock seedlings, on the other hand, are capable of growing under shady conditions; over time, they will crowd out the Douglas-firs. The Douglas-firs thus represent a transitional phase in the life of the forest, but because individual Douglas-fir trees can live for more than a thousand years, it is a long and vibrant phase. Once the western hemlocks have established themselves, however, they will dominate the stand until some cataclysmic event, such as a great fire or landslide, creates a large enough opening in the canopy for Douglas-fir seedlings to gain a foothold. A disturbance of this magnitude may occur only once every few hundred years.

Logging in the Pacific Northwest took off after World War II. Throughout the 1960s, 1970s, and 1980s, literally thousands of square miles of old-growth forests were leveled. Virtually all of this harvesting was done via clearcutting. The cleared sites were then replanted with seedlings or allowed to regenerate naturally. Thus, the primary ecological effect of the timber industry in the Northwest has been a severe and sudden change in the age distribution of the forests—from a landscape dominated by ancient stands to one that now consists largely of much younger ones. Studies conducted by The Wilderness Society reveal that nearly 90 percent of the old-growth forests west of the Cascades in Washington and Oregon have been logged. The remaining 10 percent are located almost exclusively in national forests.

Because of logging, the plants and animals that depend upon older stands are now at considerable risk of extinction.

The most famous denizen of the ancient forests is, of course, the northern spotted owl, a bird of considerable charm and controversy. Studies initiated as far back as the 1960s revealed the affinity of these owls for older forests; few of the birds live in the younger stands, and none can abide the clearcuts. Moreover, much to the chagrin of the loggers, each pair of owls requires an inordinate amount of old-growth forest for the purposes of staking out a territory and raising their young. The territory of a single pair can easily contain 600 to 2,500 acres of ancient forest, a veritable Fort Knox of wood.

Given these attributes, the spotted owl quickly became the focal point of many of the legal battles waged in the Pacific Northwest during the 1980s and early 1990s. But it is hardly the only species tied to the old-growth forests. The marbled murrelet, a small relative of the puffins, leads a remarkable dual existence: it spends most of its time on the ocean, catching small fish and crustaceans, but nests within the branches of the tallest trees in the oldest forests. These little seabirds will fly 15 or more miles inland to find a suitable forest for nesting. Both the murrelet and the northern spotted owl have been added to the endangered species list due to the loss of old-growth forests. Scientists have identified 1,000–8,000 other species that appear to be tied to the old-growth forests. The vast majority are mosses, insects, mollusks, fungi, and other small creatures, very few of which have been studied in detail. Further research may reveal that some of these creatures are capable of surviving in younger stands; it may also uncover still more species that require old-growth forests for their survival.

It is surely not the age per se of the forests that matters to these plants and animals. Rather, they are drawn to the old-growth forests by certain structural features associated with age, such as a multilayered canopy, snags, decaying logs, and moss-covered branches. Few of these features are present in younger stands, especially those that are planted and maintained by timber companies for the purposes of wood production. But, as the exception that proves the rule, in a few places in northern California, large numbers of spotted owls occur in redwood forests that are only 50 to 80 years old. In these places, a long growing season combined with highly productive soils, abundant rainfall, and the ability of redwoods to resprout from their stumps means that young forests assume many of the structural characteristics of old-growth stands at an early age. Although some people have argued that the presence of spotted owls in these young redwood stands is "proof" that the owls do not require old-growth forests, it only means that the owls can survive in young forests that look like old forests—which most young forests do not.

Fortunately for the spotted owls and other denizens of the old forests, much of their remaining acreage has been declared off-limits to further logging. In 1994, the Clinton administration decided that it would no longer permit logging in nearly 4 million acres of older forests on federal lands in Washington, Oregon, and northern California. (An additional 3 million acres had been protected by previous administrations and Congress.) The decision to spare these forests, given their immense value as lumber, surely ranks as one of the great conservation victories of the past half century. It also marks a dramatic and welcome step in the evolution of the Forest Service from an agency focused myopically on timber cutting to a far more responsible and sophisticated steward of the land and its natural resources.

Many conservationists now speak of the desirability of restoring some of the younger, cutover forests to a condition approximating their original character. In the case of the spotted-owl forests, the key ingredient is probably patience: it will take centuries for many of today's clearcuts to regenerate forests approaching the primeval stands in diversity and complexity. In the arid interior, patience alone may not be sufficient. Restoring the current crop of overcrowded young trees to open, park-like stands of ponderosa pine will require risky, controversial steps, such as selectively thinning some stands and then burning them. Whether the public is willing to accept such actions (and whether those actions will work) is anyone's guess. In the meantime, many western legislators and forestry officials speak of a forest health "crisis," as though the changes in these forests have come about suddenly or unexpectedly, when in fact they are the product of over a century of ecological insensitivity and exploitation.

By accident and by intent, we have profoundly altered many of the forests of the West—not in the crude, even brutish way we "altered" the eastern forests by cutting them down to create farms and cities, but in a subtler fashion. With a combination of hubris and zeal, Westerners sought to eliminate two key elements of their landscape—predators and fire—to make the world safer for livestock and timber. To a remarkable degree, they succeeded, if one measures success by the billions of board feet of timber and billions of cattle and sheep that have been extracted from the land. If, on the other hand, one values the number of grizzlies as highly as the number of cows, if one wishes to hike through an old-growth ponderosa pine forest, catch a cutthroat trout in a clear, cold stream, or see a spotted owl, then these traditional measures of success have little meaning.

In fact, the industries that once played such a crucial role in the settlement and development of the West, such as logging, mining, and ranching, are no longer the engines driving the economies of most western states. On the contrary, a growing number of people now view the continued exploitation of these forests and other wildlands as a threat to their quality of life and in some cases their livelihoods. Laws and policies that have long encouraged and even subsidized the exploitation of natural resources are under assault from conservationists. Yet traditions die hard in the West, and those who would maintain the status quo—the people who earn an honest living cutting timber, extracting minerals, and raising cattle—have launched a spirited counteroffensive, giving rise to some of the nation's most contentious environmental battles. These battles often assume the form of arguments about numbers—How many acres of wilderness should be protected in Montana? How much money should the Forest Service charge for the timber it sells to logging companies? How many cattle should be allowed to graze in the national forests?—but no arithmetic can solve the fundamental problem: The West just isn't big enough to satisfy everyone anymore.

CHAPTER THREE

A Sea of Grass

I f the West is now the front line for many of the nation's conservation battles, it is partly because we have all but raised the white flag when it comes to defending an equally fascinating but far more imperiled landscape: the once vast grasslands of the mid-continent. Lacking the raw physical beauty of the West or the soothing forest cover of the East, the central plains have never captured the public's imagination the way those other places have. For all too many people, the central plains are merely a transition zone—a place to get beyond en route to somewhere else. Sealed within an air-conditioned car on a broiling July afternoon, crossing miles upon miles of corn, soybean, and wheat fields, a visitor can be forgiven for hurrying onward to Yellowstone, the Grand Canyon, or Disneyland. But there was a time not too long ago when this same land harbored herds of grazing mammals comparable to those of the Serengeti, an abundance of birds and wildflowers, and a sizable and diverse community of American Indians.

Today, most of the parts—the individual species—are still around, but the whole has been shattered. The grasslands that once stretched from the Mississippi River to the foothills of the Rockies and from Canada to the heart of Texas have been plowed and paved and splintered into countless pieces; the great herds of bison and pronghorns have been supplanted by cattle and corn; the frequent wildfires that helped to maintain the open grasslands have been suppressed; the surface water and groundwater have been redistributed to facilitate intensive agriculture; and the productivity of the land has been redirected toward nourishing a single species: us.

Small wonder, then, that grasslands are among the most underrepresented ecosystems in our national park system, or that a child can grow up in Illinois or South Dakota and have no idea what a bona fide prairie looks, sounds, and smells like. Under siege and underappreciated, the central plains qualify as one of America's most abused ecosystems.

Biologists traditionally divide the central grasslands into three regions—tallgrass, mixed-grass, and shortgrass—distinguished by differences in the height and composition of the vegetation. Although this three-part classification is rightfully considered by many ecologists to be a rather crude way to represent the diversity of grassland types in the mid-continent, it makes a certain amount of sense to the eye, and it highlights a number of important ecological differences between the eastern and western portions. I shall stick with it for that reason.

The tallgrass prairie once occupied the eastern third of the central plains, a region of approximately 148 million acres extending from southern Manitoba to southern Texas and from Kentucky to Nebraska. With soils well suited for farming, the tallgrass prairie has been all but obliterated, with less than 4 percent remaining, mostly in the form of tiny, isolated patches surrounded by a sea of corn and soybeans. To the east, the tallgrass merges into the eastern deciduous forests; to the west, it merges into the mixed-grass prairie, a band of drier, shorter grassland that once stretched from Alberta to Texas. And in the driest and westernmost portions of the central plains, from the western Dakotas to the northern part of Texas, the mixed grass merges into the shortgrass. Estimates of the original extent of the mixed-grass and shortgrass prairie are clouded by disagreements among ecologists as to which acres belong in which category. Together, the two types once covered over 400 million acres of the United States and Canada, of which about 25 percent is still intact, according to one recent estimate. Arguably the most interesting of the three from an ecological perspective, the shortgrass prairie may also be the most intact; some scientists estimate that as much as 60 percent of it remains today, although much of that acreage has been invaded by non-native plants.

The North American grasslands have been described as a young and turbulent ecosystem—young because open grasslands did not take over the mid-continent until approximately 8,000 to 12,000 years ago, after the glaciers had receded and the land had dried, and turbulent because ever since, two types of disturbance—fire and grazing—have kept woody trees and shrubs at bay and redistributed important nutrients. Historically at least, the fires were caused by lightning and the incendiary practices of the Indians, whereas the grazing was a product of the immense numbers of herbivores—ranging from roundworms to grasshoppers to bison—that inhabited the grasslands.

Fire and grazing, however, do far more than merely prevent woody plants from taking over the grasslands. Both help to create a mosaic of different habitats within the grasslands, ranging from bare ground in a freshly burned site or bison wallow to tall, rank grasses in spots overlooked by bison, missed by flames, or too wet to burn. As we shall see, it is this diversity of habitats within the prairie ecosystem that enables so many different plants and animals to coexist.

Like most ecological phenomena, fire and grazing have an important spatial dimension. Fires need room to burn; bison need room to roam. Now that the central grasslands have been chopped into pieces, dissected by roads, plowed and disked, they no longer can sustain the wildfires and herds of grazing mammals that are so critical to the health of the ecosystem. Thus, the domestication of the central plains is a case history demonstrating what happens when important natural processes are disrupted, a variation on a theme we encountered in the longleaf pine forests of the Southeast and the ponderosa pine forests of Arizona. To understand why the pieces of the prairie come apart when the land is abused, one must first understand how those pieces come together—in other words, how the system operated.

Let us begin with fire. Data on the extent and frequency of fires in the presettlement or "natural" prairie ecosystem are few and far between because grasslands, unlike woodlands, retain no lasting evidence of past fires. In the case of forests, ecologists can use the scars on tree rings to reconstruct the region's fire history, but the grasses and forbs (plants without woody stems, other than grasses) of a prairie are quickly consumed in a fire and leave no enduring signs. Thus, ecologists must infer the presettlement fire history of the central grasslands either by extrapolating backward from contemporary fire events or by relying upon the writings of early explorers. Neither approach is without its problems. Today's prairies, for example, are highly fragmented by roads and other unnatural firebreaks that presumably limit the extent of any burn. And the historical record is sparse and of dubious accuracy, at least by current scientific standards.

Moreover, humans have been occupying the central grasslands for thousands of years, and undoubtedly have been setting fire to them for most of that time. It would be ludicrous to exclude the pyrotechnics of the Indians from our calculation of fire frequency. But the tribes we would want to include in our baseline were themselves being changed by the arrival of white settlers, whose records form the basis for our estimates of "natural" fire frequencies. Foreign diseases such as smallpox and persecution by settlers caused the deaths of thousands of Midwestern Indians in the late eighteenth and early nineteenth centuries. The introduction of horses into the central plains by the beginning of the eighteenth century greatly increased the mobility of the tribes and, therefore, their ability to track bison herds and set fires. The bottom line is that we have no way of knowing precisely what the baseline conditions were like in the central plains, assuming we could even reach agreement on which time period to pick as the baseline.

That said, ecologists generally agree that fires in the central grasslands were frequent, perhaps as often as every 2 to 5 years in the tallgrass or every 4 to 5 years in the mixed grass, and that a significant fraction of those fires were set by Indians. In fact, the early explorers and settlers in the northern Great Plains attributed the majority of fires they encountered to Indians, rather than lightning. Most of those fires were scattered, single events of short duration that burned a small area. Only about 10 percent of them lasted more than a day. The accounts suggest that Indians in the northern Great Plains set fires in virtually every month of the year, including the winter, but did so most often in the spring and fall. In contrast, lightning-sparked fires are most common in mid- to late summer, when the summer thunderheads roll across the plains.

It is tempting to attribute the fires set by the Indians to an early and enlightened knowledge of game management. The movements of the bison herds were a matter of great importance to the tribes who depended upon this resource, and they quickly learned how to direct those movements by altering the grasslands. An autumn burn, for example, would bring tender young growth the following spring and increase the likelihood that bison would pause in the area to dine. But as prairie biologist Kenneth Higgins has noted, there were many other reasons why the Indians burned the grasslands. Fire was a means of communicating across the open spaces; it was also a tool of warfare and a way to improve travel corridors. And some fires began accidentally when children or adults got careless. Higgins found no evidence that Indians purposely burned large areas of forest to increase the acreage of prairie or even burned large areas of the grasslands for the benefit of wildlife; the really big burns he attributes to lightning or accidents.

Depending upon one's location at the time, few spectacles in nature are more awe-inspiring or frightening than a prairie wildfire. Early writers speak of a wall of flames sweeping across the grasslands, of wolves howling and panicked bison stampeding through the smoke. In the aftermath, they describe the desolation in near-Apocalyptic terms: "Not a single weed—not a blade of grass, was left. . . . In every direction, barrenness marked the track of the flames." But this was an ecosystem nourished by flames, an aggregation of plants that could reconstitute themselves again and again with remarkable speed. And once the plants regenerated, the animals returned—provided there were other prairies nearby to provide colonists for the newly regenerated site.

In addition to fire, the other crucial ingredient in the prairie ecosystem is grazing. Images of immense herds of bison naturally spring to mind, and it would be difficult to overstate their importance in the prairie ecosystem. But the central grasslands were quite literally filled with grazers of all different shapes and sizes. The millions of bison that once inhabited the grasslands were matched by an equal number of pronghorn and an unknown but presumably large number of elk.

Topping all of these mammals in sheer numbers were four species of prairie dogs. By far the most numerous was the black-tailed prairie dog, which once occupied more than a hundred million acres of the central plains along the eastern side of the Rockies, from Canada to Mexico. At an average density of between 4 and 22 black-tails per acre, the total population of this species alone must have numbered in the hundreds of millions, if not billions. A single dog town in the Texas Panhandle stretched 250 miles in length by 100 miles in width. Given that 256 prairie dogs will eat as much grass in a year as a single cow, their overall effect on the ecosystem must have rivaled that of the bison. Largely unrecognized and unappreciated were the countless grasshoppers, crickets, and other little creatures that, in aggregate, may have consumed as much or more greenery than all of the mammals combined.

The thought of this many grazers living together might provoke some sympathy for the vegetation, were it not for the fact that much of the grassland flora is superbly adapted to handle the pressure. Grasses, for example, will regrow after being grazed, provided the bite occurs above the apical meristem, the point from which cell growth is initiated. In many kinds of grasses, especially grasses that have evolved in the presence of large grazing mammals, that meristem is located underground, protecting it from most aboveground mouths (as well as fire). Thus, light to moderate grazing can actually increase the productivity of some grasslands, as the grazed plants produce a flush of tender new shoots, which in turn attract more grazers, who also dine on the plants, causing them to send up still more shoots. There are, of course, limits to the resilience of any plant. A plant under extreme grazing pressure will drain its root reserves in order to produce more leaves, thereby making it less able to compete for water and nutrients in the soil. But in the central plains, light grazing probably promotes something akin to a positive feedback loop between the plants and the animals that eat them. A recent study in Yellowstone National Park, which lies outside the central plains but contains many of the same plants and mammals, found that grazing by elk and bison increased the aboveground productivity of the vegetation by nearly 50 percent.

Even more remarkable, perhaps, are the complex and often mutually beneficial relationships that have developed among the grazers. This phenomenon was first studied in the Serengeti grasslands, which contain the most diverse and abundant community of large grazers left on earth. In East Africa, rainfall is highly variable with respect to location, timing, and amount. Areas only 3 to 6 miles apart will experience very different patterns of rainfall in a given year. As a result, forage within the Serengeti is patchily distributed, and the millions of wildebeest, zebras, and gazelles must adopt a nomadic lifestyle to find it, especially during the leaner days of the dry season.

In his famous studies of the Serengeti, ecologist Sam J. McNaughton observed that wildebeest were usually the first to arrive at a given site, where they promptly homed in on their favorite food plants, leaving behind tall clumps of the plants they chose not to eat. When zebras passed through the site a few days later, they dined on the patches the wildebeest had avoided. Gazelles, in turn, favored the young, nutritious shoots that grew up in spots where the wildebeest had been grazing earlier in the season. This orderly utilization of the grasslands has been termed a "grazing succession." It permits a far greater diversity of grazing mammals to occupy the ecosystem than would otherwise be possible. Moreover, the herds actually increase the diversity of the vegetation by selectively consuming certain plant species, thereby opening up space for other plants to grow.

Sadly, North America's grasslands have been so completely altered by humans that we cannot piece together nearly as complete a picture of how they functioned. The little evidence we have, however, suggests a rich tapestry of interactions. Of course, a visitor passing through one of the few pieces of American prairie that still contains a diversity of large mammals is unlikely to notice much interaction among them. The bison go about their business—eating and belching, mostly—seemingly oblivious to the prairie dogs and all else around them. The prairie dogs yip at each other, scan the skies for hawks, and pop into and out of their burrows. A small herd of pronghorn prance across the grass in their wonderfully affected, almost prissy, manner. It all seems so peaceful, so placid, so disconnected. In fact, the lives of these animals are anything but disconnected.

Prairie dogs, for example, continually manipulate the vegetation around their colonies. Mounds of bare soil mark burrow entrances, which in an active dog town may number well over a hundred per acre. The little rodents also clip and eat the grass surrounding their towns, enabling other types of plants—chiefly forbs and shrubs—to gain a foothold. Eventually, forbs and shrubs come to dominate the land around the towns, much to the benefit of the pronghorn, which prefer forbs to grasses and consequently spend much of their time near the centers of dog towns, munching forbs. On the other hand, it's hard to imagine any advantage accruing to the prairie dogs from sharing their land with pronghorns, except perhaps by having some additional, taller eyes around to detect predators.

At the edges of their colonies, prairie dogs clip but do not necessarily consume the grass, presumably to keep it short in order to spot approaching predators such as badgers and coyotes. This continual clipping generates an abundance of younger, more nutritious shoots, which draws in the bison. In one study in South Dakota, biologists found that bison spent approximately 40 percent of their time on prairie dog towns, primarily along the edges, even though dog towns occupied only 12 percent of the landscape. The prairie dogs may actually benefit from the presence of the bison, because the bison help to keep the grass short, which improves both forage quality and predator detection.

Prairie dogs, like beavers, are keystone species: The diversity of habitats generated by a prairie dog town supports a tremendous variety of animals. In 1980, an indefatigable team of biologists surveyed prairie dog colonies along an 828-mile transect from northeastern New Mexico to the Utah-Wyoming state line. They recorded over a hundred species of mammals, birds, reptiles, and amphibians associated with the prairie dog colonies. Some, such as burrowing owls, swift foxes, and rattlesnakes, find shelter in prairie dog burrows. Others, such as mountain plovers and sage grouse, seek out the bare ground and short grass found on dog towns.

Both the central grasslands of North America and the Serengeti, lying at opposite ends of the earth and containing virtually none of the same species of plants or animals, operate in somewhat similar ways. In both ecosystems, a community of grazers creates a mosaic of habitats within the grasslands by virtue of where they eat and what they eat. This mosaic sustains a richer diversity of life than would otherwise occur. The presence of some animals—be they wildebeest or prairie dogs—creates conditions favorable for others. And the productivity of the land is increased by grazing (although this last point is much less certain for the central plains than for the Serengeti). But there are also some notable differences. The Serengeti, for example, represents a grazing succession, characterized by a sequential use of the grasslands by different species. In the central plains—or in those small portions of the central plains that have been reasonably well studied—the grazers are part of a grazing association, not a succession. They appear together at the same time, but choose different parts of the habitat mosaic—a mosaic that they have helped to create. (On the other hand, given that the immense migratory herds of bison were destroyed well before any ecologist could study them, it may be premature to conclude that a bona fide grazing succession did not occur in at least a portion of the central plains.)

It is also worth emphasizing that the relationships among bison, pronghorn, and prairie dogs represent facilitation, not dependence. Bison once roamed as far east as the Atlantic coast and as far south as Florida, well beyond the ranges of prairie dogs. Even today, there are thriving herds of bison and pronghorn in places devoid of prairie dogs and prospering colonies of prairie dogs in places without bison. None of these species "needs" the others to survive; rather, natural selection has shaped their behaviors to more efficiently exploit the abundant—but patchy—resources of the central plains in places where they co-occur.

Much of the preceding discussion has focused on the western portion of the central plains (the region often referred to as the Great Plains), where the trio of bison, pronghorn, and prairie dogs commingle. But even in the easternmost portions of the central grasslands—in the tallgrass prairies of Illinois, Iowa, and Missouri—fire and grazing are the ingredients that produce the habitat mosaic essential to so many species. The habitat preferences of grassland birds in Illinois, for example, fall along a gradient of vegetation height and density. Some, like the Henslow's sparrow, seek out the tall, dense vegetation found in places that have not been burned or grazed for several years; others, like the upland sandpiper and vesper sparrow, prefer the very short, sparse vegetation of recently burned or recently grazed sites. Only a landscape containing patches that have been burned or grazed at different times is capable of sustaining both sparrows and sandpipers. When the grasslands extended for hundreds of miles in all directions, the right mix of habitats was assured. Inevitably, some patches of vegetation would be burned or grazed, while other patches would escape the flames and bison. This dynamic equilibrium was profoundly and permanently altered by people.

Humans began changing the central plains almost upon arrival. As noted in the Introduction, the demise of the fabulous fauna of the Pleistocene epoch—the giant bison, camels, horses, and mammoths that made this region the equal of the Serengeti—was aided and abetted by the migration of Paleoindians across the Bering landbridge and into the central plains region. By the time white settlers arrived, thousands of years later, the Indians had settled into a somewhat more sustainable relationship with the remaining fauna and flora, primarily as hunter-gatherers who tracked the herds of bison and other large game. This is not to suggest that they were always frugal in their consumption of wild game—accounts of bison herds driven over cliffs suggest otherwise—but simply to note that anthropologists can find no evidence of a second, post-Pleistocene wave of extinctions attributable to depredations by nonwhite settlers.

But with the arrival of white ranchers and farmers came the era of slaughter and settlement. Early explorers extolled the lush grass that brushed against the bellies of their horses in the east, the immense herds of bison, pronghorn, and elk they encountered in the west, and the sense that such a rich landscape would surely reward those who chose to live there. Others—the more careful observers, perhaps, or at least the more pessimistic—noted the increasing aridity and decreasing forage as one moved farther west and doubted the land could sustain great numbers of people. But the people came nonetheless, bringing guns and horses, cattle and plows, and eventually the missing water itself. In a remarkably short time, the central plains, including the arid western portions, were transformed into productive agricultural lands.

The defining event of that transformation may have been the slaughter of the bison. No one knows precisely how many of the shaggy beasts roamed the continent prior to the arrival of Europeans. They once occupied most of the continent, but the densest numbers—the legendary herds—were confined to the grasslands. "Between the Rocky Mountains and the states lying along the Mississippi River on the west, from Minnesota to Louisiana, the whole country was one vast buffalo range, inhabited by millions of buffaloes," wrote W. T. Hornaday in 1889.

> One could fill a volume with the records of plainsmen and pioneers who penetrated or crossed that vast region between 1800 and 1870, and were in turn surprised, astounded, and frequently dismayed by the tens of thousands of buffaloes they observed, avoided, or escaped from. They lived and moved as no other quadrupeds ever have, in great multitudes, like grand armies in review, covering scores of square miles at once. They were so numerous they frequently stopped boats in the rivers, threatened to overwhelm travelers on the plains, and in later years derailed locomotives and cars, until railway engineers learned by experience the wisdom of stopping their trains whenever there were buffaloes crossing the track.

Based on written accounts and a little back-of-the-envelope arithmetic, Hornaday calculated that a single herd sighted in the vicinity of the Arkansas River may have totaled over 4 million individuals.

It fell to naturalist Ernest Thompson Seton to attempt an estimate of the original bison population of the entire continent. Approaching the problem from a variety of angles— dividing the area of the continent by the acreage necessary to support one bison, extrapolating the number of bison from the number of horses, cows, and sheep that the range could sustain, and using Hornaday's herd of 4 million as the basis for an overall density estimate—Seton calculated that between 65 and 75 million bison once occupied the continent, with over 90 percent of those occurring on the central grasslands. Some scientists would later question the accuracy of Seton's estimate, but no one disputes that millions, and most likely tens of millions, of bison once roamed the mid-continent.

In the space of a few decades, they would all be gone, the greatest aggregation of large mammals on earth destroyed for food, for fun, and even for spite. As early as 1843, no less an authority than John James Audubon was sounding a warning about the future of the bison: "Even now, there is a perceptible difference in the size of the herds, and before many years the Buffalo . . . will have disappeared; surely this should not be permitted." It was. A systematic slaughter was under way, propelled first by need, then by blood sport, and ultimately as a way to break the Plains Indians, whose dependence on the animals had not gone unnoticed by land-hungry whites. The completion of the first transcontinental railroad in 1869 marked the beginning of the final chapter in the sad history of the bison. Now, in addition to the depredations of the settlers and the Indians, the dwindling herds had to weather the attacks of professional hunters, eager to ship the meat, hides, and even the bones eastward, much as their counterparts in the Midwest were shipping the last great colonies of passenger pigeons in barrels to the eastern cities. "Buffalo Bill" Cody bragged of personally killing over 4,000 bison in the course of a year—and he was but one of many such hunters. The numerically minded Hornaday would calculate that over 3.1 million bison were killed by white men in just the 3-year period from 1872 to 1874, with more than half of that total simply left to rot. By 1883, the bison had been all but erased from North America, with only a few small, scattered herds in Alberta, Yellowstone, and Colorado left. The Colorado herd would soon fall to the bullet, but the other two herds were eventually protected, and they, combined with animals reared in captivity and released to the wild, would form the nucleus of a subsequent restoration effort.

Even before the bison and the Indians were gone, the cattlemen moved in. A brief, frenzied cattle boom took place in the southern portions of the Great Plains in the last quarter of the nineteenth century, but it quickly subsided in the face of overgrazing and harsh winters. One imagines it came as a shock to some of these ranchers to discover that there were limits to the amount of grazing the grass could take, and that a land once capable of supporting millions of bison could be denuded by a lesser number of cattle. But the bison, unlike the cattle, were migratory, and their peregrinations had given the range time to recover. The cattle, on the other hand, had nowhere to go, and bite by bite, they managed to push the more arid portions of the central grasslands closer to the desert conditions that were always lurking in the shadows.

The cattlemen also succeeded in eliminating the remnants of the fine assemblage of carnivores that once stalked the herds of bison, pronghorn, and other grazers. The government-sponsored extermination campaign that would spread like a plague over the entire West fulfilled its mission in the Plains states, too, eliminating the wolves and grizzlies (but making few inroads against the wily coyotes). Another target of the ranchers' wrath were the ubiquitous prairie dogs, which were seen as competitors for forage. The little rodents were shot and poisoned by the millions, often by agents of the federal government, in an effort to improve the range for cattle. Even today, dog towns continue to be destroyed, despite the fact that the black-tailed prairie dog has already suffered close to a 98 percent reduction in its range, and another species, the Utah prairie dog, has been added to the endangered species list.

As the prairie dogs disappeared, so too did the other animals that depended directly or indirectly on them, the most notable being the black-footed ferret. First described by Audubon and John Bachman in 1851, this sleek brown weasel with a dashing black mask preys almost exclusively on prairie dogs. Always something of a mystery to biologists, who rarely saw it, the black-footed ferret must have been an unimaginably terrifying presence to the prairie dogs, slipping down their burrows in the dark of night and attacking them in their sleep. Never the direct target of the ranchers' ire, the ferret nonetheless suffered as its sole food source was eradicated. By the early

1970s, after several years without a sighting, conservationists were ready to declare it extinct. Then, in 1981, a farm dog near Meeteetse, Wyoming, killed a strange animal that was raiding its food dish. The animal turned out to be a black-footed ferret, and the bizarre circumstances of its death led biologists to the discovery of a small but thriving ferret population living amid a colony of white-tailed prairie dogs.

For a year or two, all seemed well, until a bout of canine distemper began killing the ferrets and an epidemic of sylvatic plague began killing the prairie dogs. In 1985, worried biologists hustled eighteen of the remaining ferrets into captivity in a last-ditch effort to save the species. The captive breeding program has been wonderfully successful, so much so that scientists have begun releasing progeny back into the wild. Unfortunately, some of these release efforts have been relatively unsuccessful to date, and those in charge are grappling with a couple of disturbing problems. First, there no longer exist many prairie dog colonies of sufficient size to sustain a viable population of ferrets. Moreover, if the dog towns are subject to periodic outbreaks of plague, a disease that can decimate prairie dog populations, then the ferrets must be able to disperse into new towns when their food supply runs low. But with prairie dogs occupying only a tiny fraction of their former range, it may no longer be possible for the ferrets to travel from town to town. The prairie dog ecosystem, in other words, has been too heavily fragmented to sustain black-footed ferrets, unless humans assume the responsibility of moving the ferrets back and forth in the equivalent of an eternal biological shuttle service. Absent a concerted effort to restore prairie dogs to portions of their usurped range—an effort that shows little sign of materializing—the black-footed ferret will remain a ward of the state.

A moment of ecological reflection should cause some ranchers to question the wisdom of the whole effort to eradicate prairie dogs. Prairie dogs, it will be remembered, prefer areas of very short grass. Overgrazing by cattle increased the amount of suitable habitat for the sociable rodents; the dog towns were, to some extent at least, a problem of the ranchers' own making. Moreover, it is not clear how seriously prairie dogs compete with cattle for forage. Bison, after all, actually prefer to forage along the edges of dog towns, and one wonders whether cattle would behave the same way. In one study, prairie dogs reduced the amount of forage available to livestock by only 4 to 8 percent. Another study found that black-tailed prairie dogs reduced the amount of forage available to livestock by 33 to 37 percent—a whopping amount. However, the researchers also discovered that steers grazing in pastures with prairie dogs did not end up weighing much less than steers from pastures without them. The presence of prairie dogs apparently improves the quality of the grass and forbs, enabling the livestock to gain nearly as much weight from a smaller amount of forage.

In the wake of the cattlemen came the sodbusters, eager to bring the land into cultivation. In pursuit of this goal, they were aided by an all-too-eager Congress, which passed the Homestead Act of 1862 and the Enlarged Homestead Act of 1909 to encourage settlement of the West. The acts enabled settlers to gain title to parcels of land by making "improvements" on some of the acres and paying a filing fee. The 1909 law in particular brought thousands of would-be farmers to the western grasslands, determined to claim their piece of America's last agricultural frontier. For at least the first three decades of the twentieth century, it all seemed to work: the demand for wheat was insatiable, both domestically and internationally; prices skipped to all-time highs; and the advent of the gasoline-powered tractor, the disk plow, and the combine meant farmers could plant and harvest more acres than they had ever dreamed possible. Not surprisingly, they rushed to bring as much land into production as they could.

The good times came to an abrupt end in 1931, when a drought that had stricken the eastern United States the year before shifted westward, clamping onto the central plains with bulldog tenacity and hanging on for the rest of the decade. Throughout the region, crops withered and soils hardened and cracked. Stripped of its natural vegetation, the land could no longer hold onto its soil. In the southern plains region, the infamous Dust Bowl, fierce winds scooped up the soil by the hundreds of millions of tons, smothering the prairie towns in thick, black clouds of dust and carrying it as far east as Boston, New York, and Washington, D.C. A single dust storm in 1935 carried away twice as much earth as men and machines had excavated to make the Panama Canal. By 1938, 10 million acres had lost at least the upper five inches of topsoil. In the words of historian Donald Worster, the dust storms created "the most severe environmental catastrophe in the entire history of the white man on this continent."

The response of the federal government in the wake of the Dust Bowl years was to shower the region with money and agricultural "experts" in an effort to keep the people on the land and keep them farming. A system of price supports and production cutbacks was put in place; farmers were encouraged to adopt techniques such as contour tillage and terracing to reduce erosion; and hundreds of millions of trees were planted as windbreaks. But when the rains returned in the 1940s and the demand for grain increased, many of the farmers grew impatient with these conservation measures and reverted to their old habits of maximum production for maximum income, overlooking the fact that rain and drought, good times and bad times, have always followed each other on the central plains. When the rains disappeared again—as they did from 1952 to 1957 and from 1974 to 1977—there were dust storms, bankruptcies, and all the old reminders of how fragile and unpredictable the grasslands could be.

Fortunately for the farmers, they have gained some measure of control over the vagaries of nature with the advent of deep-well irrigation. Although attempts were made to irrigate the arid portions of the central grasslands as long ago as the late 1800s, the idea did not gain momentum until the 1930s, when farmers began to tap into the vast reservoirs of water deep beneath the earth. By the late 1950s and 1960s, they were tapping into these aquifers as feverishly as they had broken the sod 30 years earlier. Today, flying over the shortgrass region, one cannot help but marvel at their handiwork. For hundreds and hundreds of miles, the landscape bears an uncanny resemblance to an abstract painting of squares and circles—neat brown squares of freshly plowed earth inlaid with perfect green circles created by center-pivot irrigation systems. The farmers know they are draining the underground reservoirs, mining finite reserves of water in a region where water is the limiting resource, and they know they eventually will pay a stiff price for their reliance on this resource. But in the meantime, there is a living to be made from doing so.

Along the eastern edge of the grasslands, in the tallgrass region, water is less of a limiting factor, and the farmers have not had to endure anything as horrific as the Dust Bowl. But because the soil there is so rich, the tallgrass prairie has been all but obliterated by agriculture. Throughout the nineteenth century sodbusters were hard at work, reducing the amount of prairie in Illinois alone from 21 or 22 million acres in 1800 to approximately 1 million acres by 1900; less than 2,500 acres remain today. Until about 30 years ago, however, a sizable por-tion of the landscape was maintained in a condition that at least approximated the original prairie, as hayfields, pasturelands, and the like. With the advent of industrial agriculture, most of these habitats have been replaced by road-to-road row crops.

Economists and social scientists endlessly debate the pros and cons of the changing character of American agriculture. From an ecological perspective, however, it has clearly been an unmitigated disaster for the grassland fauna. Here again, we must turn our attention to birds, for they represent the only group of animals that is consistently monitored across the continent. According to data compiled by the Department of the Interior, over the past quarter century grassland birds have shown "steeper, more consistent, and more geographically widespread declines" than any other group of North American birds. Between 1966 and 1991, for example, populations of Henslow's and grasshopper sparrows declined at average annual rates of 4.2 and 4.6 percent, respectively. The mountain plover, despite its name a denizen of the shortgrass prairie, declined at an average annual rate of 3.6 percent. These may seem like small numbers, but if an annual decline of 3.6 percent continues for 25 years, it results in the cumulative loss of 60 percent of the population. Small wonder, then, that the mountain plover is a candidate for protection under the Endangered Species Act. Indeed, throughout the central plains, populations of most grassland birds are a fraction of those that existed just a few decades ago. Comparable data are lacking for most other types of animals, but a growing roster of imperiled prairie butterflies and plants suggests a widespread problem. Even the regal fritillary, a grassland butterfly whose disappearance from the eastern United States was traced to the regrowth of forests, is vanishing from its strongholds in the Midwest, almost certainly as a result of prairie destruction.

Notwithstanding such facts and figures, a curious natural historian might well wonder what exactly we have done to the prairies that qualifies as destruction. Is there any reason why cows can't fill the niche left vacant by the extirpation of the bison? And why don't farm crops, especially crops such as hay, substitute for native grasses?

The first of these questions has received surprisingly little attention from ecologists, and few of the studies completed to date provide anything approaching a clear answer. Cattle and bison are certainly more similar to each other in terms of the amount and types of food they eat than either is to pronghorn, elk, or prairie dogs. This fact alone would suggest some fundamental similarities. And cattle, like bison, can create the patches of very closely cropped grass that are such important habitats for many native plants and animals, thereby contributing to the diversity of the central plains. Indeed, one ornithologist has speculated that with the bison now largely gone, a complete removal of cattle from the national grasslands (a popular idea with some environmentalists) could jeopardize the mountain plover, which lives in the shortest of the shortgrass prairies. Even the native dung beetles, industrious little insects that lay their eggs within meticulously crafted orbs of dung, have survived the disappearance of the bison by switching to cattle dung for their handiwork.

But cattle are not bison, and it would be foolish to assume the two are ecological equivalents. Cattle, for example, tend to have a higher-quality diet than bison; they consume a lower proportion of grasses and a higher proportion of forbs than their wild brethren. Thus, cattle may not contribute as much to the vegetative diversity of the grasslands as bison because they remove less of the dominant grass cover, thereby opening up less space for other plant species. Cattle also spend more time congregating around water than bison, a habit that has led to extensive and chronic damage to riparian habitats throughout the United States. And they do not wallow in the dirt or paw the ground the way bison do. These two seemingly minor habits of bison, when replicated by tens of millions of individuals across the central plains, contributed significantly to the diversity of habitats. Even today, a visitor to the prairies can pick out the old bison wallows, still distinctive elements of the landscape more than a century after the last itchy bison rolled around in them.

Most important, cattle are not nomadic. They live in a world subdivided into discrete little sections by endless miles of barbed wire. How long they stay in a given area is determined by ranchers, not by ancient migratory behaviors crafted over the course of millennia by natural selection. Two centuries ago, there was a dynamic quality to the landscape of the central plains. Areas were grazed intensively by bison herds and then left alone for long stretches of time. Today, those same areas may be grazed year-round by a resident herd of cattle, producing a different, less variable set of habitats. Even the remaining bison herds today live more like cows than bison. They are kept behind fences, herded from pasture to pasture, even rounded up and culled. The bison may not be extinct as a species, but it is essentially gone as an ecological phenomenon.

For many years, ranchers have experimented with different grazing regimes, varying the number of cattle and the length of time they are allowed to stay in a given pasture, with the goal of producing more beef or reducing environmental damage, or both. None of these approaches provides a panacea for the problems caused by the extirpation of the bison and the arrival of cattle, but some have resulted in marked improvements in the health of riparian areas and rangelands. These regimes offer useful and practical topics for research, inasmuch as bison will never replace cattle in most of the central plains, and cattle can be an important tool for recreating some of the habitats produced by bison. But no amount of innovation on the part of the ranchers can change one fact of life: Unlike bison, a herd of cows grazing by the roadside will never cause the children inside a passing car to point excitedly and insist that their parents pull over for a closer look.

To answer the second question—can farm crops substitute for native grasses?—we must turn to a remarkable set of data that were gathered in Illinois over the course of 50 years. From 1906 to 1909, ornithologists Alfred O. Gross and Howard A. Ray conducted a series of statewide, cross-country counts of birds. They visited representative examples of virtually every habitat in Illinois, including croplands of different types, and counted the birds within them. Fifty years later, from 1956 to 1958, Richard R. Graber and Jean W. Graber repeated Gross and Ray's census, also crisscrossing the state and counting the birds in different habitats. These two studies provide a unique look at the birds associated with natural grasslands versus croplands and how their numbers have changed over time.

Summer bird populations in the ungrazed grasslands representing the last, best remnants of tallgrass prairie averaged 1.5 birds per acre. Among the common breeding species were meadowlarks, bobolinks, red-winged blackbirds, and grasshopper sparrows. Comparable densities of birds were found in many of the faux-prairie habitats that had replaced the native grasslands. For example, mixed hayfields containing both grasses and legumes harbored 1.5 birds per acre, including lots of meadowlarks and other grassland birds; red clover fields had an even higher density of 1.9 birds per acre. Some species even seemed to prefer the human-created habitats to the more natural ones. Bobolinks were ten times more common in mixed hayfields than in ungrazed grasslands.

What all of these man-made grasslands have in common is that they look more or less like native grasslands. The structure and density of the vegetation approximate what one might encounter in parts of the tallgrass prairie, even if some or all of the grasses and legumes are non-native species. In contrast, the most monotonous, most unnatural-looking croplands contained very few grassland birds. Cornfields, which in early summer consist of little more than rows of shoots poking out of the dirt, harbored an average of only 0.2 birds per acre; plowed fields fared little better, with 0.4 birds per acre. Of course, any change in land usage invariably creates winners and losers among wildlife. In this particular case, the winner may well be the horned lark, a little brown bird that prefers open habitats with patches of bare earth. Row crops provide just this type of habitat. The Grabers estimated that the horned lark population in Illinois tripled between 1907 and 1958, from 1.5 million to 4.5 million. It showed the greatest population increase of any Illinois bird during this period.

The distinction between cultivated grasslands, such as hay or clover fields, and row crops, such as corn or soybeans, is the key to understanding population trends among grassland birds. In recent decades, many farmers have converted their hayfields and pasturelands to the more profitable row crops, a change that has decimated populations of some birds. Comparing their counts with the earlier counts of Gross and Ray, the Grabers calculated that the population of bobolinks in Illinois had increased from approximately 1.2 million pairs in 1909 to 1.4 million pairs in 1958, even though the amount of prairie and pastureland in the state had declined during this period. The birds had apparently adjusted by moving into hay and oat fields. Yet according to the U.S. Fish and Wildlife Service, bobolink populations in Illinois proceeded to decline by a staggering 93 percent between 1966 and 1991. This sudden decline can be attributed to two factors: the conversion of pasturelands and hayfields to row crops and a trend toward cutting hayfields earlier in the season, when bobolinks are still nesting. More and more farmers are switching to new varieties of alfalfa that grow faster and can be cut earlier. As a result, the timing of the first cutting has been pushed forward so that it now coincides with the nesting season, and a high proportion of bobolink eggs and young are being destroyed by the mowing, raking, and baling. Those nests that somehow survive the harvest suddenly find themselves bereft of cover and exposed to predators.

Sadly, the bobolinks have plenty of company in their decline. In 1958, for example, the Grabers estimated a statewide population of 850,000 grasshopper sparrows. "The future for this species appears to be reasonably bright," they concluded. "Pasture acreage in Illinois continues to decline, but the hayfields offer a good reservoir habitat." Unfortunately for the sparrows, the hayfields were soon to be replaced by corn and soybeans. By 1991, the grasshopper sparrow population had declined by 85 percent. Other species suffering major declines during this time in Illinois include meadowlarks, savannah sparrows, Henslow's sparrows, and bobwhites.

It would be desirable, of course, to have similar data from other portions of the central plains, but I am aware of no other surveys of bird populations in agricultural and grassland habitats comparable to what has been done in Illinois. Nonetheless, the general conclusions that can be drawn from the work of Alfred Gross, Richard Graber, and others should apply to other parts of the central grasslands where the same changes in agricultural practices are happening. In short, the answer to our second question—can farm crops substitute for native grasslands?—is a weak and qualified yes. Hayfields, pastures, and other cultivated grasslands can attract many of the same birds that occur in native grasslands. Row crops, by and large, cannot.

We must be careful, however, not to assume that what works for birds will work for other organisms. What little evidence there is suggests that small mammals respond to agriculture in a manner similar to birds. In Nebraska and Kansas, for example, most of the mice, voles, and shrews associated with prairies also inhabit roadside ditches, which resemble native grasslands in appearance but consist largely of exotic plants. Insects, on the other hand, tend to be more finicky about the species of plants in their environment. Regal fritillaries lay their eggs on violets, which serve as food for their caterpillars; they cannot survive in grasslands lacking violets, regardless of how attractive those grasslands may seem to our eyes. The Ottoe skipper, another rare prairie butterfly, lays its eggs only on grasses in the genus *Andropogon*. Thus, we should expect many prairie insects to have a harder time adjusting to agricultural habitats than has been the case with most birds, and indeed, the available evidence supports this idea. Of 1,100 species of insects captured in various natural and degraded habitats in the Chicago region, nearly a quarter were found to be closely tied to the remnant prairies and were either scarce in or absent from hayfields, roadside ditches, and other degraded habitats that can serve as prairie substitutes for other animals.

Recent studies have uncovered yet another problem that may be contributing to the declines of grassland birds, namely, habitat fragmentation. Some species seem to shun smaller prairie fragments, occurring only in the larger patches. In the Midwest, for example, prairie fragments smaller than 75 acres are unlikely to be occupied by grasshopper sparrows, and those smaller than about 150 acres are ignored by bobolinks and Henslow's sparrows. The situation is analogous to what is happening in the eastern forests, where many species of song-birds no longer nest in the small woodlots left standing after developers have razed the rest of the forest. Not surprisingly, the problem is most serious in the tallgrass region, where over 96 percent of the native prairie has been destroyed. In Illinois, for example, fewer than a fifth of the state's 245 remaining patches of prairie are larger than 25 acres, and only 9 are larger than 100 acres. Small wonder, then, that the little Henslow's sparrow is now classified as a threatened species in a state where its population numbered in the hundreds of thousands earlier in the century.

Exactly why fragmentation is harmful to these birds remains something of a mystery, but a few studies suggest that rates of nest predation and parasitism are much higher in the smaller fragments than in the larger ones—precisely the pattern we saw with respect to forest-dwelling songbirds in the East. With their high proportions of edge to interior, small patches of prairie may be overrun by nest-plundering birds and mammals living along their borders. Tallgrass insects, on the other hand, seem to be less sensitive to fragment size than birds—or so the current evidence would suggest. Even fragments as small as 5 acres routinely support a few prairie-restricted species. Their greater tolerance of fragmentation may be a function of the higher densities at which insects typically occur. An acre of grassland may support, at most, a single pair of grasshopper sparrows, but thousands of grasshoppers.

Given all that has happened to the central grasslands, it seems nothing less than miraculous that relatively few grassland animals have become extinct. Some—the whooping crane and black-footed ferret being obvious examples—teeter on the brink, while others, such as the mountain plover and lesser prairie-chicken, are marching steadily toward that precipice. But the fact remains that the tallgrass, mixed-grass, and short-grass prairies combined have nowhere near as many critically endangered species as some other ecosystems, such as the Florida scrub and southern Appalachian rivers. There is still time to save virtually all of the prairie animals.

We owe this fortunate situation to two factors. First, as noted earlier, grasses did not take over the mid-continent until approximately 8,000 to 12,000 years ago, well after the glaciers had receded. Most of the plants and animals inhabiting the central plains came from adjacent ecosystems, where they still occur. The central grasslands are not their only homes. Conversely, the relatively small number of animals truly restricted to the central grasslands are disproportionately represented on federal and state endangered species lists, as evidenced by the plight of the black-footed ferret, mountain plover, and prairie chickens. Second, the central plains cover an enormous area, much of which has proved difficult to bring under cultivation. Thus, substantial portions of the mixed and shortgrass prairies remain, notwithstanding all our efforts to turn them into wheatfields and row crops. As damaged and degraded as these remnants are, they are nonetheless capable of sustaining much of the original fauna, at least for now.

The good news, then, is that most of the pieces of the grassland fauna are still with us. The trick is to prevent them from disappearing and, if possible, reassemble them into an intact and functioning ecosystem. A reassembly of this sort occurred more or less by default in the forests of the eastern United States at the turn of the twentieth century, when farmers abandoned the land they had cleared and the forests and most of the associated animals returned. But a similar resurrection of the central grasslands is unlikely to occur unless people serve both as purveyors of fire and as dispersal agents who bring back the native plants and animals.

Fortunately, a small but dedicated band of prairie enthusiasts has been willing to do just that. On a growing number of carefully tended acres, their efforts have yielded wondrous results: purple coneflowers, white prairie-clovers, and yellow compass plants again commingled under a deep blue sky. Not uncommonly, once the vegetation has been partially restored, long missing plants and insects reappear on the site, as though summoned from the earth by some preternatural power. Much of this work, however, has taken place on a scale too small to make a difference in the lives of grassland birds and other animals that require large amounts of habitat. For such species, help has come from an unlikely source: the U.S. Department of Agriculture, the very agency whose policies and programs have facilitated the destruction of the grasslands.

This unusual and welcome alliance has its origin in a series of laws created over the past four decades by Congress to curb the overproduction of crops, which was eroding both topsoil and farm income. One such law, the Food Security Act of 1985, contained a provision authorizing the Department of Agriculture to establish the Conservation Reserve Program, or CRP, which pays farmers to retire highly erodible soils from crop production and plant them with cover. These contracts run for 10 to 15 years. By the fall of 1996, the Department of Agriculture had enrolled over 36 million acres in the CRP— more land than is contained within all of the national wildlife refuges and all of the state-owned wildlife areas in the lower 48 states combined.

Although designed to combat soil erosion, the CRP has also proved to be a blessing for some grassland birds. Approximately

88 percent of the land enrolled in the program has been planted to grass, providing new nesting habitats for Henslow's sparrows, lark buntings, savannah sparrows, bobolinks, and other declining species. Were it not for the CRP, most, if not all, of this land would continue to be farmed, providing little in the way of nesting habitat for most of these birds. Whether the program produces comparable benefits for other prairie denizens, such as regal fritillaries and Ottoe skippers, is open to question, but in an era of destructive federal subsidies for logging and mining, a government program that simultaneously prevents erosion and protects vanishing birds is worth celebrating.

Much of the success of the CRP is due to its large scale. It can restore expanses of grassland large enough to support populations of vulnerable songbirds. But no existing program, public or private, is big enough to bring back the free-roaming bison herds, the wildfires, the vast prairie dog towns, and the wolves and grizzlies that once combined to make the central plains a grassland ecosystem without equal in the world. A few visionaries have pondered the unsustainable nature of modern agriculture in the western portions of the central plains—the declining aquifers, the disappearance of ancient topsoil, the small towns that are hemorrhaging people as their younger residents seek employment elsewhere—and proposed grand schemes to tear down the fences, remove the cattle, restore the vegetation, and bring back the bison. Their schemes have been met with scorn and open hostility by most of those who live and work in the region.

Political reality suggests we are a long, long way from enacting anything so bold, and perhaps we never will. In the short term, at least, the best hope for the central plains lies in the recognition that much of its fauna can and will coexist with agriculture—a kinder, gentler agriculture, to be sure, but agriculture nonetheless. There is room for both cattle and prairie dogs, both alfalfa and bobolinks, but it will require some adjustments on our part. The wildlife of the central plains has already adjusted about as much as it can.

CHAPTER FOUR

Troubled Waters

The key to breaking apart the American wilderness—the soft underbelly in that prickly body of forests, mountains, and deserts that confronted the early settlers—was its vast, intertwining network of lakes and rivers. Adventurers quickly seized upon this network as a pathway for exploration and colonization, and subsequent generations used it as a source of food, energy, and water to fuel the development of the continent. In doing so, they inflicted inestimable harm on the wildlife associated with those lakes and rivers. Arguably the most dramatic evidence of this abuse came on June 22, 1969, when Cleveland's Cuyahoga River, awash in garbage and toxic chemicals, caught fire. It was not the first time the river had burned—fires had been plaguing the Cuyahoga since 1936—but this particular fire caught the attention of the national media. The Cuyahoga, declared *Time*, was a river that "oozes rather than flows," one in which a person "does not drown but decays." Three years later, Congress enacted the Clean Water Act, which set a goal of "restor[ing] and maintain[ing] the physical, chemical, and biological integrity of the Nation's waters." The act mandated tough new measures to control water pollution, and as a consequence, the nation's lakes and rivers grew progressively cleaner. But beneath the surface, in their capacity as habitats for fish, mussels, crayfish, and other aquatic species, these waters have shown little improvement. In fact, no other group of organisms has suffered more from development or benefited less from environmental laws than our freshwater fauna. Yet, until recently, the depth of their plight was little known to most environmentalists, let alone the public at large.

In 1990, The Nature Conservancy published a remarkable analysis of the status of various types of animals. It revealed, perhaps for the first time, the extent to which freshwater species were disappearing in the United States. According to the Conservancy, more than a third (40 percent) of North American fishes are extinct or vulnerable to extinction. The comparable figure for North American crayfishes is 51 percent, while for freshwater mussels it jumps to a staggering 67 percent. In contrast, the percentage of birds considered extinct or at risk is only 15 percent; the figure for mammals is 17 percent, and for reptiles 18 percent. Aquatic species, in short, are suffering much higher losses than terrestrial species. Even more ominous, perhaps, is the accelerating rate of loss. Among fishes, for example, the rate of extinction has doubled over the course of the twentieth century.

Such high percentages of imperiled species would be troubling under any circumstances, but they are especially so in this case because they represent the loss of an extraordinarily diverse assortment of species. Over 800 different kinds of fish inhabit North America's fresh waters; the Mississippi River drainage alone contains nearly as many fish species as are found in all of Europe. And no other place on earth could match the diversity of native snails that once occurred in the Coosa River drainage or the numbers of species of freshwater mollusks in the Tennessee River drainage. For all sorts of freshwater animals—from crayfish to caddisflies—the United States is the center of diversity. To an extraterrestrial ecologist visiting this planet at the end of the nineteenth century, the most notable feature of the American landscape might well have been its rich assortment of freshwater animals.

Driving these changes in our aquatic ecosystems has been a suite of activities as vast as the scale of human enterprise itself. People have altered the physical structure of rivers by constructing everything from simple weirs to massive dams. They have straightened streambeds, smoothed bottom contours, constructed dikes, inserted culverts, and otherwise rebuilt hundreds and hundreds of rivers to suit their fancy. Pollutants, both organic and inorganic, pour into our waters from cities, industrial complexes, power plants, farmlands, pasturelands, mines, and quarries. Many are what are called "point-source pollutants," traceable to individual factories, sewage treatment plants, strip mines, and the like. Others, such as pesticides, silt, and fertilizers, fall into the category of "nonpoint-source" pollutants, which wash into rivers from sources spread across the landscape. Water is diverted and drained from lakes and rivers for drinking and irrigation, while throughout the country new species of plants and animals are introduced, some to entertain anglers, some to control imagined or real pests, and some by accident or carelessness. All these activities (and many others) have been harming fishes, mussels, and other aquatic species for a long, long time.

We tend to think of water pollution and overfishing as the primary culprits behind the loss of freshwater biodiversity, but in fact, neither problem has endangered as many species of fish, mussels, amphibians, and crayfish as has habitat destruction. It is only because our terrestrial imaginations prevent us from perceiving the extent to which we have damaged rivers as habitats—by altering their shapes, their flows, and their flood-plains, and by filling them with alien species—that we overlook the leading role that habitat destruction has played in the loss of freshwater life.

Perhaps the most telling indication of the extent to which we have altered aquatic habitats comes from the National Rivers Inventory, completed in 1982. The inventory was designed to identify U.S. streams or stream segments that might qualify as national wild, scenic, or recreational rivers. To do so, a stream segment had to be free-flowing and relatively undeveloped, and possess outstanding natural and cultural values. Of the 3.2 million miles of streams in the contiguous 48 states, only 2 percent met these requirements. Dams, water diversion projects, and other forms of development had essen-tially destroyed the natural character of the other 98 percent. The survey also revealed that only 42 free-flowing river segments of 125 miles or longer remain in the lower 48 states.

The number of dams alone is staggering—2.5 million in the United States, according to the National Research Council, obstructing almost 20 percent of the nation's river miles. A recent study concluded that only one of the large river systems in the coterminous United States—the Pascagoula River in Mississippi—was not significantly fragmented by dams. From the point of view of many fish and mussel species, the differ-ence between a free-flowing stream and one regulated by dams is so profound that they quickly die out when a dam is built, or are replaced by others better adapted to the more placid, deeper waters. At the beginning of the twentieth century, biologist A. E. Ortmann catalogued 63 species of freshwater mussels in (aptly named) Muscle Shoals, a narrow, rapid stretch of the Tennessee River in northwestern Alabama. It was the most diverse assemblage of mussel species ever known. In 1924, Ortmann returned to Muscle Shoals after a dam had been constructed. "The beautiful islands, and the general features of the river itself are gone," he wrote, "as well as a large portion of the fauna, chiefly that of the mussels." A survey in 1963 would confirm Ortmann's observation: only 30 of the original 63 species remained.

Were it not for their dull exteriors and lackluster behavior, the freshwater mussels might engender greater sympathy, because no organisms have suffered more as a consequence of our behavior. Among aquatic animals, they stand out as perhaps the most sensitive indicators of habitat degradation and pollution. Most species cannot abide the slack, silt-laden waters upstream from a dam, and they are acutely sensitive to certain pollutants, particularly metals such as copper or zinc. They are readily harmed by concentrations of dissolved metals well below those that would affect humans; water that is good enough for us to drink may be bad enough to kill them. Mussels are also relatively immobile, living for decades within a few square yards of stream bottom; they cannot move out of the way of an oil spill or seek cleaner waters upstream. Finally, their peculiar reproductive behavior makes them highly dependent upon other aquatic species for their survival.

In the early spring, male mussels release clouds of sperm into the water. Downstream, females collect the sperm through their siphons and use it to fertilize their eggs. When the eggs hatch, the larvae, called glochidia, are expelled into the water, and must find their way to a host fish. Depending upon the species, they attach themselves to either the gills or the fins of the fish, where they reside for 1 to 3 weeks. When they have metamorphosed into juvenile mussels, they drop from the fish and fall to the river bottom, where, if they are fortunate enough to land on a suitable substrate, such as the clean cobblestone bottom of a riffle, they will develop into adults. Each species of mussel seems to be able to grow on only one or a few fish species; if the host fish disappears, so does the mussel. Adult mussels do not reach sexual maturity until they are 3 to 5 years old, and some individuals may live as long as 100 years.

As if the steady degradation of their habitats were not enough, mussels and fish must contend with the inevitable human disasters that seem to befall all water bodies. In 1967, for example, a large storage pond for fly ash (a waste product of coal refining) at the Appalachian Power Company's electric generating station at Carbo, Virginia, gave way, spilling vast amounts of polluted alkaline water into the Clinch River, one of the nation's biologically richest rivers. The spill killed fish, mussels, and other aquatic animals for 90 miles downstream. With time, most of the affected portions of the river have recovered from the accident. Recovery, however, has been painfully slow in the 12-mile stretch directly below the power plant, where, three decades later, mussels are just beginning to reappear. Acutely sensitive to pollution and poor at recoloniz-ing vacant habitat, mussels are typically the first to go and the last to return when a river is damaged.

If there is a mecca for freshwater aquatic life in the eastern United States — or, more accurately, an Alamo — it is Pendleton Island, in extreme southwestern Virginia. To our terrestrial eyes, it is an unremarkable place: a wooded island of about 35 acres located only a few yards from the banks of the Clinch River, flanked on both sides by farmland and forest. While the above-water portions of Pendleton Island are unexceptional, the gravel bars and riffles along its shores harbor the richest collection of freshwater mussels left on earth, a diversity of species matched only in years past by Muscle Shoals. Surveys in the early 1980s turned up over 40 species of freshwater mussels, including over 20 imperiled species. Decades earlier, many of these rare species occurred much more frequently in the upper Tennessee River system, but a long history of deforestation, industrialization, farming, mining, dam and road construction, and water pollution has taken its toll, reducing the mussels to scattered remnant populations in places like Pendleton Island.

In 1984, The Nature Conservancy purchased Pendleton Island, thereby removing the threat of development along its shores. It has worked closely with farmers to prevent cattle from damaging the riverbanks and polluting the water with sediment and manure. But the Conservancy cannot control everything that happens upstream, and something is killing the rare mussels of Pendleton Island. Recent surveys have turned up only 30 to 35 species, and many of these show little evidence of successful reproduction. No one is certain what pollutant is responsible for the mussels' demise; in fact, there probably isn't a single factor driving them to extinction. Rather, a potpourri of widespread pollutants, from sediments and nutrients washing off farm fields to toxic chemicals embedded in the mud, is slowly but surely poisoning them. A mussel that is already stressed by one toxic compound may be killed by the addition of another, even if the concentration of that second compound is so low that, by itself, it would have little effect.

The Commonwealth of Virginia's response to the plight of its endangered mussels and fishes has been desultory at best, negligent at worst, and probably little different from that of many other states. The Clean Water Act requires every state to adopt water quality standards to protect established stream uses, which at a minimum include the protection of aquatic life. This provision permits a state to designate particular rivers or river segments as waters of exceptional ecological importance and to develop more stringent discharge standards for those waters. Virginia, however, did not begin to address the issue of controlling the toxic discharges that might be harming the Clinch River mussels until the mid-1980s, well after the Clean Water Act was passed. The Virginia Water Control Board (now part of the Department of Environmental Quality) focused first on chlorine, which is used in sewage treatment and power plants and is very toxic to mussels. After much wrangling with local constituencies, it begrudgingly banned the discharge of chlorine and other halogenated compounds into waters containing federally protected endangered species, providing a needed break to the beleaguered mussels of the Clinch River.

The board next focused on copper, another element toxic to mussels, and after years of study and argument, imposed a stricter standard for copper for portions of the Clinch River below the scene of the infamous fly ash accident. Unfortunately, it chose to apply the stricter standard only to the 12 river miles immediately below the site of the spill—the 12 miles that are currently almost devoid of mussels. And when it comes to controlling sediment pollution due to farming and logging operations, the state has done little more than ask farmers and loggers to abide by a set of weak, voluntary guidelines.

One might expect the Endangered Species Act to come to the rescue, but this noble law has been notoriously ineffective at protecting aquatic species. The Fish and Wildlife Service has been slow to add vanishing aquatic species to the official list of endangered species, and it has had relatively little success in recovering their populations when it has done so. Thus, in a 1994 assessment of its endangered species program, the Service concluded that 89 percent of protected mussels were still declining, 9 percent were of unknown status, and only 2 percent were improving.

Part of the problem may be the difficulty of identifying threats to aquatic biodiversity. A dam that threatens to inundate the last refuge for a rare fish or mussel is hard to overlook, and the Fish and Wildlife Service can justifiably block its construction, or at least force the dam builders to modify the design. But where should the Service draw the line when the "threat" is dozens of pollutants that individually may or may not be harming aquatic life, but together form a deadly witch's brew? And what should it do in cases in which no individual factory or farmer is breaking the law, but the cumulative effect of all of their activities is slow, progressive habitat degradation that is harmful to a rare fish or mussel? Stepping on any one interest group's toes—be it farmers or power plant operators or manufacturers—inevitably brings forth cries of "Why us and not them?"

Precisely this problem has bedeviled all efforts to control the most widespread and damaging pollutant in American rivers today, silt. This seemingly innocuous substance, essentially dirt washed into rivers, is deadly to a wide range of aquatic life. Excessive amounts of suspended sediments can clog the gills of fish and mussels, leading to death or respiratory distress. When it settles to the bottom of the river, silt buries riffles composed of clean, smooth stones, thereby destroying a key habitat for many types of aquatic organisms. It smothers the eggs and larvae of all manner of fish and invertebrate animals. It can even bury sedentary adult mussels. Silt also acts as a delivery vehicle for toxic chemicals, which bind to individual dirt particles and may be washed into a nearby lake or river during rainstorms. Wherever soil is exposed to the elements in proximity to water—in a recently plowed field, an overgrazed pastureland, a fresh clearcut, or a road under construction—siltation is likely to occur. The contribution of any one site to the overall problem may be small, but the cumulative effects can be deadly. According to the Environmental Protection Agency, sedimentation is the most important cause of river and stream pollution in the United States today.

The most effective remedies for sediment pollution are surprisingly straightforward: Prohibit construction near stream banks, keep cattle out of riparian zones, and restrict farming and timber cutting alongside lakes and rivers. Most states and counties have enacted regulations along these lines, but the magnitude of sediment pollution in American lakes and rivers suggests such rules are nowhere near as stringent as they need to be. Strengthening them, on the other hand, means stepping on a multitude of toes, something state and county legislators are loath to do.

One cannot visit a place like Pendleton Island without experiencing a mixture of emotions. The richness of aquatic species is dazzling; the variety of endangered species is matched by few other places in North America. But the knowledge that they are slowly, inexorably dying adds an element of melancholy that seems inappropriate for a sunny June afternoon. When I was taken there by scientists from The Nature Conservancy, we prowled along the banks of the island, looking for muskrat middens. Muskrats love to eat mussels, and the piles of shells they leave behind are an invaluable (albeit gruesome) source of information about which mussels live nearby. In one midden alone, we found the shells of nearly twenty species of mussels, including two very rare ones. Toward the end of our visit, we sifted through the gravel in the riverbed and found a bumpy, fan-shaped shell about 2 inches in width. It had once belonged to a green-blossom pearly mussel, a species last seen alive in 1982 and now believed extinct.

Although the prognosis for freshwater mussels is grim, scattered evidence gives us hope the declines can be halted and even reversed. Scientists are beginning to learn how to breed these strange little animals in captivity—no small feat given the mussels' complicated life histories. This newfound skill may enable biologists to hold onto the rarest species until more is known about the reasons for their declines in the wild. It may also allow conservationists to replenish depleted populations in rivers once those rivers have been cleaned up.

There is even evidence that mussel populations can rebound naturally if their habitats are allowed to heal. One of the more remarkable examples of such progress comes from the Duck River in central Tennessee, which once harbored an impressive assemblage of mussels. That assemblage was largely intact until the mid-1970s, when the Tennessee Valley Authority (TVA) proposed to build two dams in the river, one in the upper reaches, to be called Normandy Dam, and the other in the middle stretch, to be called Columbia Dam. Normandy Dam was finished in 1976, destroying the last known population of the turgid-blossom pearly mussel. As that dam was completed, the Fish and Wildlife Service added the turgid-blossom pearly mussel and two other species, the birdwing pearly mussel and the Cumberland monkeyface pearly mus-sel, to the endangered species list. This protection, of course, came too late for the turgid-blossom pearly mussel, but the other two species still inhabited the middle stretches of the Duck River, where construction of Columbia Dam was well under way.

In preparation for the filling of the reservoir that would occur when Columbia Dam was finished, the TVA purchased about 16,000 acres of land in the Duck River watershed, includ-ing extensive buffers along the banks of the river. By doing so, the TVA essentially precluded development along the margins of the river, permitting only light farming. Also, most of the remaining landowners in the watershed ceased to develop their lands, anticipating the rising water levels.

The Fish and Wildlife Service found itself in a dilemma. Completion of Columbia Dam would surely destroy the populations of the two endangered mussels. But the TVA had already purchased the land and was nearly done with the dam. Unwilling to block the project, the Service instead allowed the construction to continue, but made final approval to close the gates and flood the reservoir conditional upon the successful completion of a two-part mitigation program: The TVA had to transplant the endangered mussels to another location where they could prosper, and it had to improve the habitat for them in two other rivers, the Clinch and the Powell. The transplantation attempts were largely a failure—the mussels never bred at the new site—as were the TVA's efforts to improve their habitats in the Clinch and Powell rivers. But something strange was happening in the Duck River. The mussels were increasing in numbers. By buying the adjacent land and limiting development along the river, the TVA had unwittingly created extensive buffer zones, thereby improving habitat conditions to the benefit of the endangered mussels.

By the end of the 1970s, the TVA's (and the nation's) enthusiasm for expensive "pork barrel" dams was waning, with the result that Columbia Dam was never completed. Today, the TVA is considering transferring the land to the State of Tennessee for use as a park. The rare mussels are still there, doing quite well by mussel standards, with the uncompleted and unwanted dam standing as a monument to the forces that have driven so many of their kin to extinction.

In the western United States, the same panoply of changes—from dams and factories to introduced non-native species—has occurred, but it has taken place in a landscape that differs fundamentally from that of the East in at least one respect: aridity. West of about the hundredth meridian, water becomes a scarce resource—too scarce to support agriculture without massive irrigation projects, too scarce to sustain cities without dams and reservoirs. When Almon Harris Thompson climbed a ridge in southern Utah and deduced the course of the Escalante River in 1872, he mapped the last unknown river in America, bringing to a close one more chapter in the story of the fast-disappearing frontier. The expedition's leader, John Wesley Powell, recognized that the key to settling the West was managing its water; the desert could be made to bloom, but not everywhere, and not easily. A rational program of water development would permit people to prosper there; an irrational program (or none at all) would set them up for eventual failure. As might be expected, we followed the latter course, occasionally adjusting it as technology and trauma dictated. Farms and ranches sprang up, flourished briefly, and died like desert flowers. An era of monumental dam construction, which began in the depths of the Great Depression and is only now ending, gave us control over the water, thereby expanding the scale of agriculture and permitting sleepy little towns to mushroom into big cities.

Of course, none of this could happen without profound changes to the rivers and lakes of the West. "Change," in fact, is much too mild a word; they were essentially redesigned. The western fishes, unfortunately, were ill equipped to survive under such circumstances. Approximately 170 of North America's 810 native freshwater fishes occur only west of the Rocky Mountain divide. They are a strange assemblage, many representing ancient lineages that have somehow persisted in the isolated river systems of the West. Others, like the tiny pupfishes and daces that occur in many of the oases and springs that dot the desert, are the products of thousands of years of isolation as lakes and streams have expanded, contracted, and changed course. In general, these fishes are superbly adapted to weather the droughts, scouring floods, high salinity, and other harsh attributes of western rivers, lakes, and springs. Unfortunately (from the fishes' perspective), these very attributes have been erased or changed by the dams, diversions, and other structures we have placed in these rivers. Moreover, because many of these western fishes have evolved in relative isolation, they appear to lack the competitive abilities and antipredator defenses exhibited by fishes from more species-rich water bodies. Thus, they are poorly equipped to compete against the hordes of non-native fishes that have been dumped into their habitats by wildlife managers.

As a symbol of the extent to which we have reconfigured the water resources of the arid West, nothing can compare with the Colorado River. From its origins in the high peaks of northern Colorado, it races southwest, joining with the Green, Dolores, and San Juan rivers as it moves through Utah. In Arizona it picks up the Little Colorado and Gila rivers before emptying out into the Gulf of California, completing a journey of more than a thousand miles, and in the process, sculpting some of the most spectacular and formidable terrain on earth. Or so it used to be. Today, the Colorado is sliced and tamed by ten major dams, which annually generate 12 million kilowatts of electricity. It provides water for nearly 25 million people and 3 million acres of farmland. It keeps cattle alive on Wyoming ranches, puts winter vegetables from California's Imperial Valley on the dinner tables of New Yorkers, and brings water-skiing and motorboating to Nevada and Arizona. In short, it enables people throughout much of the West to forget they are living in an arid and unforgiving land and to ignore for the time being the inevitable limits to growth that have always accompanied this landscape of incomparable beauty.

In its pristine state, the Colorado River basin harbored only about thirty-one species of fish, a relatively small number for such a big river system. Four are now among the nation's most imperiled and controversial species. The Colorado squawfish is the largest minnow in North America, occasionally growing as large as 5 feet and weighing over 80 pounds. The humpback chub and bonytail chub are also rather impressive members of the minnow family, with adults exceeding a foot in length. The fourth species, the razorback sucker, belongs to the group of fish known (regrettably, from a public relations perspective) as suckers. The endangered status of these four fishes and the bitter dispute over what must be done to save them mirror past and present battles over water use throughout the arid West.

A century ago, these four species were the dominant fishes throughout the main branches of the Colorado River basin, thriving in an environment that few other fish could tolerate. In its natural state, the Colorado is a river with two personalities, the aquatic equivalent of Dr. Jekyll and Mr. Hyde. In the late spring and summer, melting snows boost the volume of water by nearly two orders of magnitude, increasing the flow rate from a few thousand cubic feet per second to a couple of hundred thousand, and turning a relatively placid river into a stampeding torrent, capable of scouring its banks, flooding adjoining lands, and sweeping tons of gravel, sediment, and other debris downstream. Somehow the chubs, suckers, and squawfish thrived under such conditions. For the three species that have been reasonably well studied (the squawfish, razor-back sucker, and humpback chub), scientists have determined that reproduction is actually timed to coincide with the spring floods. The young fish subsequently mature in the gentler eddies and backwaters that form after the floodwaters have subsided and been replaced by the low, stable flows of the late summer and fall.

The ten dams now placed along the Colorado have funda-mentally altered its behavior, reducing the spring and summer floods, lowering water temperatures, trapping sediment, and changing the structure and vegetation of the banks. This domesticated Colorado no longer produces the awesome spring surges that served to create the backwater nursery habitats. Moreover, fisheries managers, myopically focused on providing more game fish for anglers, have introduced sunfish, catfish, walleye, pike, trout, and bass into the reservoirs formed by the dams. Today, over 90 percent of all fish in the Colorado River system are non-native species introduced for recreational fish-ing. Many of these exotic species compete with and prey upon the native fishes. As a result of all these changes, the native squawfish, chubs, and suckers have disappeared from large portions of the basin. Some populations now consist entirely of aging adults, with little or no evidence of successful recruitment. Of seventy razorback suckers collected in Lake Mohave between 1981 and 1983, for example, none was thought to be less than 24 years old, and the oldest individual was estimated to be 44 years old.

The Colorado squawfish and humpback chub appeared on the first official list of endangered species compiled by the Department of the Interior in 1967. When the department subsequently tried to add the other two, it ran into a wall of resistance from western water developers and the Colorado River Water Conservation District (the agency responsible for promoting water development within the State of Colorado's portion of the basin). The department nonetheless classified the bonytail chub as endangered in 1980. Unfortunately, protection may have come too late for this species. Only a few old individuals have been sighted in recent years, with no evidence of successful reproduction in the wild. The razorback sucker was not added to the endangered list until 1991.

The U.S. Fish and Wildlife Service has identified the Green and Yampa rivers, which come together in the upper portion of the Colorado River basin, as the key areas for saving the four native fishes. The Yampa is the only large river in the entire basin whose flow patterns have not been substantially altered by dams or other obstructions. The Green River, on the other hand, was irrevocably changed in 1963 with the completion of Flaming Gorge Dam, a 3.75 million acre-foot hydropower dam that has created a huge reservoir in northeastern Utah and southwestern Wyoming. Predictably, it has dampened springtime floods and lowered water temperatures on the Green River. For years, environmentalists have urged dam operators to change the flow patterns so they mimic natural conditions—in other words, to release more water in the late spring and summer to simulate the floods that once scoured the basin, and to release less water at other seasons when the rivers were traditionally less turbulent. Doing so would restore habitat for native fish along the river, and it might reduce populations of non-native fish, most of which are not adapted to the rough-and-tumble world of the unregulated Colorado. But in the eyes of many water users and state officials, such a request amounts to heresy. To them, every gallon of water that spills through the dam without generating power is wasted.

The Fish and Wildlife Service, true to form, has attempted to find a middle-ground solution to the controversy. It has forced dam operators to develop a power-generating schedule more closely aligned with the natural flows of the river, but it has refused to demand that Flaming Gorge be managed as a "run-of-the-river" dam that allows water to move freely and takes whatever power is generated whenever it is generated. Whether this moderate course will be enough to protect the native fishes remains to be seen. For the most critically endangered species, the path of moderation may amount to little more than a gentler path to extinction.

Introduced fishes are a vexing problem not only in the Colorado River system but throughout the United States. Eager to provide anglers with a diverse and abundant supply of game fish, fisheries managers have reared, transported, and released uncountable billions of fish into rivers, lakes, and ponds where they never occurred naturally. Some, like the brown trout, have been brought in from other countries; others, like the rainbow trout, are native to certain parts of the United States, but have been widely transplanted outside their native ranges. In addition to these government-sanctioned transplantation efforts, individual anglers have dumped "extra" baitfish into water bodies, and aquarium owners have released unwanted pets, adding to the roster of introduced species.

The cumulative effect of these introductions on native fishes has been nothing less than disastrous. In reviewing the reasons why various species and subspecies of North American fishes have disappeared over the past century, a committee of the American Fisheries Society concluded that introduced species were a contributing factor in two-thirds of the cases; only habitat loss exceeded introductions in its frequency as a factor contributing to extinction. Today, approximately half of the endangered fishes in the United States are threatened to some degree by introduced species, as are a number of rare mussels and crayfishes. In Arizona and New Mexico, for example, the Apache trout, desert pupfish, Gila trout, loach minnow, Little Colorado spinedace, spikedace, Virgin River chub, woundfin, Yaqui catfish, and Yaqui chub are threatened by a panoply of non-native fishes, including brown trout, rainbow trout, largemouth bass, smallmouth bass, various catfishes and sunfishes, red shiners, and crappies.

One can understand the mindset of old-time fisheries managers, especially those working in the West, without necessarily endorsing their actions. Stuck with a native fish fauna consisting of minnows and suckers and a few trout, they were keen to "improve" their fisheries. Their visions of western waters filled with sunfish, catfish, bass and other popular species became a real possibility when the great dams suddenly created vast lakes and reservoirs that were unsuitable for many of the native fishes, but potentially prime habitat for a host of exotics. And so, with zeal and persistence, they proceeded to remake the fish communities of a continent.

In one infamous case, fisheries managers from Wyoming and Utah teamed up in 1962 to poison over 400 miles of the Green River. A new dam was about to be completed, and the managers intended to stock the new reservoir with rainbow trout. The fish then living in the Green River (a collection of native and introduced species) were considered undesirable for sportfishing; more important, they were seen as potential competitors and predators of rainbow trout. That there was virtually no scientific evidence to support this claim appeared to have little effect on the decision. Over the protests of numerous scientists and environmentalists, the poisoning went forward, a massive operation involving vehicles, airboats, a helicopter, and more than a hundred people. Among the native fishes living in the path of the poison were Colorado squawfish, razorback sucker, humpback chub, and bonytail chub—even then recognized as vanishing species. Aware of the possibility that the poison could reach the protected waters of Dinosaur National

Monument, the organizers set up a detoxification station 16 miles upstream from the park boundary. They unfortunately underestimated the concentration of poison and had difficulty preparing the detoxicant. The poison swept past the detoxification station and into the park, killing the rare fish and causing an uproar. Letters of protest from scientists and influential congressmen caused Secretary of the Interior Stewart Udall to reconsider the conditions under which poisoning and stocking activities should take place. "Whenever there is a question of danger to a unique species," he concluded, "the potential loss to the pool of genes of living material is of such significance that this must be a dominant consideration in evaluating the advisability of the total project."

The introduced rainbow trout did fine for a while, but eventually declined in numbers. Two other introduced species, lake trout and kokanee salmon, have prospered in the reservoir, and today they draw most of the anglers. Meanwhile, the squawfish, chubs, and razorback cling to existence. And the dam that precipitated all of this controversy? It was none other than Flaming Gorge Dam, the very one whose current operations are now being changed to help the native fishes.

The poisoning of the Green River may have marked a turning point in our attitudes toward aquatic ecosystems. Environmentalists used it as an example of state and federal indifference to native fishes. State and federal agencies began to pay a little more attention to rare native fishes; passage of the Endangered Species Act 11 years later ensured that they would continue to do so. But the tradition of stocking fish in waters outside their natural ranges is deeply entrenched in fisheries management. Since 1950, one of the primary funding sources for sport fisheries management has been the Federal Aid in Sportfish Restoration Act. Through an excise tax on fishing equipment and motorboat fuels and import duties on fishing equipment, pleasure boats, and yachts, the federal government collects funds, which it distributes as matching grants to the states for the management of sport fisheries. Over the past four decades, the Sportfish Restoration Act has provided over half a

billion dollars to the states, and annual revenues now exceed
$200 million.

What is striking—and perhaps inexcusable, given the sorry
state of American lakes and rivers—is how little of this money
is spent in ways directly beneficial to aquatic ecosystems. In
1991, for example, the federal government gave out $184 mil-
lion in Sportfish Restoration Act funds. Only 4 percent of this
was spent to improve aquatic habitats, while 16 percent went
to build user facilities such as boat docks and piers, and 15 percent went to fish stocking programs. Much of the money allo-
cated for fish stocking was used to stock non-native species.
Fisheries managers are more careful these days about where
and when they release exotic fishes, but they have yet to abandon a practice that has already inflicted immeasurable harm on
aquatic ecosystems throughout the country, and will continue
to do so as long as species are moved around like pawns on a
chessboard.

In at least one respect, our treatment of aquatic species has
been the exact opposite of our treatment of terrestrial species.
For centuries, Americans strove mightily to rid the land of its
largest predators, shooting, trapping, and poisoning countless
wolves, grizzlies, mountain lions, coyotes, and eagles under the
belief that doing so would create a safer world for deer, elk,
cattle, sheep, and other tasty vegetarians. For almost as long,
we have been adding large predatory fishes—bass, pike,
salmon, trout—to lakes and rivers that never had them, with
little concern for the creatures they would consume. Today, the
practice of controlling populations of terrestrial predators is far
less popular and widespread than it was at the turn of the
century, but in aquatic ecosystems, predator augmentation,
otherwise known as fish stocking, is still practiced with gusto.

It undoubtedly strikes many people as silly to worry about
the fate of razorback suckers, Cumberland monkeyface pearly
mussels, and other obscure aquatic creatures, or worse yet, to
stop the construction of dams and bridges for their sake. When
the debate is framed in such stark and narrow terms, what is
missing is any sense of the ultimate significance of such losses.

Over time, the cumulative losses of aquatic life can become great enough to alter the very structure of the food webs within water bodies, even to the point of damaging or destroying productive fisheries and other benefits of healthy aquatic ecosystems. No lake or river is too big or too deep to escape harm. For more than three decades, this fact has been painfully clear to the federal, state, and municipal governments that are struggling to restore the Great Lakes. Spanning more than 750 miles from east to west, and covering an area of 94,000 square miles, these five water bodies constitute the greatest expanse of fresh waters on the surface of the planet, equal to 18 percent of the world's supply of fresh water. They are also among the most damaged aquatic ecosystems in the nation.

Commercial fishing in the Great Lakes began around 1820 and expanded rapidly, reaching a peak in 1899, when 147 million pounds of fish were harvested. Among the mainstays of the fishing industry were lake trout, blue pike, and approximately eight species of salmonlike fish in the genus *Coregonus*, variously named ciscoes, chubs, whitefish, and bloaters. Today, the Great Lakes still produce about 110 million pounds of fish per year (about three-quarters of the turn-of-the-century total), but the value of the catch is greatly reduced because its composition has changed so dramatically. No less than four of the eight *Coregonus* are now extinct, and two of the surviving species are classified as endangered. The blue pike is gone as well, and lake trout are too rare to sustain more than a token commercial harvest. Commercial fishermen have had to turn their attention (and their nets) to smaller, less valuable species, such as bloaters, perch, smelt, and alewives.

Determining the reasons for these changes is akin to solving a decades-old murder: Many of the clues have perished, most of the witnesses have vanished, and the remaining evidence is fragmentary and circumstantial. Adding to the confusion are intrinsic ecological differences among the lakes, complex interactions among fish species, and the sheer magnitude and extent of human activities occurring within each watershed. The declines in fish stocks began as early as the nineteenth century as a result of overexploitation of the most valuable species coupled with pollution of their habitats. As a given species grew scarce, the fishermen would switch their attention to the next most valuable species, until it too became unprofitably scarce. In this way, they depleted stock after stock of successively smaller, less desirable species, a practice known as "fishing up." Beginning in the 1920s and 1930s (and continuing to the present time), non-native fishes began to spread across the Great Lakes, competing with and preying upon native species. The growth of cities and industries in the Great Lakes region in the 1940s, 1950s, and 1960s created additional problems for some native fishes in the form of pervasive pollution.

In Lake Michigan, for example, the fishermen initially focused their attention on the lake whitefish (one of the *Coregonus* species), which retained a good flavor when salted. So intense was the harvest that by 1860, some of the fishing grounds for this species were already depleted, and by the 1870s, complaints about the scarcity of whitefish were widespread. During this same period, a booming timber industry was stripping away much of the region's forest cover, creating sediment pollution, and sawmills were dumping immense quantities of sawdust into streams, smothering some of the spawning grounds of the whitefish.

With whitefish harvests dropping, fishermen turned their attention to lake trout, ciscoes, and lake herring. The lake trout, a magnificent predatory fish that can exceed 40 pounds, became the most valuable commercial species in Lake Michigan from 1890 until the mid-1940s. Harvest figures for lake trout fluctuated considerably throughout this period, but in general, they show a gradual decline. From 1890 to 1911, for example, the catch averaged 8.2 million pounds per year; from 1927 to 1939, it averaged only 5.3 million pounds. Lake trout appeared to rebound in the early 1940s, before the population suddenly and irrevocably crashed in 1945. By 1954, the commercial catch was all of 34 pounds, and two years later, the lake trout was extinct in Lake Michigan. The cause of this final (and fatal) decline was almost certainly the spread of the sea lamprey, a ghoulish, eel-like fish that attaches itself to other fish, rasps a hole in their bodies, and feeds on their body fluids. The sea lamprey is native to the Atlantic coast. It arrived in Lake Ontario in the 1830s, when shipping canals linking the Great Lakes with Atlantic coast river systems were being constructed, and gradually spread to the other lakes. It reached Lake Michigan in 1936, where it found the big trout an irresistible target.

The *Coregonus* ciscoes fared as poorly as the lake trout, their demise serving as a textbook example of the practice of "fishing up." In the first half of the twentieth century, fishermen targeted the largest species, such as the blackfin and deepwater ciscoes, using nets with a mesh size of $4\frac{1}{2}$ inches. Several million pounds were taken each year. By 1950, depletion of the large ciscoes had forced most fishermen to switch to a mesh size of $2\frac{1}{2}$ inches, suitable for capturing the intermediate-sized species. By the end of the decade, they were using nets with a mesh size of only $2\frac{3}{8}$ inches to snare even smaller individuals.

Remarkably, the smallest of the ciscoes, the bloater, enjoyed something of a population explosion in Lake Michigan in the 1940s and 1950s. It may well have benefited from the extirpation of the lake trout, which had been one of its major predators. For the larger ciscoes, however, life continued to get worse. With lake trout scarce, the sea lampreys began attacking them instead. Moreover, the growing population of bloaters made it difficult for the few remaining blackfin, shortnose, and deepwater ciscoes to find suitable mates; many appear to have hybridized with the ubiquitous bloaters. The increasing amount of pollution in the Great Lakes also may have reduced populations of the aquatic insects upon which they fed. "The ciscoes of the Great Lakes," lamented the U.S. Fish and Wildlife Service in 1974, "probably represent the most significantly endangered fishery, the most significantly endangered fish populations, and the most significantly endangered combination of fish species in the freshwaters of the United States."

Even the bloaters' resurgence was short-lived, with numbers declining steadily in the 1960s. The cause of this decline is not clear, but a likely factor is the introduction of the alewife, a member of the herring family. Native to the Atlantic coast and perhaps Lake Ontario, alewives were blocked from entering the other Great Lakes by Niagara Falls. Construction of the Welland Canal enabled them to get around that barrier and reach the other lakes, where they became spectacularly abundant. First recorded in Lake Michigan in 1949, alewives increased so rapidly that fishermen were able to harvest 41.9 million pounds of them in 1967 alone. Alewives feed on the same tiny, free-floating animals, called zooplankton, that young bloaters eat, and it is difficult to imagine that Lake Michigan could support so many alewives without a concomitant reduction in bloaters. Alewives also eat the eggs of other fish, a habit that may have spelled trouble not only for the bloater but for the other ciscoes as well.

More or less the same story can be told about the other Great Lakes, although there are important differences among the lakes in terms of their ecology and history of abuse. In Lake Erie, for example, the commercial fishery underwent the same transformation that occurred in Lake Michigan, from an industry focused on high-value fish to one subsisting on low-value species. At the beginning of the twentieth century, the core of the Lake Erie fishery consisted of lake trout, blue pike, sauger, whitefish, and lake herring. That fishery is now dominated by smelt, yellow perch, and to a lesser extent, walleye, and is far less profitable for the fishermen. The same troika of abuses—overexploitation, alien species, and pollution—that transformed Lake Michigan drove the changes in Lake Erie as well.

Overfishing unquestionably played an important role in the demise of Erie's lake trout, sauger, whitefish, and herring. Advances in fishing technology, including the development of nylon nets and the conversion of steam-powered boat engines to gasoline and diesel fuel, enabled fishermen to catch more fish even as stocks declined. The effects of water pollution were felt as far back as the end of the nineteenth century, when sedimentation due to logging and farming began to smother the spawning grounds of Erie's whitefish and lake trout. Curiously, however, the sea lampreys and alewives that have plagued the other Great Lakes appear not to have taken as great a toll on Erie's fish. Lampreys were detected in Lake Erie as early as 1921, but they never became particularly common there, perhaps because Erie's watershed contains few suitable spawning streams for them. Alewives also failed to explode in numbers, perhaps because Lake Erie's shallow waters are too cold for them in the winter and spring.

Although the shallowness of Lake Erie may have kept the number of alewives in check, it has made the lake highly sensitive to certain types of pollutants, most notably inorganic nutrients such as phosphorus. When present in excess amounts, phosphorus can foster a condition known as eutrophication. High concentrations of it cause phytoplankton and algae to grow profusely. When these plants die, they sink to the bottom and decompose, a process that exhausts the dissolved oxygen in the water and creates anoxic conditions that are fatal to a wide range of aquatic organisms. Eutrophication became a serious problem in the Great Lakes in general, and Lake Erie in particular, during the 1950s and 1960s, when concentrations of phosphorus climbed, largely because of the widespread use of phosphate detergents. Throughout the 1950s, more than 225 tons of phosphates entered Lake Erie each year, creating a nutrient-rich soup in which a few plants, animals, and bacteria thrived, but many other species suffocated. Newspaper stories described Lake Erie as a "dead lake," but the opposite was true: Erie was too much alive, far too fecund for its own good.

Recognizing that lakes such as Erie would remain eutrophic as long as phosphate pollution continued, the governments of the United States and Canada signed the Great Lakes Water Quality Agreement in 1972, which called for sharp reductions in phosphorus levels. This was to be accomplished in large part by restricting the sale of phosphate detergents in the Great Lakes watershed. In addition, the two governments invested billions of dollars to upgrade municipal waste facilities throughout the region. As a result of these actions, annual discharges of phosphorus from U.S. and Canadian cities dropped sharply. For Lake Erie, this reduction in phosphorus amounted to a turning back of the clock. The phytoplankton and algae decreased dramatically, aquatic insects that had almost disappeared years ago became abundant once again, and fishermen began catching more walleyes.

This turnaround came too late for a few species, most notably the blue pike. Native to Lakes Erie and Ontario, the blue pike was one of the mainstays of the fishery. Between 1885 and 1962, over a billion pounds of marketable blue pike were landed, with annual harvests from Lake Erie alone exceeding 20 million pounds in good years. Blue pike populations, however, had a history of fluctuating wildly. The catch could drop from 20 million pounds to 2 million pounds in the space of a few years, and rebound just as fast. Perhaps because good years had always followed bad ones, fisheries managers were not too concerned when blue pike numbers dropped precipitously in 1958. But this time there was no rebound, only further declines. In 1967, the U.S. Fish and Wildlife Service declared the blue pike an endangered species, but by then it was too late—the last sighting came in 1974. The timing of the blue pike's demise strongly suggests that eutrophication was an important factor, probably because it decimated the aquatic insects upon which blue pike fed. Overfishing may have played a role as well, reducing the blue pike population to such a low level that many of the remaining individuals ended up mating with walleyes (a close relative) instead of each other.

With conditions improving in the Great Lakes due to environmental regulations, fisheries experts set about rebuilding the once-great commercial and recreational fisheries. The discovery of a chemical that kills larval sea lampreys enabled biologists to bring populations of that pest under control. Lake trout were subsequently reintroduced to all five lakes, although at the present time, only Superior boasts a self-sustaining population. All too predictably, the experts also turned to alien species to provide new sportfishing opportunities, in this case chinook, coho, and pink salmon brought in from the Pacific Northwest.

The abundant (and alien) alewives provide a ready source of food for the salmon, and the stocking program has been understandably popular with anglers, but one wonders about the wisdom of tinkering further with a system that has already been so profoundly altered by alien species.

By design and by accident, alien species continue to fill the Great Lakes. This trend, more than the accumulated industrial wastes, pesticides, and other pollutants, probably poses the greatest long-term threat to these ecosystems. Nearly 30 percent of the alien species in the Great Lakes have been discovered since 1959, and new ones are arriving at a rate of one per year. The most notorious of the recent arrivals is surely the zebra mussel, a fingernail-sized mollusk from the Old World that arrived in Lake St. Clair in 1986 as a stowaway in the ballast water of a ship. With the force of a Biblical plague, the little mussels managed to sweep through all of the Great Lakes by 1990, reaching densities as high as 24,885 individuals per square foot in some places, clogging the intake pipes of power plants and municipal water facilities, and forming piles 2 feet deep on the bottoms of the lakes. By the spring of 1997, zebra mussels had been detected in twenty states and two Canadian provinces, supporting earlier predictions that they eventually would occupy two-thirds of the nation's waterways. The Department of the Interior estimates that the cost of dealing with them could run into the billions of dollars in the Great Lakes region alone by the turn of the century.

How this explosion of zebra mussels will affect the ecology of the Great Lakes is a lively topic of discussion within the scientific community. Like all clams, oysters, and mussels, the zebra mussel feeds by pumping water through its body in order to extract particles of organic matter. Because a single zebra mussel can filter a quart of water per day, the uncountable billions of zebra mussels in the Great Lakes today clearly are capable of removing an immense amount of organic matter from the water column. Water clarity has increased remarkably in portions of the Great Lakes where zebra mussels are abundant. Because we tend to equate clear water with healthy water, this change would appear to be a positive development, but in fact, it is deeply troubling. The organic matter in the water column—the plankton, the zooplankton, the edible bits and pieces—forms the basis for the food chain. What goes into the gut of a zebra mussel cannot go into the gut of a native fish, worm, or other organism. In this sense, the zebra mussels may be outcompeting native species and thereby altering the entire food chain. Moreover, their profoundly obnoxious habit of settling on any hard surface poses an additional threat to native snails and clams. In the Lake Huron-Lake Erie corridor, it is possible to find native clams with 7,000 zebra mussels attached to their shells. This many hitchhikers can kill their host by preventing it from eating and breathing. Predictably, native mussels have declined dramatically in some areas following the arrival of zebra mussels.

At the present time, scientists know of no way to control this invading army of zebra mussels, although a number of them are studying the species in its native range (where it is far less of a nuisance) to ascertain what keeps it in check there. In the meantime, an ecological "experiment" of immense proportions is unfolding before our eyes. The zebra mussel is a reminder that two opposing forces are at work in the Great Lakes. One is the expensive, sometimes contentious, ongoing effort by federal, state, and local governments in two countries to reverse the effects of a century and a half of use and abuse; the other, nearly as powerful, is the pace of development and commerce in the Great Lakes watershed, which guarantees that new pollutants and new species will seep into the waters over time. The Great Lakes today bear little resemblance to the Great Lakes of a century ago, and what they will look like in another hundred years is anyone's guess.

A second Brobdingnagian effort to restore freshwater ecosystems and the fisheries they sustain is under way in the Pacific Northwest, where the harvest of seven species of salmon and seagoing trout has been a mainstay of the culture and economy for as long as people have lived there. Snippets of information from early explorers provide clues to how abundant these fish once were. "The multitudes of this fish are almost inconceivable," wrote the explorers Meriwether Lewis and William Clark after visiting the Columbia River in 1805, while records from the mid-nineteenth century describe streams almost choked with salmon. Even after intensive exploitation in the latter half of the nineteenth century, the great runs persisted, albeit in somewhat reduced numbers. Tons of salmon were routinely thrown overboard because the canneries could not keep up with the fishermen. Estimates of the number of salmon in the Columbia River prior to arrival of white settlers range from 7.5 to 16 million fish per year. Today fewer than a million fish make the journey, and most of these are born and raised in hatcheries.

What happened in the interim was the industrialization of the Northwest, from the construction of dams, great and small, that provide abundant and cheap hydropower and have turned landlocked Lewiston, Idaho, into a virtual seaport, to the spread of irrigated agriculture, to the development of a world-class timber industry that has cut most of the region's world-class forests in less than a century. These developments plus countless others have literally shrunk the world of the wild salmon, reducing the number of river miles they can reach and eliminating spawning and rearing habitats in even those places still accessible to them. A recent study estimated that Pacific salmon have disappeared from about 40 percent of their historical breeding range in Washington, Oregon, Idaho, and California over the past century, and in many areas where they still occur, their populations are much reduced in numbers.

For many years, a few people—a handful of biologists, some Indian tribes, some commercial fishermen—had complained about declining salmon populations, but until about a decade ago, the attitude of most political leaders was one of apathy. That changed abruptly on April 2, 1991, when the National Marine Fisheries Service announced its intention to place the Snake River sockeye salmon on the federal list of endangered species—the first northwestern salmon to earn that distinction. Now that the power of the Endangered Species

Act was about to be invoked, the plight of the Northwest's salmon could no longer be ignored.

Historically, few salmon traveled as far or climbed as high as the intrepid sockeyes of the Snake River, which for countless generations had journeyed 900 miles from the Pacific Ocean through the Columbia River and up the Snake River to their ancestral spawning grounds in Idaho's Redfish Lake. A difficult journey even in the best of times, the trip from the ocean to the lake (or, for the young salmon, from the lake to the ocean) had become a virtual impossibility in recent decades. Eight enormous hydropower dams now hindered the salmon's progress at various points along the Columbia River system; use of water for irrigation meant lowered water levels; and extensive logging and grazing throughout the watershed had damaged the habitat and polluted the water. Even the ocean, where the fish spend most of their lives, had become a more hostile environment as the scale of commercial fishing operations increased.

Indeed, by the time the Snake River sockeye was granted protection under the Endangered Species Act, it was unclear whether any still survived. In 1990, not a single fish had made the journey to its ancestral spawning grounds. Fortunately, the following year, four sockeyes returned to the lake, whereupon they were promptly captured and artificially spawned so that their progeny could be raised in captivity. In succeeding years, the number of returning adults ranged from a high of eight (1993) to a low of none (1995). The future of the Snake River sockeye (to the extent it has one) now rests with a captive breeding program that is churning out eggs and youngsters by the thousands in the hope that a few will survive to maturity and make that long and increasingly treacherous voyage to the sea and back.

What is at stake here is not the survival of a species per se—there are still plenty of sockeye salmon in the Pacific Northwest and Alaska—but the survival of a specific population of sockeye—in this case, the population that moves up the Snake River to spawn in Redfish Lake. Biologists use the term "stock" to refer to the discrete populations of each species that spawn in different rivers or at different times of the year. Thus, the sockeye that spawn in the Deschutes River constitute a separate stock from those in the Snake River. Similarly, the winter run of chinook in the Sacramento River is considered a separate stock from chinook that make the same journey in spring or summer. This differentiation of salmon populations is much more than an exercise in hairsplitting. Each stock potentially carries unique genetic adaptations to the environment in which it lives. A Deschutes River sockeye may differ in fundamental physical, behavioral, and physiological ways from a Snake River sockeye—not enough, certainly, to warrant calling them separate species, but enough so that they cannot be considered interchangeable, a point that has important ramifications with respect to the use (and abuse) of hatcheries.

In 1991, the American Fisheries Society published a report assessing the status of salmon stocks in the Pacific Northwest. The Society classified 106 stocks as already extinct and an additional 159 as facing a moderate to high risk of extinction. Among the leading causes of extinction or endangerment were dam construction, logging, agriculture, and overharvesting. The number of vulnerable stocks did not come as a surprise to longtime students of salmon, but it must have horrified legislators, farmers, timber industry executives, power company officials, and others who suddenly had visions of dozens of other stocks joining the Snake River sockeye on the list of federal endangered species. For those who make their living catching and processing salmon, the American Fisheries Society numbers raised an even bleaker vision: unemployment. Commercial fishing in Washington, Oregon, and northern California is directly or indirectly responsible for 65,000 jobs. The commercial salmon industry represents a small and fading fraction of this total, with the number of workers declining in synchrony with the stocks. Another economically important activity threatened by the disappearing stocks is sportfishing, which pumps millions of dollars into the regional economy each year. In 1994, for example, the annual sport catch of salmon in Washington was the lowest since record-keeping began in

1964, a consequence of "widespread closures and drastically shortened seasons" due to declines in salmon populations.

Each alleged despoiler of salmon habitat likes to blame the other despoilers for most of the damage, leading to unproductive rounds of finger pointing, but in fact, their relative responsibilities vary from watershed to watershed. In the Columbia River basin, most observers would point to the more than 1,000 hydropower dams, irrigation dams, diversion dams, and other obstructions that now confound the movement of salmon, and in particular, the eight massive Army Corps of Engineers dams on the lower Snake and Columbia rivers. Yet when the big dams were being built half a century ago, engineers and scientists expressed supreme confidence that the needs of the salmon had been taken into account. After evaluating the hatcheries and fish ladders that were an integral part of the design plans, a committee of the American Fisheries Society concluded in 1937 that "[n]o possibilities, either biological or engineering, have been overlooked in designing a means to assure perpetuation of the Columbia River salmon."

What went wrong? First, no fish ladder works flawlessly. Sometimes the adult fish cannot find them; other times they get lost in the reservoir or fall back from above the dam. More important, perhaps, the Army Corps of Engineers initially designed the ladders so that adult fish could get up them, but not so that juveniles could get down them. Consequently, up to 90 percent of the juveniles were killed, shocked, or lost in the reservoirs as they moved from their birthplace to the sea. "This fundamental engineering error was made not once but eight times over 40 years. It was not made in ignorance—fish advocates pointed it out from the beginning. It was made despite laws, policies and repeated assurances that anadromous fish runs would be preserved." And for those few fish that can find their way through the maze of dams, bypasses, and spillways, the journey downstream has become a much longer, more dangerous, and more stressful one.

Correcting these problems has been an expensive, contentious undertaking, involving adjustments to the dams themselves, changes in flow rates, and even the creation of a salmon "taxi service," in which young fish are collected, loaded onto barges, and transported below the dams. Unfortunately, the number of returning adults remains low, prompting some to question the efficacy of these efforts. A number of environmentalists, Indian tribes, and state officials have asked the power authorities to lower the reservoirs, which would enable the young fish to complete their journey downstream in a shorter time. Scientists, however, are uncertain whether doing so would be any better for the young salmon than barging, and it might interfere with river traffic, hinder irrigation, and entail some loss of hydroelectric power—objections that are raised loudly and often by industries, farmers, and power companies.

For over a hundred years, the predominant response to the decline in salmon has been a technological one: hatcheries. In the Columbia River basin alone, over eighty major hatcheries are currently in operation, churning out millions of fish each year. Without them, there would be virtually no salmon. Over 95 percent of the adult coho that make their way up the Columbia River basin each year are hatchery-reared, as are 80 percent of the summer chinook, 70 percent of the spring chinook, and 70 percent of the steelhead.

One might argue that distinguishing between hatchery-reared and wild-reared fish is merely ichthyological snobbery. If there are enough salmon to satisfy commercial fishermen, anglers, and environmentalists, why obsess over their origins? The answer is twofold: First, there simply aren't enough salmon to satisfy everyone, and second, hatcheries may ultimately accelerate rather than reverse the declines. In most cases, the brood stock used to start up hatchery production came from a different river system; it was not the native stock. The genetic differences between stocks often translate into important differences in physiological, behavioral, and other traits that make each stock uniquely adapted to its home river. Once they are released into the wild, hatchery-reared fish can mate with the indigenous wild stock and dilute its gene pool, often to the wild stock's detriment. They also compete with wild fish for food and other resources. When the U.S. Fish and Wildlife Service reviewed efforts to rebuild dwindling or vanished wild stocks with captive-reared fish, it concluded that less than 10 percent were successful.

That finding, however discouraging it may be to hatchery advocates, is not especially surprising. The ultimate problem with hatcheries is that they draw people's attention away from the ultimate problems facing the fish: habitat degradation and overfishing. If a spanking new hatchery can churn out millions of young salmon every year, it becomes all too easy to overlook the big hydropower dams, the cows grazing along the riverbanks, the soil washing off the freshly plowed fields, the clearcuts on the slopes above, and the fleet of fishing vessels lurking offshore. "We can replace the wild salmon with hatchery salmon," noted one Oregon environmentalist, "but having made that decision, we cannot protect the salmon ecosystem."

Which is how it has always been. Scientists usually can find a way to breed a rare fish in captivity; they are even discovering ways to raise rare mussels in aquariums, providing a glimmer of hope for these most imperiled animals. But with respect to the tougher and vastly more important goal of preserving aquatic ecosystems, we have hardly begun to crawl, much less hit our stride. The fault lies not with the scientists, who have worked diligently to identify the problems, but with those who created the problems in the first place by using rivers for transportation, irrigation, manufacturing, waste disposal, and hydropower—in other words, all of us.

CHAPTER FIVE

The Coastlines of a Continent

I have never understood the appeal of a day at the beach, at least not the congested, noisy beaches my friends and family enjoy. The thought of spending a day beneath the sweltering sun, sandwiched among hundreds, maybe thousands, of other people, holds no attraction for me. It's not that I dislike beaches; in fact, a few (but only a few) rank among my favorite places. One such beach is Mustang Island, near Corpus Christi, Texas. Undeveloped and almost inaccessible, it has retained much of its wild character.

A couple of years ago, a biologist from the National Audubon Society took three of us from the Environmental Defense Fund on a boat tour of Mustang's nooks and crannies. Birds were everywhere. Thousands of aptly named laughing gulls lined the beaches and mudflats, their maniacal cries providing a constant background noise. Squadrons of black skimmers, elegant black-and-white birds with long red bills, passed overhead, their staccato call notes reminding me of puppies barking at each other. And snowy plovers scurried up and down the sandy beaches like officious little businessmen racing to catch a train.

I also remember the garbage: a line of detritus encircling the entire island, composed of old tires, plastic bags, soda bottles, discarded toys, cups and containers from fast-food restaurants, and every other manner of debris that a person could possibly toss into the sea. Although it did not pose an immediate threat to any of the birds we saw that day, the wrack line of garbage was offensive to the eye, a omnipresent stain on an otherwise wild landscape. When I expressed my disgust to our guide, he replied, "I guess I think of it as a sign of a healthy beach. If there's no garbage, it means someone is raking the sand every day, and if someone is doing that, then the beach has been developed." What he said made a lot of sense, in a twisted sort of way. The beaches of Venice, California, and Fort Lauderdale, Florida, have very little garbage, but they also have very few plovers, skimmers, or other shorebirds. What they do have, in abundance, are sun-loving residents and tourists, and to keep them happy, an army of custodians is paid to remove the debris that washes ashore every day.

For as long as people have lived in North America, from the Paleoindians of the Pacific Northwest to the current residents of Key West, a large fraction of the population has chosen to live or work near the sea. Approximately 42 percent of the U.S. population currently resides in counties bordering the Atlantic or Pacific oceans. The impacts of so many people and so much activity are apparent not only in the beach houses, boardwalks, industrial ports, and "scenic" highways that line both coasts, but also in a variety of more subtle ways, including a hyperabundance of gulls and a scarcity of roseate terns along the Atlantic coast, a growing roster of alien species in San Francisco Bay, and the many beach-dwelling birds, mammals, reptiles, and insects that have made their way onto the endangered species list.

At the same time, however, rebounding populations of sea otters and elephant seals off the West Coast, ancient sea turtles that still lumber ashore to lay their eggs on a few beaches in Florida, Georgia, and Texas, and least terns that now build their nests atop the flat gravel roofs of shopping malls (instead of the overcrowded beaches) are a testament to the innate resilience of many coastal animals—a resilience that seems to emerge whenever the wildlife is given a modicum of respect. It may well be an adaptation to life in an inherently unstable world, an environment in which hurricanes and nor'easters erase beaches and marshes overnight, where El Niño can turn productive waters into biological deserts for months on end, and where sand dunes advance and retreat across the landscape. Not all species exhibit this resilience, and even among those that do, there are clear limits to what they can tolerate. But it does create an interesting dynamic: a collection of scrappy survivors trying to get by in an environment that is increasingly dominated by one rather overbearing species. In the discussion that follows, I shall focus on those animals that use land for at least a portion of their lives (e.g., sea turtles, seals, shorebirds) and are therefore tied to the actual coastlines, as opposed to whales, sharks, and most other exclusively marine species.

Not surprisingly, all five "mindless horsemen" of environmental degradation—overkill, habitat destruction, alien species, disease, and pollution—have left their mark on the fauna of both coasts. But the one that seems to have arrived first is overkill. Well before the Civil War, several birds and mammals had already disappeared from both the Atlantic and Pacific coasts, victims of a comparatively small but voracious human population. The great auk, a large and flightless relative of the puffins, once bred in colonies on coastal islands in the North Atlantic, but its innate tameness, combined with its inability to fly, made it an all too easy target for hungry fishermen. From bones recovered from Indian middens, ornithologists have deduced that the great auk once nested from the west coast of Greenland to Massachusetts, as well as off the coast of northern Europe. The only eyewitness accounts of its presence in the United States, however, are to be found in the journals of a few seventeenth-century explorers. It seems likely, therefore, that whatever breeding colonies existed in New England were destroyed by the beginning of the eighteenth century (and perhaps much earlier). The great auk survived in Canada and Greenland for perhaps another century, until fishermen located and destroyed those colonies, too. The last European specimen was obtained in 1834, and a pair killed 10 years later off the coast of Iceland is generally considered the last record of the species anywhere on earth.

Along the Pacific coast, the first animals driven to extinction by European explorers lived in precisely the region where the very first humans of any kind entered the New World: the Bering Sea. In 1741, Czar Peter the Great dispatched Admiral Vitus Bering to explore the Siberian frontier and to determine whether there was a land linkage between the Siberian coast and the North American continent. Although Bering was about 10,000 years too late to find the landbridge, the naturalist on board his ship, Georg Wilhelm Steller, found two unique animals: a manatee-like creature of elephantine proportions and a large black cormorant. The former, named the Steller's sea cow in honor of its discoverer, grew to 30 feet in length and dined on the lush "forests" of kelp (a type of algae) growing in the Bering Sea. Steller's spectacled cormorant was nowhere near as impressive as his sea cow, but within the family of cormorants, it too was something of a giant, weighing in at 12 to 14 pounds. To hungry explorers, both species represented a ready source of food during long sea voyages. Within 26 years of Bering's expedition, the sea cow was gone; the cormorant may have survived until the mid-1800s before it, too, was eaten to extinction.

Bering's explorations opened up a new world—literally and figuratively—for the fur trade. The cold, gray waters of Alaska and Siberia teemed with sea otters and fur seals, and there was money to be made—lots of it—from this seemingly limitless supply of animals. In reality, of course, the supply was anything but limitless, and the Russian sailors soon found themselves heading south in search of more pelts, establishing settlements as far as present-day California. In the meantime, growing numbers of Spanish, British, and American sealers were advancing up the Pacific coast from Mexico and California, exploiting the populations of sea otters and fur seals that lived farther south. Their discovery of thousands of giant elephant seals along the Baja and California coasts created a new market for a different kind of product: oil. From the blubber of a single 18-foot male elephant seal, a sealer could extract approximately 210 gallons of oil, which was used as lamp fuel. One such hunt off the coast of California in 1852 was graphically described by the ship's captain:

> The sailors get between the herd and the water; then, raising all possible noise by shouting, and at the same time flourishing clubs, guns, and lances, the party advance slowly toward the rookery, when the animals will retreat, appearing in a state of great alarm. Occasionally an overgrown male will give battle, or attempt to escape; but a musket-ball through the brain dispatches it; or some one checks its progress by thrusting a lance into the roof it its mouth, which causes it to settle on its haunches, when two men with heavy oaken clubs give the creature repeated blows about the head, until it is stunned or killed. After securing those that are disposed to show resistance, the party rush on the main body. The onslaught creates such a panic among these peculiar creatures, that, losing all control of their actions, they climb, roll, and tumble over each other, when

prevented from farther retreat by the projecting cliffs. We recollect in one instance where sixty-five were captured, that several were found showing no signs of having been either clubbed or lanced, but were smothered by numbers of their kind heaped upon them.

By the beginning of the twentieth century, sea otters and elephant seals teetered on the brink of extinction. At that point, only about 1,000 to 2,000 sea otters were left worldwide, less than 1 percent of the estimated population at the time of Bering's voyage. Most of the survivors lived in remote sections of the Russian and Alaskan coasts. In the United States south of Alaska, the animals were thought to be extinct until a small population was discovered off central California in 1938. Northern elephant seals fared even worse, having been reduced to fewer than 100 individuals by the early 1890s. At that point, their rarity may have become their saving grace, for sailors no longer found it profitable to seek out and slaughter the last few individuals.

In contrast to the situation along the Pacific coast, the Atlantic fur-bearing seals by and large lived north of the U.S. border, in the Maritime and Arctic provinces of Canada. The two species that regularly ranged as far south as New England—the harbor seal and the gray seal—were not especially valued for their fur, oil, or meat, and consequently were not subjected to a commercial harvest. Thus, the Atlantic coast of the United States never became a prime locale for the fur and oil trades (at least not oil derived from seals—whales were a different story). But it did become the epicenter of a very different type of market, one centered around flesh and feathers. The presence of immense numbers of waterfowl, shorebirds, and sea turtles so close to many of America's largest cities sparked an intense and wide-ranging recreational and commercial harvest that lasted until the beginning of the twentieth century. "Harvest," in fact, is a grotesque euphemism; "slaughter" more aptly describes the frenzy of shooting, trapping, and egg collecting that decimated a multitude of species.

The killing was motivated by several factors. Many of the participants were simply recreational or subsistence hunters, people who enjoyed hunting or depended upon wild game to supplement their diets. Others were commercial hunters, who shot vast quantities of birds or collected buckets of wild bird eggs to supply markets in the growing East Coast cities. Commercial hunting was hardly restricted to the coast—recall the barrels of passenger pigeons shipped out of the Midwest in the late nineteenth century—but the coastal birds, by virtue of their proximity to the cities, were especially vulnerable. The absence of game laws and bag limits enabled these hunters to operate with complete disregard for the welfare of the species they shot. Last but not least, at the close of the nineteenth century, the apparel industry managed to create a nearly insatiable demand for the feathers (and sometimes the whole carcasses) of wild birds to adorn women's hats. The convergence of these three different demands resulted in several decades of ceaseless harassment and killing of American waterfowl, sandpipers, plovers, herons, terns, and even gulls.

Among these birds, the sandpipers and plovers in particular were poorly suited to intensive, uncontrolled hunting. Most of them breed on the tundra of northern Canada and Alaska, where the brief Arctic summer allows them at most a few weeks to establish territories, lay a single clutch of eggs, and fledge offspring. If a predator takes their young (an all too common occurrence in the harsh Arctic environment), there is rarely time to renest, and an entire season's reproductive effort may be lost. Such birds have a difficult time rebuilding their populations in the face of excessive hunting because their rates of reproduction are so low. Moreover, many of these shorebirds engage in spectacularly long and difficult migrations. Semipalmated sandpipers, smaller than sparrows, migrate from the north coast of Alaska to northern South America and back again; 6-inch sanderlings circumnavigate the Western Hemisphere by moving across the top of North America and down the Atlantic coast to their wintering grounds in Chile and Peru, and then up the Pacific coast to their breeding grounds in the Arctic. For many shorebirds, their time in the coterminous United States amounts to little more than brief rest and refueling stops, where large numbers of birds congregate en route to or from the Arctic. Hunters quickly learned to stake out these stopover points, with the result that these birds were shot and harassed throughout their spring and fall migrations.

All were fair game, from the stately curlews to the tiny sandpipers, because they occurred in flocks (which pleased the market hunters), responded readily to decoys or imitations of their calls, and were good to eat. As the larger species dwindled due to overkill, the gunners increasingly turned their attention to the smaller ones, much as the fishermen of the Great Lakes would later pursue and deplete successively smaller fish species using nets with finer meshes. The greater the aggregations of a given species of shorebird, the more likely it was to be overharvested, a circumstance that drove one species, the Eskimo curlew, to extinction and nearly eliminated two or three others.

A 12-inch bird modestly colored in shades of brown and buff, the Eskimo curlew followed two distinct migratory paths between its breeding grounds in the Canadian Arctic and its wintering grounds in the pampas of Argentina. In the spring, the birds headed north across the Great Plains; in the fall, they moved south along the Atlantic coast. The curlews were so numerous that settlers in the Great Plains sometimes called them "prairie pigeons," a reference to the flocks of passenger pigeons that filled the eastern forests. And, like the pigeons, the curlews were shot by the bushel. Wrote one observer:

> Hunters would drive out from Omaha and shoot the birds without mercy until they had literally slaughtered a wagonload of them, the wagons being actually filled, and often with the sideboards on at that. Sometimes when the flight was unusually heavy and the hunters were well supplied with ammunition their wagons were too quickly and easily filled, so whole loads of the birds would be dumped on the

prairie, their bodies forming piles as large as a couple of tons of coal, where they would be allowed to rot while the hunters proceeded to refill their wagons with fresh victims. The compact flocks and tameness of the birds made this slaughter possible, and at each shot usually dozens of the birds would fall.

Eskimo curlews remained abundant until the 1870s, when both hunters and ornithologists noticed a sudden drop in their numbers. By the turn of the century, the species had become extremely rare, and a single bird seen along the Texas coast in the spring of 1963 and another shot in Barbados in the fall of that year were the last unimpeachable records. Perhaps a lone curlew or two, the last of their tribe, still make that fateful journey from the high Arctic to Argentina, but if so, they have managed to elude legions of birdwatchers who search for them in vain.

Populations of many other shorebirds were decimated during this period, including golden plovers, buff-breasted sandpipers, long-billed curlews, willets, dowitchers, knots, godwits, and even the little sanderlings and semipalmated sandpipers. A few, such as the buff-breasted sandpiper and Hudsonian godwit, became so rare that some ornithologists predicted their imminent extinction—which, fortunately, did not come to pass.

The market gunners took a heavy toll on the nation's ducks as well, and populations of canvasbacks, redheads, scaup, and other waterfowl that congregate in coastal estuaries declined during the late 1800s. Fortunately, waterfowl tend to be more prolific than shorebirds. Most ducks lay more eggs and enjoy a longer nesting season than sandpipers, and are therefore better able to withstand the pressure of hunting. Consequently, with one exception, none of the ducks came close to extinction. The exception was the Labrador duck, a peculiar little black-and-white duck that appeared each winter off the Atlantic coast from New England south to Chesapeake Bay. Never common, it was nonetheless hunted for food and sold in the markets.

Beginning around 1850, Labrador ducks grew steadily scarcer, until they finally disappeared altogether. An individual shot in the fall of 1875 off the coast of Long Island became the last record of the species.

The growing popularity of feathers as adornments on women's hats during the last quarter of the nineteenth century spurred a new round of shooting directed at different groups of birds. Most prized were the white egrets and other herons that sport long, graceful plumes during the breeding season. But as heron populations declined, the plume hunters turned their attention to other species. Terns became a favorite target, and before long, most of the accessible nesting colonies of common, roseate, and least terns along the Atlantic coast had been destroyed. Even gulls were not immune to the pressures of the market, where both their feathers and eggs were much in demand. By the end of the nineteenth century, great black-backed gulls had disappeared entirely from New England, while herring gulls, once a common nesting bird in Maine and Massachusetts, persisted in only a few remote areas.

Along the West Coast, the millinery trade was not as big an enterprise as it was in the East, but market hunters were still a force to be reckoned with. At least one naturalist in California was bemoaning the decline of game birds as early as 1880, a decline he attributed to overhunting. In 1913, scientists from the Museum of Vertebrate Zoology in Berkeley, California, sent a questionnaire about the status of various game birds to "responsible observers" throughout the state. Virtually all of the respondents reported major declines in populations of ducks and geese, averaging 50 percent for ducks and 75 percent for geese. Estimates of the number of ducks sold annually in the markets of California ranged from 350,000 in 1911 to 125,000 in 1916. Rails and shorebirds were also shot for the market, leading to noticeable reductions in the populations of several species, including California clapper rails, dowitchers, and long-billed curlews. "Sale of game on the open market has been fundamentally the most important factor in reducing California's supply of game birds," declared the eminent ornithologist Joseph Grinnell in 1918.

As the nineteenth century came to a close, birds "were being consumed so fast that spokesmen in their defense, heretofore shrill, solitary voices, began at last to band together and to conscript others to the cause." The ensuing public outrage fueled the creation of the American Ornithologists' Union in 1883 and the National Association of Audubon Societies, progenitor of the National Audubon Society, in 1902. State and federal laws essentially ended the plume trade by 1913, and passage of the Migratory Bird Treaty Act 5 years later gave the federal government the authority to determine bag limits and hunting seasons for migratory species. The unregulated slaughter of America's wild birds had come to an end. In subsequent years, hunters would become some of the strongest supporters of wildlife conservation in the nation, backing up their considerable political muscle with cold hard cash in the form of hunting license fees and excise taxes on hunting gear, which has funded the purchase of important wildlife habitat.

For the beleaguered seals and otters of the Pacific coast, relief came at about the same time. The federal government prohibited the taking of sea otters in Alaskan waters in 1910, and a year later, the United States, Great Britain (representing Canada), Russia, and Japan signed a treaty limiting the harvest of fur seals. Also in 1911, the Mexican government finally took steps to protect the few remaining elephant seals.

If there is a bright side to overexploitation, it lies in the fact that once the slaughter has stopped, the affected species may be able to recover—assuming, of course, that a large enough population remains and the habitat is still there. In some cases, the animals return on their own (recolonization); in others, people nudge the process along by moving animals from surviving populations to now vacant habitats (translocation). Either way, recolonizations and translocations constitute important "ecological experiments." By observing what happens to an ecosystem when a missing species returns, ecologists retroactively learn about the role of that species within the ecosystem. (One can also deduce the role of a species by observing what happens when it is removed. In the United States, however, the "removal" of many species took place in the nineteenth and early twentieth centuries, long before there were ecologists around to study the consequences.)

Fortunately, a number of coastal mammals and birds have made extraordinary comebacks since the era of market hunting, and the insights scientists have gained from studying these animals have been among the most important in conservation biology. In the case of the sea otter, the surviving populations in Alaska and California increased steadily and resettled much of their former range once they were protected. Otters have also been translocated to parts of British Columbia, Washington, and Oregon in an effort to jump-start the recovery process there. Subsequently, in almost all of these locales, scientists have noted a remarkable transformation in the marine environment: Sea urchin populations have plummeted, and lush undersea "forests" of kelp have sprung up.

The explanation for these changes lies in the complex relationship between otters, urchins, and kelp. Sea otters are voracious consumers of marine invertebrates, including crabs, abalone, and especially sea urchins. A 50-pound adult otter may eat 25–30 percent of its weight daily in urchins and other creatures. Sea urchins, in turn, are equally voracious consumers of kelp. When otters were driven to the brink of extinction in the eighteenth and nineteenth centuries, the urchins found themselves living in a much safer world, one lacking their main mammalian predator. Their numbers exploded, and they quickly devoured the kelp. The return of the otters reversed that change, often with stunning speed. In some areas, the once abundant sea urchins all but disappeared shortly after the otters arrived; in other places, the only urchins that survived were the ones too small to be of interest to the otters.

The effect of the otters extends well beyond sea urchins and kelp, however. Kelp forests constitute a distinctive and important ecosystem in the North Pacific, providing food and shelter for a wide range of organisms. As kelp decays or is broken apart by waves, it releases organic matter into the marine environment— organic matter that is readily consumed by mussels, anemones, crabs, and other organisms, which are themselves consumed by fish, birds, sea otters, and other top predators. Studies in the Aleutian Islands of Alaska have shown that the presence of kelp (made possible by the presence of otters) results in a richer, more productive ecosystem due to this input of organic matter. Mussels and barnacles grow faster and larger in places with kelp (and otters) than in places without it. Rock greenlings (a type of fish) are 10 to 100 times more common in kelp forests than they are in areas grazed by sea urchins. The extraordinary effect that sea otters have on marine environments fully justifies calling them keystone species.

Up and down both coasts, many of the other mammals and birds that were heavily persecuted at the turn of the century have staged comebacks as spectacular as that of the sea otter, but the ecological ramifications of their decline and subsequent recovery are largely unknown. Northern elephant seals, for example, have increased from fewer than 100 individuals at the start of the twentieth century to more than 125,000 today. Given that an adult male elephant seal eats approximately 42,000 pounds of squid, fish, and other sea life per year, and an adult female over 10,000 pounds, one may reasonably assume that today's rebounding elephant seal population ingests hundreds of millions of pounds of marine life annually. What, then, was happening to all the marine organisms that were not being eaten by elephant seals during the period when they were almost extinct? How did marine food webs change in the absence of this enormous predator, and what have been the consequences of its recovery? Because elephant seals spend so much of their lives at sea, diving to incredible depths in search of prey, scientists do not know how the disappearance and reappearance of this animal has affected other species in the deep waters where it feeds.

By the 1920s, some ornithologists were reporting a resurgence in populations of sandpipers, curlews, and plovers. Gulls and terns, too, began to return to the nesting grounds they had abandoned during the height of the shooting. Looking back, it seems almost miraculous that so few birds or mammals were driven to extinction as a result of the carnage of the late nineteenth century, although many came close. Second chances are an all too infrequent phenomenon in the history of wildlife conservation, yet that has been the story on both coasts.

It would be wrong to conclude, however, that the era of overexploitation has come to an end. Marine mammals and birds are now reasonably well protected, but for a host of other, less charismatic animals, commercial harvests continue to exceed what their populations can tolerate. The "poster child" of contemporary overexploitation may well be the white abalone, a large marine snail that lives in deep underwater reefs along 700 miles of coastline in southern California and Baja. Thirty years ago, white abalone were truly abundant along certain reefs, reaching densities as high as 4,000 individuals per acre. When divers began harvesting the species commercially in 1965, state officials restricted the take of smaller individuals in order to maintain a healthy, sustainable abalone population. The idea was to give the animals enough time to grow and reproduce before they were harvested. Yet the white abalone fishery collapsed nonetheless in just 9 years.

At that point, with the snails no longer subjected to a commercial harvest, one would have expected their numbers to increase slowly. Instead, the opposite occurred. Abalone populations continued to decline, and today the species appears to be on the brink of extinction. What the regulators apparently overlooked were some critical facts about the white abalone's breeding behavior. Males and females release their sperm and eggs into the water column; fertilization cannot take place unless the two sexes are very close to each other, usually within a yard. Divers apparently reduced the density of white abalone below the threshold for successful fertilization, such that sperm and egg never meet. Based on the ages of the few remaining individuals, some scientists believe that the last successful breeding season occurred as far back as 1969, and that the species has been in a downward spiral ever since. There is some hope that more white abalone will be found in deeper waters, where commercial divers rarely ventured, but absent such a discovery, the species seems destined for extinction, as the last few aging individuals release their eggs and sperm in futile little clouds that slowly dissipate in the immense void.

The spiny lobster is another victim of overexploitation, although it is nowhere near as imperiled as the white abalone. Spiny lobsters, like sea otters, are voracious predators of sea urchins, and they may well play a comparable role in protecting the Pacific coast's kelp forests. They also make a singularly delicious entree at fine restaurants, and as a consequence, their numbers have been greatly depleted in recent years. Whether their decline will eventually spell trouble for the kelp forests is anyone's guess.

Even when animals are protected against commercial or recreational harvests, they can fall victim to the fishing industry's mad scramble for other species. A striking example of this phenomenon may be unfolding in the Aleutian Islands, where the number of sea otters has plummeted by 90 percent since 1990 (this coming after decades of growth). With their arch-predator in abeyance, sea urchin populations have exploded, causing great damage to the region's kelp forests. Scientists attribute the decline of the otters to increased predation by killer whales. The whales, in turn, are eating the otters because their preferred prey—sea lions and seals—have become much scarcer in recent years in the Bering Sea. Why the sea lions and seals have declined is controversial, but the most likely explanation involves a reduction in their prey (fish) due to the region's burgeoning commercial fisheries.

A more direct example of conflict between commercial fisheries and native wildlife involves the five species of sea turtles found along the Atlantic coast of the United States. Individuals of all five species—Kemp's ridley, hawksbill, loggerhead, green, and leatherback—come ashore to nest on select beaches along the southern Atlantic and Gulf coasts, although only the loggerhead and green now do so in any numbers.

How common sea turtles were prior to the arrival of European settlers will never be known. Ecologist Jerome B. C. Jackson has used historical accounts and some back-of-the-envelope arithmetic to estimate that somewhere between 33 and 660 *million* green sea turtles may have lived in the Caribbean Sea prior to Columbus's arrival. At those numbers, the weight, or "biomass," of green sea turtles would have rivaled or exceeded that of bison on the central plains, an analogy made all the more fitting by the fact that green sea turtles, like bison, are grazers, dining on sea grasses and algae. It is therefore entirely reasonable to conclude, as Jackson does, that green sea turtles had as great an effect on their environment as bison did on the grasslands. The turtles cropped the sea grasses, thereby helping to create a mosaic of habitats, and they redistributed nutrients via their urine and feces. How the presence of so many turtles affected populations of other marine grazers, such as sea urchins and fish, must remain a mystery, however, because European settlers had decimated turtle populations in much of the Caribbean by 1800. (Indeed, as early as 1620, the Bermuda Assembly felt compelled to pass a law protecting the younger green sea turtles from harvest.)

In the United States, early naturalists such as Mark Catesby and Audubon reported nesting aggregations of green sea turtles in Florida, but gave no indication of their numbers. The memoirs of General William T. Sherman, on the other hand, suggest that turtles were abundant in eastern Florida in 1840, when he was stationed there: "They were so cheap and common that the soldiers regarded it as an imposition when compelled to eat green turtle steaks instead of poor Florida beef or the usual mess-pork. I do not recall in my whole experience a spot where fish, oysters, and green turtles so abound as at Fort Pierce, Florida." Within five decades, however, Floridians were complaining about a lack of sea turtles, which they attributed to bad weather, steamboats (which were alleged to frighten the animals)—indeed, anything but the real culprit, which was surely overexploitation.

Leatherback, Kemp's ridley, and hawksbill sea turtles were placed on the U.S. endangered species list in 1970, green and loggerhead sea turtles in 1978. In the years that followed, however, sea turtle populations in much of the Southeast did not increase. On the contrary, growing numbers of dead turtles were washing up on beaches in the Gulf of Mexico and along the Atlantic coast. The cause was quickly identified as entrapment and drowning in the trawl nets used by fishermen to catch shrimp. The shrimp fishery is extraordinarily wasteful: For every pound of shrimp that is caught, 2 to 8 pounds of other sea life are killed and shoveled overboard. Included every year among that "by-catch" (as the wastage is called) were thousands of sea turtles.

The drowning of sea turtles in shrimp nets constituted a violation of the Endangered Species Act, but the National Marine Fisheries Service (which has jurisdiction over endangered marine species) did not wish to prohibit trawling in the Gulf of Mexico and elsewhere where sea turtles lived. Instead, it committed itself to finding a technological solution to the problem. That solution emerged in 1980 in the form of a Turtle Excluder Device, or TED, a boxlike structure that, when attached to trawl nets, enabled most of the trapped sea turtles to escape unharmed. Although the Fisheries Service conducted numerous studies showing that TEDs did not significantly diminish the shrimp catch, the shrimpers were nonetheless skeptical and declined to use them. And the Fisheries Service, feeling political heat from Gulf Coast politicians, declined to make their use mandatory.

The growing numbers of dead turtles appearing on beaches, coupled with pressure from environmentalists, finally forced the Fisheries Service to reconsider its decision, and in 1986 it proposed to make the use of TEDs mandatory for some boats in some places at certain times of the year—a far more timid response than environmentalists had wanted. For several years thereafter, the shrimpers tried, with little success, to challenge the new rules in court. They were more successful in persuading Congress to pass stopgap laws to delay the TED regulations, which resulted in still more turtle deaths.

When the rules were finally allowed to go into effect in the summer of 1989, the shrimpers quickly claimed that the TEDs were becoming clogged with seaweed, which was reducing the shrimp harvest. An all too obliging Commerce Department (which oversees the National Marine Fisheries Service) suspended enforcement of the regulations while a study was undertaken. When that study demonstrated unequivocally that seaweed was not a problem, the Commerce Department reinstated the regulations. The shrimpers then tried civil disobedience, blockading the Houston Ship Channel. In response, the Commerce Department once again suspended enforcement of the TED rules. Environmentalists sued to have the rules reinstated, and won. In the fall of 1989, under court order, the TED regulations were finally implemented.

For 5 more years, environmentalists and shrimpers engaged in a kind of trench warfare in the halls of Congress, in the offices of federal regulators, and in the courts, with the former pushing to make the use of TEDs mandatory in all sea turtle habitats throughout the year, and the latter resisting any expansion of the regulations they detested. Science and the law were on the side of the environmentalists, however, and on December 1, 1994, the Commerce Department made the use of TEDs mandatory on all shrimp trawls operating from North Carolina to Texas. The rule came almost 24 years to the day after the Kemp's ridley sea turtle was added to the endangered species list.

With the two most immediate threats—overexploitation and drowning—finally under control, the sea turtles seem poised for a comeback comparable to that of the sea otters and elephant seals. And, indeed, there is some recent evidence that their numbers are building. But another, even more intractable threat may yet frustrate efforts to save these ancient reptiles. It is that most ubiquitous of threats, habitat destruction.

Sea turtles demonstrate remarkable intergenerational fidelity to their nesting beaches. After spending 10 to 50 years at sea, most females return to the place where they were born to lay their own eggs. How many of these ancient nesting sites now lie buried under asphalt or overbuilt with summer houses is anyone's guess. Still more sites literally washed away when overzealous engineers installed seawalls, riprap, and jetties to protect beachfront property. Such structures usually accelerate beach erosion, and when they collapse (which they inevitably do), the resulting debris can pose an insurmountable obstacle to an adult turtle seeking higher ground for nesting or a hatchling racing for the sea.

Beach replenishment, which consists of trucking or pumping sand onto eroding beaches, might appear to be a simple way to improve the lives of sea turtles, but it usually has the opposite effect. For several years after treatment, replenished beaches tend to be harder and more compacted than natural ones, which makes it difficult for the females to dig their nests. Moreover, the new material may differ from the "native" sand in its consistency, which can affect the temperature of the eggs, their ability to respire, and ultimately, the rate of hatching. Add to these factors the hubbub of the trucks and pumps that deliver the sand, and the result is rarely beneficial for the turtles.

Artificial lighting is another, less widely recognized form of habitat degradation for sea turtles. Most sea turtles come ashore to nest at night, and they avoid brightly lit areas. When the hatchlings emerge from their nests, they use natural light as a cue to orient themselves toward the sea. The ensuing scramble to the ocean is an exceptionally dangerous moment in their lives, with gulls, crabs, raccoons, and other predators creating a deadly obstacle course between the nests and the relative safety of the water. The hatchlings are easily disoriented by porch lights, streetlights, automobile headlights, and other artificial sources of illumination, which cause them to meander aimlessly, or head inland, until exhaustion or predators take their toll. Even the glow on the horizon of a distant city can be enough to confuse the hatchlings. Fortunately, a number of communities where sea turtles nest have instituted lighting ordinances that either prohibit artificial lights close to nesting beaches or mandate the use of low-pressure sodium lights, which seem not to distract the turtles.

Even plastic debris, such as the garbage that spoiled the beauty of Mustang Island, poses a threat to the largest of the sea turtles, the leatherback. Leatherbacks feed exclusively on jellyfish and other soft-bodied sea creatures. They apparently mistake floating plastic bags and deflated balloons for jellyfish, an understandable error that all too often results in fatal stomach obstructions. Nearly half of the adult leatherbacks sampled worldwide had plastic in their stomachs, a statistic that says as much about our own species' carelessness as it does about the leatherbacks' lack of discrimination.

The sea turtles are just part of a growing roster of imperiled beach dwellers. On the Atlantic coast, they are joined by piping plovers, roseate terns, Puritan tiger beetles, northeastern beach tiger beetles, and at least eight varieties of beach mice, all of which have been placed on the endangered species list because of habitat destruction. On the Pacific coast, the western snowy plover and California least tern have been added to the list for much the same reason. Even some of the commoner sandpipers, which seemed to be doing so well after the market hunting era came to a close, have suffered major population declines since the 1970s, perhaps because some of the key beaches where they congregate during migration have been developed.

For all of these species, the nature of habitat destruction goes well beyond the physical destruction of the beaches to include their recreational use. Plover eggs and tiger beetles are crushed beneath the wheels of dune buggies and sport-utility vehicles; joggers and strollers flush incubating terns, leaving the eggs and nestlings exposed to predators and the sun; dogs chase down and kill flightless young plovers and terns. Such damage may be unintentional, but it is deadly nonetheless.

Of course, what is habitat destruction for one species often turns out to be habitat enhancement for another, and therein lie the roots of one of the most serious problems facing coastal wildlife today. On both coasts, the past half century has seen an extraordinary rise in the numbers of gulls, raccoons, foxes, rats, and other animals that thrive in close association with humans. For these opportunists, expanding human populations along the coast have meant more landfills, garbage cans, picnic grounds, and other rich sources of food plus few, if any, of their own predators to worry about. In addition to feeding on our left-overs, these animals also prey upon the eggs and nestlings of plovers, terns, sea turtles, and other beach dwellers. Add to this mix the cats and dogs that people keep as pets and often allow to roam, and the world of a piping plover or Alabama beach mouse begins to look depressingly similar to that of a forest-dwelling songbird in the East—little available habitat, but lots of predators.

Consider, for example, the problems posed by gulls. Few other animals have benefited more from a growing human population than these garbage-loving birds. Our landfills and fishing fleets (which dump millions of tons of by-catch over-board each year) have created a food bonanza for them. Once nearly extirpated from the United States by egg harvesters and shooters, herring gulls have filled to capacity virtually all of the available nesting sites in New England and have expanded their range southward. Today, they nest abundantly from Canada to North Carolina. A second species, the great black-backed gull, has experienced an equal if not greater population expansion. Essentially unknown as a breeding species in the United States at the end of the nineteenth century, black-backs now nest alongside herring gulls from Maine to North Carolina.

The effect of these large numbers of gulls is twofold. First, these large, aggressive birds literally usurp the nesting spaces of smaller species such as terns and plovers. Second, herring and great black-backed gulls are voracious consumers of the eggs and chicks of other birds (not to mention beach mice, hatchling sea turtles, and pretty much anything small enough to stuff down their throats). At site after site, an increase in gulls has coincided with a decrease in terns. In New England alone, roseate terns abandoned at least thirty important nesting sites between 1920 and 1979; in at least thirteen cases, a hostile takeover by gulls was identified as the cause. And in Massachusetts, Rhode Island, and Virginia, piping plovers have disappeared from sites to which herring and black-backed gulls have spread. A combination of too many gulls, too many people, and too little habitat has reversed the major population gains that terns and plovers made in the early decades of the twentieth century, after the era of market hunting came to a close.

Efforts to control expanding gull populations in New England began as far back as the 1930s. Various strategies, ranging from puncturing eggs to poisoning adults, were tried, but none made a permanent dent in their numbers. State and federal officials found they could control gull numbers in a few discrete places at best. Patience waned and budgets shrunk, with the result that most of these efforts were abandoned by the early 1970s. Passage of the Endangered Species Act in 1973 and the subsequent designation of roseate terns, piping plovers, and other coastal animals as protected species rekindled interest in reducing gull populations. More recently, however, gull control programs have come under attack from the animal rights movement, an unfortunate development because, in the short term at least, these programs may be essential to the survival of a number of beleaguered species.

Along both coasts, wildlife managers have been forced to employ a variety of techniques to protect sensitive plants and animals. They have erected fences around tern and plover colonies to prevent dogs, cats, and other animals from disturbing the birds, and they have poisoned or trapped predatory animals such as raccoons and foxes. In one bizarre case, the Fish and Wildlife Service allowed a developer to build 753 condominiums in prime habitat for the endangered Alabama beach mouse, but insisted that none of the residents be permitted to own cats—apparently a politically more palatable decision than simply refusing to allow the construction in the first place.

Lest one think these sorts of problems are confined to beaches, with their hordes of tourists, retirees, and sunworshippers, it is worth noting that most, if not all, coastal ecosystems, including marshes, bays, and estuaries, have been heavily altered by human activities. The San Francisco Estuary, consisting of San Francisco Bay and the delta of the Sacramento and San Joaquin rivers, once sustained one of the grandest wildlife spectacles on the continent, featuring sea otters, tule elk, and millions of waterfowl and shorebirds. The sea otters and tule elk disappeared by the middle of the nineteenth century, the victims of overexploitation. An influx of settlers to California, caused in part by the Gold Rush, brought a new threat to the estuary's flora and fauna: habitat destruction. Much of the bay's productivity depends upon a delicate balance between the fresh water exiting from the Sacramento and San Joaquin rivers and the incoming salt water of the Pacific Ocean. Beginning in the latter half of the nineteenth century and continuing to the present time, Californians have dammed and diverted the rivers that feed into the bay in order to sustain a fabulously productive agricultural empire in the Central Valley. Between 1860 and 1930, they diked and drained 97 percent of the freshwater marshes of the Sacramento-San Joaquin delta. They also diked and drained the brackish and saltwater marshes fringing the bay in order to create salt ponds (for commercial salt production), pastures, and dry land for commercial development. Today, approximately 80 percent of these tidal marshes have been destroyed, while over half of the fresh water that would otherwise reach San Francisco Bay in an average year is stored or diverted upstream.

The effects of these changes on the bay's fauna and flora can be measured in numerous ways—in the diminished runs of salmon that make their way up the few free-flowing river segments, in the smaller numbers of ducks and sandpipers that settle in for the winter, in the demise of the estuary's commercial fisheries, and most notably, in the growing number of Bay Area plants and animals that have been added to the endangered species list. Two species in particular, the California clapper rail and the saltmarsh harvest mouse, stand out as unwitting symbols of how difficult it has become to protect native wildlife in the remnants of this once glorious ecosystem.

Both the mouse and the rail are dyed-in-the-wool marsh dwellers. Their habitat can be divided into three zones—low, mid-, and upper marshes—that vary slightly in elevation and are therefore subjected to different degrees of flooding as the tides ebb and flow. Each zone also tends to exhibit its own distinctive vegetation. The rail is a devotee of the cordgrass and pickleweed that grow in the low and mid-marshes, while the mouse prefers pickleweed. However, both animals use all three zones over the course of a year, spending much of their time in the productive low marshes but retreating to the upper zone during unusually high tides. But much of that upper zone has been lost to commercial and residential development, while extensive portions of the mid- and low marshes have been converted to pastures and salt ponds. In the southern reaches of the bay, additional acres of mid-marsh habitat have subsided due to groundwater withdrawals, becoming de facto low-zone marshes. Thus, the rails and mice find themselves living in an environment where approximately four-fifths of their original habitat has been destroyed and a sizable portion of what is left is no longer suitable.

To add to the rails' woes, red foxes were introduced accidentally into the interior of California and spread to the coast, whereupon they took to the salt marshes "like Labrador retrievers take to a duck pond," and began preying on the rails. Their depredations nearly drove the birds to extinction in the late 1980s, until state and federal agencies initiated a trapping program. The foxes have also demonstrated a keen gastronomic interest in California's least terns and western snowy plovers, both of which are on the endangered list.

The San Francisco Estuary, in fact, has the dubious distinction of being perhaps the most extensively invaded estuary in the world, with a higher proportion of its habitats dominated by non-native species than is the case in any other comparable aquatic ecosystem. According to a recent study, at least 234 non-native species of plants, animals, and microorganisms have established populations in the bay and delta. No shallow-water habitat has been spared from invasion, and in some parts of the estuary it is difficult to find any native species in abundance. Entire food webs have been disrupted and reconfigured by alien species. Fish from the eastern United States and clams and mussels from Asia and the Mediterranean now dominate many portions of the estuary. Equally troubling is the fact that the rate of invasion has increased dramatically in recent decades — from an average of one new species established every 55 weeks from 1851 to 1960 to an average of one new species every 14 weeks from 1961 to 1995. Not even the Great Lakes can match the San Francisco Estuary in the degree to which it has been overrun with alien plants and animals.

Two factors in particular have conspired to make the bay such a haven for alien species. The first is opportunity. The bay is a hub of human activity, with countless ships, planes, trains, trucks, and automobiles arriving and departing every day, some small fraction of which carry and deposit unwanted plant and animal hitchhikers. Still other species have escaped or been released from hatcheries, ornamental ponds, and aquariums, and now run amok in the estuary. The second key factor is disturbance. As noted before, habitat alteration invariably creates winners and losers. All of the dikes, dams, landfills, and other structures that have made San Francisco Bay a worse place for clapper rails and saltmarsh harvest mice have made it a more habitable place for alien plants and animals.

The alien invasion of San Francisco Bay is an extreme manifestation of a widespread coastal phenomenon. Up and down both coasts, non-native species are increasing steadily in numbers and variety, with no immediate prospects of a slowdown. A few are conspicuous and easy to monitor — the 25-pound mute swans along the East Coast being a prime example — but most are obscure worms, isopods, and the like that can go undetected for years. Rarely do ecologists have any real sense as to how these invaders are affecting native species or the ecosystems in which they reside. Every year their ranks are swelled by new arrivals, some fraction of which will eventually prove to be harmful to our native fauna and flora.

Although habitat destruction and alien species are the most pervasive threats to coastal wildlife, they rarely receive as much attention (or vilification) as a third menace: oil pollution. When a tanker runs aground, or an offshore well suffers a major blowout, images of oil-soaked seabirds and fouled beaches fill the evening news and fuel public outrage. The names of the offending ships — *Torrey Canyon, Amoco Cadiz, Exxon Valdez* — are seared in our memory like the names of notorious gangsters, and understandably so: The loss of marine life immediately following a catastrophic spill can be staggering. But how significant are these losses over the long term? Are the affected species capable of recovering from a catastrophic spill, and if so, how long does the recovery process take?

Unfortunately, our ability to answer these basic questions is severely limited for two reasons. First, there are rarely any "baseline" data on plant and animal populations from before the spill. This gaping information hole can make it difficult, if not impossible, for scientists to determine the extent of the injury, much less what constitutes recovery. Even in cases in which baseline studies have been conducted, they are rarely comprehensive in nature. A few conspicuous species of birds or mammals may have been monitored prior to the spill, but there is little chance that any biologist was counting barnacles, mussels, or polychaete worms prior to the accident, even though these little creatures may suffer as grievously from a spill as their larger brethren. Second, each spill represents a unique event, making generalizations dangerous. The location of the accident, the amount and type of oil, the time of year, and the weather conditions all influence which species are harmed, how they are harmed, and (perhaps) how quickly they recover.

That said, what limited evidence we have suggests that oil spills are neither the apocalyptic disasters described by some environmentalists nor the minor, erasable moments portrayed by oil industry spokesmen. The damage that is done to wildlife and marine ecosystems is quite real, and some of it can be long-lasting. But many of the affected species show a remarkable ability to rebound from a major spill.

One of the few cases in which baseline data were available prior to an oil spill involved the 1990 Arthur Kill spill in New York Harbor. On January 1 of that year, a refinery pipeline in the harbor ruptured, sending 567,000 gallons of fuel oil into the tidal creeks and marshes of the Arthur Kill ("kill" is a Dutch word for creek), which separates Staten Island from New Jersey. Over 300 gulls and 200 ducks perished immediately following the spill, along with much smaller numbers of muskrats and black-crowned night herons. What makes this case particularly interesting is the fact that researchers had been studying mussels, fiddler crabs, and other invertebrate animals prior to the accident. In heavily oiled areas, almost all of the mussels died, and even in places several miles away from the spill, some mortality was detected. The fiddler crabs had nestled into their burrows for the winter when the spill occurred, but oil seeping through the mud drove many of them to the surface, where they quickly succumbed to freezing temperatures and surface oil.

Six years later, populations of ducks, gulls, night herons, and muskrats around Arthur Kill were back to pre-spill levels. Mussels had increased as well, but were not yet up to pre-spill levels. The population of fiddler crabs had more or less recovered, but scientists noted some lingering behavioral abnormalities: Crabs in creeks near the spill site exhibited more aggressive behavior than those from unoiled creeks. Because the spill had occurred in the dead of winter, a number of migratory birds—chiefly herons, egrets, and ibises—were absent from the Kill at the time, which undoubtedly spared many of them an untimely death. When they returned the following spring, however, their feathers were quickly soiled by the lingering oil.

Adult birds transferred this oil to their eggs and young during incubation, killing embryos and nestlings. In the case of the snowy egret, an elegant white bird with long black legs and yellow toes, reproductive rates remained low for several years thereafter. These lingering problems notwithstanding, six years after the spill xthe Arthur Kill was a cleaner and livelier place than anyone had expected it to be.

Even the wildlife around Prince William Sound, Alaska, site of the *Exxon Valdez* fiasco, has demonstrated a surprising resilience. When it ran aground on March 24, 1989, the *Exxon Valdez* spilled over 11 million gallons of crude oil, killing an estimated quarter million seabirds (mostly murres), along with 3,500–5,500 sea otters, 300 harbor seals, and an unknown number of fish. How many crabs, mussels, limpets, isopods, worms, and other marine invertebrates perished along with the vertebrates is anyone's guess, but the number was surely immense.

As is typically the case with oil spills, intensive monitoring of wildlife populations did not begin until after the accident. The absence of baseline data has made it very difficult for scientists to determine how badly the affected species were injured and whether they have recovered. The murres are something of an exception. They nest in large colonies on offshore islands, a few of which had been surveyed prior to the spill. Biologists did not detect a statistically significant decline in murre populations in most of these areas in the years following the accident, but what to make of this finding is unclear. An actual decline could have occurred, but might not have registered as statistically significant (as often happens when only a few sites are monitored and sample sizes are small). Similarly, any change (up or down) in the population could have been obscured by natural year-to-year variability. Some, but not all, of the colonies produced markedly fewer chicks for a few years after the spill; the extent to which this decrease was a result of the oil or a reflection of other, extrinsic factors remains unclear. Scientists generally agree that the murres of Prince William Sound are recovering from the events of March 24, 1989, but whether everything is back to normal—and even what "normal" means for murre populations—is still in dispute.

A variety of other birds, including loons, harlequin ducks, cormorants, black oystercatchers, pigeon guillemots, and bald eagles, declined in and around the spill zone. Populations of some (e.g., bald eagles) appear to have recovered, but others have not, based on surveys through 1996. The sea otters have also rebounded, although as of 1997, they had not fully recovered in the most heavily oiled areas. Harbor seals were already in decline before the spill; their numbers are still declining.

I have dwelt on the *Exxon Valdez* spill because it was by far the worst such disaster in American history, and because it is also one of the best studied. The fact that some of the affected species are well on the road to recovery demonstrates their considerable resilience to such events. At the same time, the lingering problems afflicting others, as well as the disputes among scientists over interpretations of the limited data, caution against making any sweeping generalizations about oil spills.

I suspect that for years to come, whenever there is an oil spill, environmentalists and oil industry spokesmen will disagree over its seriousness. Three conclusions, however, strike me as indisputable. First, the greater the demand for oil, the greater the probability of future oil spills, simply because of the increasing number of tankers and miles of pipeline needed to service that demand. Second, oil spills occur against a backdrop of other natural and human perturbations to coastal environments. An oil spill in an ecosystem that is already stressed by pollution, habitat destruction, winter storms, or El Niño events may have disproportionately large and lasting effects on wildlife. Finally, to the extent that any oil spills stem from carelessness, neglect, or successful efforts by the oil industry to delay new safety standards, they represent needless tragedies, regardless how long their effects last.

Perhaps because catastrophic spills attract so much attention, we have come to think of them as the principal sources of oil pollution in marine environments. In fact, the effects of chronic oil pollution due to leaky pipelines and storage tanks, minor spillage from tankers and offshore rigs, bilge washings, and countless other sources may match or exceed the ecological damage from major accidents. The Environmental Protection Agency estimates that 175 million gallons of oil end up in U.S. landfills each year just from people changing the oil in their cars; some proportion of this oil then makes its way into streams and creeks and ultimately into the ocean. Lots of little spills can kill as many birds (or other animals) as a single big one, and even birds exposed to sublethal amounts of oil can suffer from diminished reproductive rates if the exposure is chronic. Field studies also have shown that when a salt marsh is exposed to multiple low doses of oil, a substantial portion of the vegetation dies. In at least one case, that loss of vegetation boosted the rate of erosion of the underlying substrate, which fundamentally altered the topography of the marsh ecosystem. One must be cautious, however, about making too many generalizations. As is the case with major spills, the effects of chronic oil pollution are sure to depend upon a host of variables that vary from place to place.

There was a time not too long ago when it seemed as though the Pacific coast would have to get by without sea otters and elephant seals, and when egrets and terns seemed destined to become rare sights along the Atlantic coast. Such fears no longer seem warranted, thanks to our own belated appreciation of these animals and to their own innate resilience. But I suspect that the opportunity to experience—to see, hear, and smell—a stretch of beach that approximates the rich and vibrant community of life that greeted the first settlers will soon be confined to a few precious places—a handful of barrier islands or mainland refuges, perhaps, where vigilant wardens chase away gulls, erect fences to keep out trespassers and their pets, and trap marauding raccoons, opossums, and other garbage-fed predators. At these special places, terns and skimmers will still congregate, beach mice will scurry among the dunes as dusk approaches, and during a few quiet evenings each summer, the last of the sea turtles will haul themselves ashore to lay their eggs. Under such circumstances, a fortunate visitor may feel as though he had stepped into the very shoes of John James Audubon—until he happens to notice the garbage at his feet or the offshore oil rigs looming in the distance.

CHAPTER SIX

A Bounty at the Border

The two seminal events in the peopling of the continental United States—the arrival of the first humans and the arrival of the first Europeans—began at opposite ends of the country and proceeded in opposite directions. The first Paleoindians crossed the Bering landbridge some 20,000 years ago and subsequently headed southward and eastward into the heart of the continent. The Europeans first explored the southern fringes of the nation at the start of the sixteenth century and eventually spread northward and westward.

Whereas the Paleoindians who settled Beringia encountered a cold and bleak landscape with relatively few species of plants and animals (apart from the abundant and edible mammals), the Spanish conquistadores, Franciscan missionaries, adventurers, and refugees who first prowled the forests, grasslands, and mountains of the Southeast and Southwest were delving into the biologically richest part of the nation. Here, at the southern fringes of the United States, the temperate zone begins to give way to the tropics. It is a subtle but significant transition, bringing mahogany trees and geckos to the Florida Keys, ocelots to South Texas, and jaguars to southeastern Arizona. In this border region, where the variety of birds, butterflies, and other creatures begins to climb, where unfamiliar species, genera, and families begin to appear, one can sense how the richness of life increases as one moves closer to the equator, building to a crescendo in the tropical forests of South America, Asia, and Africa.

There is another gradient that parallels this north-to-south rise in species richness: a north-to-south rise in the number of endangered species. Southern Florida, southern Texas, Arizona, and southern California all qualify as endangered species "hot spots"—a dubious distinction to be sure, and one that has become increasingly troublesome for the developers, farmers, and ranchers who find their activities in this part of the country increasingly constrained by the Endangered Species Act and other wildlife protection laws.

This second gradient, unlike the first, fits no general rule in ecology. Instead, it is most likely the result of three factors. First, many species reach the northernmost limits of their distribution along the southern fringes of the United States. Consequently, their populations within this country tend to be very small and localized, making them vulnerable to extirpation. There may be no more than a couple dozen pairs of red-billed pigeons or rose-throated becards in the United States—to name two species that bring a smile to the face of any birdwatcher fortunate enough to see them—although both species are quite common south of the border. Second, this region contains a variety of strange and delightful ecosystems supporting plants and animals that occur nowhere else on earth; the small ranges of these species make them comparatively easy to exterminate through habitat destruction. Finally, the southern fringes of the United States have been heavily used, abused, settled, and developed by Europeans and their descendants for nearly half a millennium. Departing from Puerto Rico, Juan Ponce de Leon reached Florida as early as 1513; Alvar Nuñez Cabeza de Vaca traveled north of the Rio Grande into what is now Texas during the late 1520s and early 1530s; and men under the command of the legendary Francisco Vazquez de Coronado marched north from Mexico, through the Southwest, to the Great Plains in the 1540s. Conquistadores, fishermen, farmers, ranchers, and retirees have all staked a claim at one time or another to this same small region of the United States. Thus, the conservation challenge along the southern border is finding room for both people and wildlife—admittedly the same challenge we face in almost every corner of the country, but one made especially difficult in this case by the fact that we are dealing with so little land and so many species.

In a region so richly endowed with wildlife, it is difficult to pick one place as the standout. But 150 years ago, that honor might have gone to the Everglades. The shallow waters of Florida Bay and the mudflats and marshes at the southern tip of the Florida peninsula once sustained a fabulous collection of wading birds, including hot-pink spoonbills, immaculate white egrets, and stately herons of assorted sizes, shapes, and colors. Only a handful of places on earth—the llanos of Venezuela, the Pantanal of Brazil—could match the bird life of the Everglades. During the last quarter of the nineteenth century and the first decade of the twentieth, however, populations of wading birds throughout the Southeast plummeted as whole colonies were shot, victims of the millinery trade's craving for plumes. When protection finally came, the birds rebounded, and in 1947, Congress established Everglades National Park to ensure that the spectacular wildlife of South Florida would be safe forever.

But after increasing in numbers from 1913 (when the plume trade ended) through the 1940s, populations of wading birds in the Everglades began a downward decline that has continued to the present time — from a peak of nearly a quarter million individuals in the 1940s to 20,000–30,000 today. No other national park has failed so miserably at protecting the natural resources it was intended to save. But the Park Service is hardly to blame. Like most aquatic ecosystems in the United States, the Everglades has been extensively and disastrously rearranged by humans, with most of the damage occurring outside the borders of the park.

Before it suffered the assaults of farmers, developers, and engineers, the Everglades functioned as a kind of glorious drain. Water from the meandering Kissimmee River, south of present-day Orlando, would flow into Lake Okeechobee. The lake, in turn, would periodically overflow its banks. This overflow, in conjunction with rain falling directly on the Everglades, created a 40- to 60-mile wide sheet of water that inched its way toward Florida Bay. So lazy was the current that water exiting the lake in March might not reach Florida Bay until the following February. This "river of grass," seldom more than 3 feet deep, was the heart of the Everglades.

This pristine Everglades was a vast wilderness with an almost storybook array of appealing animals, including river otters, mountain lions (panthers), alligators, and "the most glorious assemblage of wading birds on the North American continent." But the aesthetics of the place were by and large lost on the white settlers of Florida, who regarded it as a hot, sticky, and dangerous wasteland. The first state legislature declared the Everglades to be "wholly valueless" and asked Congress for assistance in converting the land to useful purposes. Congress obliged, turning control of 20 million acres of Everglades land over to the state in 1850, with the express desire that it be sold and drained, and the proceeds used to drain more land. So began the construction of a series of canals to carry water from the Everglades to the Atlantic Ocean and (eventually) the Gulf of Mexico.

Once drained, the mucky soils of the Everglades proved to be wonderfully rich for growing crops, especially sugarcane and vegetables. Congress enhanced the profitability of sugarcane production by enacting a sugar price support program in 1981. By limiting sugar imports from other countries, the federal government ensured that domestic sugar prices would remain high and sugarcane farming would remain profitable.

In 1928, a hurricane caused a massive overflow from Lake Okeechobee that killed over two thousand people and prompted calls for better flood control. The federal government obliged with a major flood control program, which included the construction of an earthen dike around the lake and the straightening and channeling of the Kissimmee River. A positive feedback loop set in: The initial drainage projects encouraged more people to move into the area and establish towns and farms; more people and more development inevitably meant more death and destruction in the wake of hurricanes, floods, and other natural disasters, prompting calls for still more flood control projects. Also, more fresh water was needed to satisfy the thirst of the growing cities along the coast and in the Keys.

Major hurricanes struck South Florida again in 1947 and 1948, causing new misery and prompting Congress to authorize a grand and comprehensive flood control program for the region. The Central and Southern Florida Project for Flood Control and Other Purposes, as it was called, literally paved the way for the ensuing decades of growth and development. It entailed the construction of a massive network of levees, water storage areas, channel improvements, and water pumps designed to control and direct water flow throughout the region. As a result of this project and the earlier ones centered around Lake Okeechobee, approximately a thousand square miles of Everglades wetlands have been drained, and a spider's web of 1,400 miles of canals and levees and 143 water control structures now crisscrosses the 'glades.

All of these changes have had serious consequences for the Everglades. In addition to the direct loss of wetlands, the hydrology of the Everglades has been profoundly altered. Less water now passes through the 'glades and into Florida Bay. Droughts are more frequent, leading to more fires; the fires, in turn, facilitate the spread of certain alien plants. *Melaleuca quinquenervia*, for example, is an Australian tree that was introduced in the beginning of the twentieth century to help dry out the Everglades. Largely unsuitable for native wildlife, it now dominates vast areas east of Everglades National Park and is spreading into the park itself. Its march across South Florida is aided by the fact that its seed capsules are opened by fire. Another invasive alien, the Brazilian pepper tree, sprouts after fires; it has infested about 100,000 acres of the park. Reduced water flow may also be responsible for the intrusion of salt water into mangrove and coastal marsh areas, which has reduced the fish populations that feed the wading birds. Stately great white herons now prowl the boat docks along Florida Bay, begging for fish from humans. Without the handouts, the birds are unable to find enough food in the bay to raise their young.

A lack of water is not the only problem facing the Everglades; how and when it gets there is equally if not more important. Prior to human tinkering, water levels in the 'glades rose in response to summer rains and gradually declined over the course of the dry winter. The magnitude of this seasonal change in water levels varied from year to year, depending on the rainfall. This natural unpredictability posed something of a challenge to the wading birds. Hunting is easiest for them at low water levels, when fish and crustaceans are concentrated in small areas. Too much water floods the pools and sloughs, dispersing the fish so that the birds cannot forage efficiently. Too little water causes shallow pools and sloughs to dry out completely. Fortunately, in the vastness of the primeval Everglades, with its countless sloughs, bays, and ponds of different sizes, shapes, and depths, the birds could usually find at least a few places that provided the right conditions. Thus, the size of the Everglades provided a reasonably secure cushion against the normal year-to-year variations in rainfall.

But in the ditched, diked, regulated, and reduced world of today's Everglades, the river of grass has been turned into "a series of pools connected by canals and pumping stations." Less water passes through the system as a whole, and whatever water does, is pumped through on a cycle largely divorced from the natural rhythms of the landscape. The result has been an unmitigated disaster for the wading birds. In dry years, much of the water is diverted to agricultural lands to the north of the park or thirsty cities to the east. In wet years, too much water is pumped into the remnant marshes, and the birds are deprived of the shallow, concentrated fishing grounds they like.

Among the species hardest hit by these changes is North America's only native stork, the wood stork. Unlike its European relative that will nest atop chimneys in quaint little towns, the wood stork prefers to nest in colonies in remote cypress swamps. On land it is tall and even a bit gawky, but in the air, riding the thermals of a warm summer day, it is a creature of considerable grace and beauty, strikingly patterned in black and white. Wood storks are tactile feeders, swishing their long, drooping bills in the water until they bump up against a luckless minnow or frog. In South Florida, they formerly began nesting around November or December, when water levels in the higher-elevation marshes in the northern Everglades were shallow enough to concentrate fish and other prey. By the time their young were ready to fledge, some 4 to 5 months later, the high-elevation marshes had dried out, but the deeper bays and sloughs to the south were now shallow enough to provide good fishing. In recent decades, however, releases of water from the region's flood control system have kept water levels unnaturally high during the winter months. As a consequence, the wood storks have been delaying nesting, sometimes holding off until the spring. Now, by the time their eggs hatch or the young fledge, the summer rains have already begun, flooding the pools, dispersing the fish, and threatening the young storks with starvation.

The U.S. wood stork population plummeted from perhaps 20,000 breeding pairs in 1930 (living primarily in Florida) to

4,000–5,000 pairs by the early 1980s. In 1984, the federal government classified the wood stork as an endangered species in the United States, making the bird a symbol of just how degraded the Everglades has become. Over the past decade, the population has slowly increased to approximately 7,800 pairs (with considerable fluctuations from year to year), but a growing proportion of the birds are bypassing the sickly Everglades and choosing instead to nest in Georgia and South Carolina, in essence voting with their wings.

As if too little water delivered at the wrong times were not trouble enough, the Everglades also faces a water quality problem. Naturally deficient in certain nutrients, especially phosphorus, the Everglades is vulnerable to agricultural runoff. Farming the muck releases stored phosphorus, nitrogen, and perhaps other elements. Fertilizers are an additional source of phosphorus and nitrogen (although sugarcane is less heavily fertilized than many other crops), as are the defecating dairy cattle that live around Lake Okeechobee. Nutrient overloads, in turn, cause algae blooms, fish kills, and the spread of cattails into areas once dominated by sedges and floating vegetation.

For decades, people have been expressing concern about the health of the Everglades, but the response from legislators has been less than enthusiastic. Federal legislation passed in 1970 and 1989 began to address the issue of water quantity by guaranteeing minimum flows into the national park. The 1989 bill also added an additional (and critical) 107,600 acres to the eastern end of the park. The long-neglected issue of water quality finally rose to prominence in 1988 when the federal government sued the state of Florida on the grounds that the nutrient-laden waters running into the national park and nearby Loxahatchee National Wildlife Refuge constituted a violation of the state's water quality laws. Legal challenges, an outraged public, and increasingly obvious signs of ecological distress have finally brought the Everglades the attention it deserves, and federal and state authorities are now in agreement that drastic steps must be taken to rescue the ecosystem.

Although the details have yet to be worked out, the goal of the rescue plan is clear: to re-create as much as possible the natural water flows that once characterized the Everglades. To that end, federal and state officials intend to undo the channelization of the Kissimmee River, freeing it to follow a more natural course, breach some of the levees that now confine or redirect the movement of water through the region, and convert approximately 40,000 acres of farmland into marshes that will soak up excess nutrients. The extent to which these efforts will succeed in restoring wildlife populations remains to be seen. It seems unlikely that an ecosystem so reduced in size can fully recapture the wildlife populations it once sustained. Moreover, bureaucratic timidity, resistance from sugar growers, and the seemingly insatiable thirst of the Atlantic coast cities may yet diminish or derail the project. But for now, the intentions are noble, even historic, and the plan amounts to one of the most ambitious ecological restoration efforts in American history. "Floridians have spent most of the 20th century trying to destroy the Everglades, and much of it trying to save the Everglades, often at the same time," observed Florida governor Lawton Chiles in 1991. "I hope to see the day, before the end of the 20th century, when we have restored as much of the Everglades as we can, when we have finally learned to live in peace with the Everglades, when we can simply allow it to be."

South and east of the Everglades, trailing away from the tip of the Florida peninsula, lies an arc of low islands that has become a second major battleground in Florida's struggle to conserve its endangered species. The Florida Keys have been described as "the only West Indies one can drive to," a statement that is only partially correct. While the vegetation of the Keys is strongly Caribbean, with red mangroves fringing the islands and gumbo limbo and mahogany trees in the uplands, the animal life is a curious blend of Caribbean and continental species. Bobcats, white-tailed deer, woodrats, and gray squirrels, all of which can be found in the Keys, are derived from the mainland. Other Keys animals, such as mangrove cuckoos and American crocodiles, are undeniably Caribbean in origin. The reason for such a peculiar assemblage of species lies in the geological and biological history of the Keys.

In a very real sense, the Keys represent life built upon a foundation of death, for they began as mounds of limestone made from the remains of old coral reefs and the decomposing carcasses of countless hard-shelled marine organisms. During the height of the Ice Age, approximately 60,000 to 80,000 years ago, sea levels dropped as a significant fraction of the earth's water accumulated around the poles as ice. The receding waters exposed first the Keys—enabling plants, birds, insects, and other mobile organisms to settle there—and then a vast plain connecting the Keys to the Florida mainland. Deer, squirrels, and other terrestrial animals spread across this natural causeway. Many thousands of years later, the warming climate caused the polar ice caps to begin to melt, raising ocean levels around the world, and by 10,000 years ago, the Keys had become separated from the mainland. The mammals, reptiles, and other species that had reached the present-day Keys across dry land now found themselves stranded.

New species evolve from isolated populations, but that process generally requires longer than 10,000 years. Consequently, most of the mammals and reptiles of the Keys are not unique species, but rather local races or subspecies of more widespread ones, differing in size, shape, or color from their continental relatives, but presumably capable of interbreeding with them, were it not for the ocean that keeps them apart. Because water is less of a barrier to most birds than it is to mammals, birds breeding in the Keys have differentiated even less from their mainland or Caribbean relatives; they tend to belong to the same races that nest on the continent or in the West Indies.

Given how old and deep the human footprint is in Florida, it should come as no surprise that some of the earliest disappearances of wildlife species in the United States occurred there. Among the most coveted species on any birdwatcher's list is the Key West quail-dove, a ground-dwelling pigeon handsomely patterned in shades of white, brown, and purple.

Although the first specimen known to science was collected in South Florida (hence the bird's name), a modern ornithologist could spend a lifetime in the Keys without seeing one. In the last century, the Key West quail-dove has been recorded no more than a handful of times in the Keys or mainland Florida, although it nests as close as the Bahamas and Cuba. But when John James Audubon visited Key West in 1832, he reported that hunters were able to shoot "as many as a score in a day." Audubon also tallied two other Caribbean doves: the zenaida dove (a close relative of the ubiquitous mourning dove) and the blue-headed quail-dove. He described the former species as nesting on a few grassy islands in the Keys, and the latter as a rare visitor in the spring. The blue-headed quail-dove has never been seen again in the United States, and records of the zenaida dove since Audubon's time are few and far between.

Why Audubon's doves vanished from the Keys will never be known with certainty, but the answer surely includes habitat loss. In the eighteenth and early nineteenth centuries, visitors from the Bahamas removed many of the prime trees for timber. During the late nineteenth century, farmers cleared portions of the uplands to grow various fruits and vegetables, including pineapples, lemons, and, of course, key limes. But the thin, rocky soils that barely covered the limestone foundations of the Keys were ill-suited for farming, making these ventures marginal at best. By the early 1900s, most of the farms had been abandoned, enabling the forest to recapture the land. The completion of a railroad causeway linking the Keys with the mainland in 1912, which was turned into an automobile highway in 1938, and the construction of a pipeline to bring fresh water from the mainland to the islands in 1940 ushered in a new era of population growth. About 84,000 people now live in the Keys, with more arriving daily. In the winter months their ranks are swelled by hundreds of thousands of tourists. The ensuing frenzy of development has consumed much of the Keys' prime ecosystems, including the tropical hardwood forests called hammocks, the scruffy pinelands of the Lower Keys, and the mangrove forests on the fringes of the islands.

The loss of quail-dove habitat in the Keys, however, is only half the equation. The Keys were always at the periphery of these birds' ranges, and their presence in the United States may well have depended on frequent immigrants from Cuba, the Bahamas, or elsewhere in the West Indies. Audubon, in fact, reported seeing small flocks of Key West quail-doves flying between Cuba and Key West. As forests were felled in the West Indies, and populations of doves in those areas declined, the frequency of colonization may have dropped to the point at which the waning U.S. populations could no longer be replenished. All of this is speculation on my part, but it does explain how a single intrepid naturalist in an age without causeways and automobiles could find three distinct species that have subsequently eluded generations of fanatical birdwatchers.

Another tropical dove, the white-crowned pigeon, continues to reside in reasonably large numbers in the Keys and on the southern tip of the Florida peninsula, with a population estimated at about 10,000 pairs. White-crowns nest in large colonies, usually on offshore islets or in remote mangrove forests where their nests are safe from predators. After fledging, the young birds undertake a treacherous flight from their nesting colonies to the main Keys or the Everglades, where they obtain food from the many fruit-bearing trees and shrubs that grow in South Florida's tropical hardwood forests. The long-term survival of the white-crowned pigeon in the United States thus depends upon the protection of two essential habitats: predator-free nesting areas, usually consisting of mangroves, and hardwood forests on the Keys and South Florida mainland. Unfortunately, both habitat types have come under assault, especially the hardwoods. A recent study estimated that more than 40 percent of the tropical hardwood forests of the Upper Florida Keys have been destroyed.

To make matters worse, the dispersal powers of the young pigeons are initially rather limited. They fly to patches of hardwoods near their nesting grounds for the first few days, until they are ready to range more widely in search of food and shelter. For this reason, a protected network of hardwood patches, running the length of the Keys, may be necessary for their well-being; a handful of reserves clustered in one section of the Keys may not be enough. Tough zoning laws have slowed the loss of the remaining native forests in the Keys, but it is anyone's guess how long these restrictions can be sustained in the face of mounting pressure from developers.

More may be at stake here than the survival of one species of pigeon (albeit a very elegant pigeon). By eating and then defecating the seeds of fruits, white-crowned pigeons function as important dispersers of fruit-bearing trees and shrubs in the Keys. Their disappearance ultimately could result in a reduction in the variety and abundance of fruiting plants, a loss that would affect countless other plants and animals within this rich ecosystem. But for the moment, one can still walk the roads of Key Largo and experience the pleasant surprise of startling a half dozen or so slate-blue pigeons that explode from the treetops and with swift, strong wingbeats disappear into the impenetrable mangroves.

Whereas the rarest birds in the Keys are from the Caribbean, the rarest mammals come from mainland populations, but have diverged to the point at which they are considered distinctive local races. The Key deer, a diminutive race of the ubiquitous whitetail, is without question the most famous and charismatic of the mammals. It currently inhabits the Lower Keys from Little Pine Key to Sugarloaf Key, although it once ranged as far south as Key West. Adult bucks weigh about 80 pounds on average and stand 27 inches at the shoulder; does typically weigh slightly over 60 pounds and stand 25 inches at the shoulder. Their small stature has been interpreted as an adaptation to the sparse food available to them on the Keys, a plausible but unproven idea. Beginning in the late 1800s and continuing through the 1950s, Key deer were ruthlessly hunted for food and sport. By 1946, the population may have numbered as few as 26 individuals (although this estimate, like most counts of Key deer, is subject to dispute). Protection from hunting and creation of a National Key Deer Refuge enabled the population to grow to approximately 300–500 individuals today. But the boom in real estate has eliminated much of the deer's native habitat and turned an increasing proportion of the animals into backyard panhandlers, a development that deeply troubles wildlife biologists. Collisions with cars have become the major source of mortality for Key deer, an inevitable consequence of crowding more people into a small area. Although the Key deer was among the first animals to be placed on the federal endangered species list in 1967, its future remains in doubt, in striking contrast to the overly successful whitetails on the mainland.

Two other mammals, the Key Largo woodrat and Key Largo cotton mouse, are both restricted to a single island in the Keys, where they are threatened by the clearing of hardwood forests for residential and commercial development as well as the island's growing population of cats. A 1988 study estimated that 2,100 acres of habitat suitable for these two rare rodents remained on Key Largo, enough to support approximately 6,500 woodrats and 18,000 cotton mice. While those numbers may seem robust, they are far from sufficient to ensure the long-term survival of these rodents. Small mammals tend to be shorter-lived and perhaps more vulnerable to environmental perturbations than larger ones, necessitating the protection of larger populations and, wherever possible, multiple populations. Under the current situation, a single hurricane could wipe out either rodent, and for this reason alone, they may well be more imperiled than the more widespread Key deer, even though the deer are much less numerous.

A hurricane very nearly did eradicate the Schaus' swallowtail, a spectacular brown, yellow, and orange butterfly that once inhabited hardwood hammocks from South Miami to Key West. By the early 1980s, commercial development, coupled with pesticide spraying to control mosquitoes, had reduced its range to just Key Largo and a few small islands to the north in Biscayne Bay. Then, on August 24, 1992, Hurricane Andrew slammed into Biscayne Bay and northern Key Largo. A butterfly census the following spring turned up only seventeen Schaus' swallowtails. As luck would have it, however, just 2 months before the hurricane struck, Dr. Thomas Emmel, an entomology professor at the University of Florida, had removed a hundred Schaus' swallowtail eggs from the wild to start a captive colony. Since 1995, descendants of the captive swallowtails have been released to bolster the wild population. Moreover, new colonies are being established on other islands where the butterflies once occurred, a necessary precaution against the next hurricane. Hurricanes have been pounding the Keys for as long as there have been Schaus' swallowtails— longer, perhaps—but until the twentieth century, the butterfly's range was large enough to ensure that some patches of habitat escaped harm. Only when the entire population was compressed into a small area at the north end of the Keys did a natural event have unnatural consequences. For the Schaus' swallowtail, and for many other endangered animals of the Florida Keys, the best hope for survival lies in the preservation of as much of their remaining habitat as possible and the serendipitous forbearance of future hurricanes.

The recent history of the Florida Keys is not entirely one of declining species. On the contrary, a variety of plants and animals have colonized the islands in recent years, with direct and indirect assistance from humans. At least five species of geckos and three species of anoles (the latter frequently but incorrectly referred to as chameleons) have gained a foothold in the Keys, probably as stowaways aboard ships. They are most likely to be seen clinging to the walls and ceilings of buildings, an endless source of delight for children and appreciative adults. Another, less welcome immigrant is the shiny cowbird, a close relative of the native brown-headed cowbird. Shiny cowbirds were first sighted in southern Florida in 1985 and are now being seen with increasing frequency across the southeastern United States. Like its brown-headed relative, the shiny cowbird is a brood parasite, laying its eggs in the nests of other birds. Its arrival in the United States is a natural event, insofar as no one actually carried it to our shores. But shiny cowbird populations have been expanding for decades throughout the West Indies and South America as deforestation creates more of the open habitats they require. Their colonization of the United States is a consequence of this population explosion, making *Homo sapiens* at least indirectly responsible for the shiny's success. The cowbirds, in fact, represent the flip side of the story of Audubon's doves. The deforestation in the West Indies that reduced populations of Key West quail-doves, blue-headed quail-doves, and zenaida doves to the point at which they no longer visit Florida has benefited the shiny cowbirds, which are now regular visitors to U.S. shores. Their presence in South Florida has sparked considerable worry among ornithologists, who wonder how our already embattled songbirds will fare under the burden of yet another species of parasitic cowbird.

Although the Everglades and the Keys have attracted the lion's share of attention from environmentalists, neither is the most imperiled ecosystem in the state, nor the one sheltering the greatest number of endangered species. That dubious distinction belongs to a very different habitat, a world of "dry sandy flats full of scruffy, stunted plants, straggly trees, bothersome insects, and assorted reptiles" called the scrub. Scrub vegetation occurs on dunes along both the Gulf and Atlantic coastlines as well as on certain sandy soils in the interior of central Florida. The interior scrub in particular has long fascinated biologists because it is an ancient ecosystem, formed 1 to 3 million years ago, at a time when the rest of Florida was under water. Before receding, the sea deposited enormous sand dunes hundreds of feet tall in a line down the center of the peninsula. Those dunes are known today as the Lake Wales Ridge, a 100 mile by 10 mile strip of high ground in an otherwise flat state.

The Lake Wales Ridge scrub is a harsh environment, characterized by hot weather, porous, nutrient-poor soils, and intense fires caused by frequent electrical storms. Yet, over the millennia, hundreds of plants and animals have adapted to living there; many occur nowhere else on earth. The dominant vegetation is an elfin forest of oaks, hickories, pines, and shrubs, interspersed with hundreds of sinkhole lakes. The fauna and flora are a Dr. Seuss-like collection of delightful oddities, including legless lizards that "swim" through the sand, thousand-year-old oaks standing 4 feet high, and little mint plants that produce a natural insect repellent.

Too dry to farm and too dense for cattle herding, the scrub escaped destruction for 400 years following Ponce de Leon's arrival. All that has changed recently, as subdivisions, shopping centers, and citrus groves have gobbled up some 80 to 90 percent of the Lake Wales Ridge scrub over the past six decades. A now-outdated estimate from 1988 places the total amount of intact native scrub left on the ridge at less than 20,000 acres. The result of this habitat loss is a growing roster of disappearing species, including over thirty plants that are either listed as endangered species or under consideration for listing by state and federal authorities, plus an assortment of rare lizards, insects, spiders, and other creatures.

Regrettably, rare plants and obscure little animals engender scant sympathy from the public, and they are poorly served by state and federal laws designed to protect endangered species. To protect such ecosystems, one often needs a more appealing symbol. Thus, if significant amounts of scrub are still around in 50 years' time, some of the credit will go to a rare bird whose bizarre behavior has intrigued ornithologists for decades: the Florida scrub-jay, which has become the flagship species of the scrub.

With its blue wings and tail, brown back, and gray underparts, the Florida scrub-jay is virtually identical in appearance to other scrub-jays that are abundant in the western United States and Mexico. Recent biochemical studies, however, demonstrate that it is a distinct and separate species and, as its name suggests, one restricted to the scrub. With only about 5,000 pairs left, the Florida scrub-jay was added to the federal endangered species list in 1987. Its protected status may help to slow the rate of destruction of Florida scrub and (one hopes) spur local authorities to establish more preserves.

Florida scrub-jays have a rich and complex social system, involving cooperation within extended families, land acquisition and inheritance, and lifetime "marriages" with occasional "divorces." A breeding pair typically bonds for life, defends a territory of approximately 20 to 30 acres, and raises one brood per year. Unlike most other songbirds, however, young Florida scrub-jays do not leave home when they fledge. Instead, they remain with their parents for 1 to 7 years and help them raise more siblings, forgoing the opportunity to find their own mates and produce their own offspring. These helpers assist their parents with feeding their younger siblings and guarding the nest.

The most likely explanation for this curious behavior is a simple one: a shortage of space. In places where Florida scrub-jays have been well studied, virtually every acre of scrub is occupied by jay families. There is rarely any vacant habitat in which a wandering young jay can settle and raise a family. Like twenty-something children in Manhattan who live with their parents while waiting for a rent-controlled apartment to come on the market, young jays are forced to stay in their natal territories and bide their time. They become breeders through one of two routes. First, they can replace a breeding jay that has suddenly died elsewhere in the neighborhood. Alternatively, they can help their parents expand the size of the family territory and eventually take over a small section for themselves, a process ornithologists call "territorial budding," but which could just as accurately be described as "inheriting the back forty."

That we can see some of our own behavior reflected in the world of the Florida scrub-jays may yet instill in us some small measure of compassion for both the jays and the scrub. To erase this strange and ancient ecosystem for the sake of more orange juice and shopping malls would be nothing less than obscene. In recent years, both the state of Florida and the federal government have spent significant amounts of money to acquire parcels of scrub, but not fast enough to stay ahead of the bulldozers.

Compared with what is happening on Lake Wales Ridge, where destruction of the scrub threatens the very survival of many species, the situation in the Lower Rio Grande Valley of Texas is somewhat less dire. Almost all of the species of concern in this region are still reasonably common in Mexico and Central America. What is at stake here is their future within the United States, where, by virtue of political boundaries, they reach the northern limits of their ranges within a 4,200-square-mile region extending from Falcon Dam to the southern tip of South Padre Island. This sliver of subtropical America once harbored a rich mosaic of habitats, including riparian woodlands, sabal palm forests, Chihuahuan thorn forests, and old oxbow lakes called resacas. Together, these ecosystems sustain over 500 species of vertebrates and 1,200 plants.

Rich in wildlife, the valley has always been poor in the things humans crave. The Spanish came north seeking gold, land, and power. The gold was nonexistent, the arid grassland and brushland incapable of sustaining large herds of cattle, and the precipitation too unpredictable for productive farming. Consequently, they made little effort to establish a presence in the region for two centuries. It was not until the second half of the eighteenth century that the first Spanish settlements began to appear on the south side of the Rio Grande. The cattle quickly overgrazed the grasslands, forcing the settlers to drive them across the river in search of new forage, into what is now Texas. Rio Grande City, the first valley town north of the river, was formed in 1757; Brownsville was not established until 1840.

Those who chose not to run cattle attempted farming, but the beans, corn, squash, and other vegetables they planted never amounted to much. Rainfall was unpredictable, and the best farmland was next to the river, where frequent floods swept away crops—and dreams—with indifference. Hurricanes and periodic outbreaks of cholera and yellow fever provided further evidence of nature's seeming hostility toward settlers.

Enter the speculators. At the beginning of the twentieth century, they began buying the parched and dying ranchlands and selling them to farmers in the Midwest. Advertisements boasted of fertile riverine lands, dependable water, and cheap labor. The developers chartered trains to bring Midwesterners to the valley for carefully staged visits to model farms. In a haze of greed, hype, and hope, deals were made, property changed hands, and the valley became a highly productive agricultural region. The key to success was obtaining water. The farmers enlisted an army of Mexican and Mexican-American laborers, who, working 14 or 15 hours a day, six and a half days a week, constructed a network of irrigation ditches and pumping stations that finally made agriculture a viable enterprise in the valley. With irrigation, cotton and citrus trees grew well, as did a variety of vegetables, including onions, cantaloupe, cabbage, bell peppers, and corn. In the ensuing decades, the scale and intensity of agriculture would continue to grow as farm operations became more mechanized and as pesticides, fertilizers, and other agricultural chemicals became readily available. Prosperity, however, has not kept pace with productivity: The Lower Rio Grande Valley remains one of the poorest regions of the United States, trailing the rest of the nation by almost every measure of poverty.

The spread of agriculture came at the expense of most of the valley's natural ecosystems. Today, the mosaic of habitats that sustains the region's extraordinary natural diversity is still present, but in tattered remnants surrounded by miles of pesticide-laden farm fields. By some estimates, more than 95 percent of the valley's native vegetation has been destroyed. The U.S. Fish and Wildlife Service has protected some fine examples of the natural vegetation in the Santa Ana and Laguna Atascosa national wildlife refuges, but most of the remaining habitat is in private hands and consists of small patches under 100 acres in size.

From an ecological perspective, the situation is analogous to—but much more extreme than—what is happening to the deciduous forests of the eastern United States. Natural areas are being fragmented into smaller, more isolated patches, the movement of animals between patches is becoming more difficult, and animal populations are dwindling. The result is a much greater risk of extinction for those species that cannot abide the vegetable fields, citrus groves, and cities that are replacing the natural vegetation of the Lower Rio Grande. A growing number of animals, including about 86 vertebrates, now find themselves "hanging on by the skin of their collective teeth." Not surprisingly, the situation is most dire for those animals that have large territories or home ranges, the most notable example being the small and large cats of the Lower Rio Grande Valley.

At the time of the first Spanish settlements, no fewer than four tropical cats—jaguar, margay, jaguarundi, and ocelot—may have prowled the thickets and forests of the valley. The jaguar and margay are now gone from this region; the jaguarundi is either extinct in the United States or down to a handful of individuals; and the ocelot is highly endangered.

The jaguar is so closely linked in our minds to the tropical rainforest that its historical presence in the United States comes as a surprise to most people. But at the time of the American Revolution, this largest, most dangerous, and most beautiful of New World cats ranged from the Tehachepi Mountains in California northeast to the Grand Canyon and southeast to the Gulf of Mexico. Like the wolf and grizzly bear, the jaguar is an animal that most people fear and, historically, most ranchers hated. It was extirpated from California by 1860 and from Texas by 1946. Although a lone animal may wander north from Mexico into the United States from time to time, giving rise to occasional sightings, the jaguar is essentially gone from the United States. Given the lack of suitable habitat both in this country and in adjacent portions of Mexico, re-establishing a viable population of jaguars is unthinkable in South Texas and probably anywhere else in the southwestern United States. But for a naturalist living in the Southwest today, there is no grander fantasy than to drive along a mountain road at dawn, round a sharp bend, and encounter a jaguar. For the briefest of moments the animal is frozen in the middle of the road, blinded by the headlights. Then it vanishes, leaving the astonished driver to wonder whether the whole episode was real or imagined.

The only confirmed U.S. record of the margay, a graceful cat resembling a miniature jaguar, is a single specimen collected in Eagle Pass, Texas, in 1852, well to the north of the Lower Rio Grande Valley. Shy and arboreal, margays have eluded biologists in places where they were thought to be relatively widespread, perhaps justifying a tiny measure of hope that this magnificent animal may occasionally wander into the United States. But it does not adapt well to disturbed habitats, making the odds of its survival here incalculably small. Although the margay was added to the federal endangered species list in 1972, it has probably been gone from within our borders for over a century. Soon to join the ranks of extirpated species may be the weasel-like jaguarundi. Once found in southeastern Arizona and southern Texas, it has become exceedingly rare in recent decades. A roadkill near Brownsville, Texas, on April 21, 1986, provides the most recent tangible evidence of its continued presence in the United States. Numerous uncon-firmed sightings each year in both Texas and Arizona sustain the optimism of the biologists who continue to search for it in vain.

The ocelot, a margay look-alike, once occurred in south-western Arkansas, Texas, and Arizona. While the last confirmed record from Arizona dates back to 1964, a small number survive in the Lower Rio Grande Valley. The size and security of this population are poorly known, but 25 to 30 individuals are thought to live in the relative safety of the Laguna Atascosa National Wildlife Refuge in Cameron County. Outside the refuge, much of the remaining thorn forest exists in patches too small to sustain ocelots, which have home ranges of a square mile or more. Yet of the tropical cats whose ranges extend into the United States, the ocelot probably has the best chance for recovery. It poses no threat to livestock, and it is adaptable, ca-pable of surviving in partly cleared forests and second-growth woodlands, provided those woodlands are not too far apart. In the crowded world of South Texas, the second biggest threat to its survival (after the obvious shortage of habitat) may be collisions with cars.

None of the subtropical birds of the Lower Rio Grande Valley, save one, is presently classified as endangered by the U.S. Fish and Wildlife Service, but many, such as the red-billed pigeon, yellow-green vireo, Audubon's oriole, and rose-throated becard, have very small populations north of the Rio Grande. Their future in the United States is clouded by the fact that not only is there very little habitat left for them, but most of what remains is highly fragmented. The same problems of nest predation and nest parasitism that plague songbirds living in forest fragments in the eastern United States also appear to be harming songbirds in the Lower Rio Grande Valley. A recent study conducted in the valley concluded that rates of nest predation and parasitism were higher for orioles, jays, sparrows, and other songbirds nesting in narrow patches of forest than for those living in wider patches.

Another, equally insidious threat to the survival of some of these rare birds may be the various water diversion structures that have been constructed along the Rio Grande, including four dams, an extensive floodway system, and a network of canals and pumping stations for irrigation. Historically, snowmelt from the Colorado Rockies caused the river to over-flow its banks as far south as Hidalgo and Cameron counties. These floods were essential to the health of the riparian wood-lands of the Lower Rio Grande Valley because they replenished the water table, swept away competing vegetation, and created favorable conditions for tree regeneration. With the construc-tion of the dams and other structures, however, flooding has all but ceased along the Lower Rio Grande. The lack of floods, coupled with recent episodes of drought and freezing weather, has taken a heavy toll on the valley's remaining scraps of ripar-ian woodland. In many places, the tall trees have died and been replaced by thorn-scrub vegetation, causing significant changes in the bird life. Over the past two decades, for example, ornithologists have monitored changes in the birds and plants of a 20-acre patch of riparian forest in the Santa Ana National Wildlife Refuge, near McAllen, Texas. During this time, the vegetation has become increasingly like that of a thorny scrubland, with fewer tall trees and a much denser understory of mesquite, acacia, and other shrubs. Remarkably, the total number of nesting birds on the site has increased sixfold, but the mix of species is now quite different from what it originally was. Three birds associated with riparian woodlands—the red-billed pigeon, rose-throated becard, and altamira oriole—have disappeared, while several others associated with scrublands have increased tremendously, including the white-winged and mourning doves, olive sparrow, long-billed thrasher, and white-eyed vireo. Throughout the valley, several riparian forest birds seem to be much rarer now than they were in the 1950s, suggesting that these forests may well be the most imperiled ecosystem in a part of the country where virtually all wild areas qualify as rare and endangered.

In the long run, the key to preserving the wildlife diversity of the Lower Rio Grande Valley lies in restoring connectivity between the remaining fragments of natural habitat and in recreating the floods that sustain the riparian forests. In 1984, the Fish and Wildlife Service unveiled a bold plan for the region in which it proposed to link together the existing parks and preserves by creating a corridor of natural vegetation along the length of the Rio Grande, from the Laguna Atascosa refuge north of Brownsville through the Santa Ana refuge south of McAllen and northwest to Falcon Dam. By means of land purchases and easements, a total of 132,500 acres could be protected for the benefit of wildlife. Included within this acreage would be a number of vegetation types that are not currently represented in the national wildlife refuge system. The corridor itself would extend at least 330 feet back from the river. Unfortunately, funding to acquire the necessary lands has not matched the pace of development in the Valley, leaving skeptics to wonder whether this vision will ever become a reality.

To recreate the floods that no longer sweep across the tamed and tethered Rio Grande, the Fish and Wildlife Service has begun to pump water from the river into floodplain forests in the Santa Ana National Wildlife Refuge. Although it is far too early to judge whether these artificial floods can replace the real ones, the preliminary results are encouraging, with numerous seedlings of native trees sprouting after the waters receded. Whether this type of intensive "hands-on" management—even if successful—can be replicated on a large enough scale to benefit the riparian birds and other animals remains to be seen.

Farther west, in southern Arizona and New Mexico, a different assortment of subtropical plants and animals sneaks across the border, to the delight of naturalists. Here, where deserts, grasslands, and isolated mountains come together to form the richest array of habitats in the nation, a far greater percentage of the landscape remains undeveloped. It may seem paradoxical, therefore, that this relatively wild region of the country experienced some of the earliest losses of animal species that can be attributed to the arrival of the settlers. But even though the landscape is largely undeveloped, much of it is highly degraded as a consequence of over a century of excessive livestock grazing and logging.

No habitat has suffered more than the perennial grasslands that once extended across eastern and central Arizona and parts of southern New Mexico. As noted previously, in the 1870s and 1880s, stockmen turned immense numbers of cattle onto the open range. Overgrazing by a million or more cows eliminated the native grasses and enabled mesquite and other woody plants to take over. When drought struck, the resulting damage to the vegetation, the native wildlife, and the cattle themselves was almost unimaginable. "During the years 1892 and 1893," wrote one witness,

Arizona suffered an almost continuous drouth, and cattle died by the tens of thousands. From 50 to 90 per cent of every herd lay dead on the ranges. The hot sun, dry winds and famishing brutes were fatal as fire to nearly all forms of vegetable life. Even the cactus, although girdled by its millions of spines, was broken down and eaten by cattle in their mad frenzy for food. This destruction of desert herbage drove out or killed off many forms of animal life hitherto common to the great plains and mesa lands of the Territory

[Arizona]. Cattle climbed to the tops of the highest mountains and denuded them of every living thing within reach. Often many miles from water and too weak to reach it, they perished miserably. I saw, later, what I had never expected to see in Arizona, Mexicans gathering bones on the ranges and shipping them to California for fertilizing purposes.

Today, most visitors to this region drive through miles and miles of dense mesquite, blissfully unaware that at one time a plush carpet of grass covered much of the land.

Among the first animals to be driven out by the cattle was the masked bobwhite, a southwestern race of the familiar bobwhite quail of the East. Male masked bobwhites look strikingly different from their eastern cousins: their heads are dark black, lacking the white stripes of the eastern birds, and their underparts are colored a rich cinnamon. But they give the same whistled call—the sharp, ascending "bob-white" that is familiar to every rural resident in the East. When heard in the arid grasslands of the Southwest, it can seem jarringly out of place. Searching for the masked bobwhite in Sonora, Mexico, at the turn of the century, naturalist Herbert Brown remarked,

It is not easy to describe the feelings of myself and American companions when we first heard the call *bob white*. It was startling and unexpected, and that night nearly every man in camp had some reminiscence to tell of Bob-white and his boyhood days. Just that simple call made many a hardy man heart-sick and homesick. It was to us Americans the one homelike thing in all Sonora, and we felt thousands of miles nearer to our dear old homes in the then far distant States.

In the United States, the masked bobwhite was once a common resident of the tallgrass plains of southeastern Arizona, from the Baboquívari Mountains east to the Upper Santa Cruz Valley. The massive influx of cattle toward the end of the nineteenth century took a swift and terrible toll on its habitat, however, so much so that by the early 1900s, the masked bob-white had been grazed to extinction in this country. The same fate nearly befell the bird in northern Mexico (where it also oc-curs), but fortunately, a tiny population has managed to hang on in what little is left of the native grasslands of Sonora.

Another possible victim of overgrazing was a little bird so rare and obscure that most birdwatchers are unaware of its very existence: Worthen's sparrow. The first specimen known to science was collected near Silver City, New Mexico, on June 16, 1884, but it has never been seen again in the United States. In northeastern Mexico, the only other place where it now occurs, Worthen's sparrow is a rare resident of mesquite-juniper and yucca-juniper grasslands, habitats that are rapidly disappearing due to farming and ranching. Ornithologists have long assumed that the single U.S. record represents a lost or wandering bird. But the date of discovery corresponds to its breeding season in Mexico, hardly the time when a wanderer would be expected. Was Worthen's sparrow once a rare summer resident of the American Southwest and, like the masked bobwhite, an early victim of the cattle? We will never know. But it is entirely possible that well before the extinction of the Carolina parakeet and passenger pigeon, a tiny sparrow had already been driven out of one of the wildest, least settled parts of the nation by the cattlemen.

Ornithologists do know that a variety of other grassland birds, including the Montezuma quail, Botteri's sparrow, Baird's sparrow, and rufous-winged sparrow, went from being very common in Arizona to being very rare during the height of the cattle era. Now that grazing has been brought under partial control, most of them have recovered slightly, but it is doubtful any of these birds will ever regain their former abundance in the United States. Too much of their historic habitat is dam-aged beyond repair.

The ecological riddle is why livestock were so harmful to the arid grasslands of the Southwest, yet had comparatively little ef-fect on the shortgrass and mixed-grass prairies of the Great Plains. The answer probably lies in the different evolutionary histories of the two regions. In the Great Plains, immense herds of grazing mammals, most notably bison, have been a part of the landscape since the Pleistocene. The native grasses evolved under intense grazing pressure from bison and other large mammals and, consequently, developed various structural adaptations that enabled them to persist and even prosper under such conditions. In contrast, there have been no great herds of bison in the Southwest. For over 10,000 years, this region supported only four big grazers, none of which lived in large herds: mule deer, elk, pronghorn, and bighorn sheep. Thus, the evolutionary pressure on southwestern plants to develop defenses against intense grazing has not been as strong, with the result that the bunchgrasses, grama grasses, and other tasty plants of the arid grasslands cannot tolerate continual, intense grazing as well as their counterparts in the Midwest can. When the cattle and sheep arrived en masse in the nineteenth century, they were a shock to the system.

Still, the situation is not beyond hope. In the case of the masked bobwhite, the U.S. Fish and Wildlife Service has launched an admirable, if uphill, effort to restore the species to Arizona. Bobwhites breed well in captivity, and the fortuitous capture of some masked bobwhites in Mexico enabled the Service to build up a sizable population in captivity. But efforts to find a place to release them in Arizona were stymied for many years by the absence of suitable grasslands. Several locations were tried, but to no avail; the overgrazed grasslands could not support a viable quail population. Then, for a period of time, the Service leased land on a private ranch and attempted to find the right balance between bobwhites and bovines. That effort also failed when a drought hit the region in 1979 and the cattle ate away the birds' cover. Recognizing at last that cows and masked bobwhites were simply incompatible, the Service purchased the ranch in 1985 and christened it the Buenos Aires National Wildlife Refuge. The Service then removed the cattle entirely (a step the ranching community greeted with wails of protest) and began once again to release masked bobwhites.

As is often the case with endangered species, the availability of suitable habitat, while essential, does not guarantee a successful restoration program. One must still find a way to prepare captive-reared animals for life in the wild. At various times in the past, the Service has experimented with releasing young birds, adult birds, and even young birds accompanied by sterilized adult common bobwhites that served as foster parents, all with relatively little success. Since 1996, it has employed a more complex release protocol. The eggs are hatched off-site and the chicks transferred to the refuge on their first day, where they are placed in indoor pens with adult masked bobwhites that act as foster parents. After three and a half weeks, the young birds are placed in outdoor pens, where they spend the summer and early fall before being released into the wild in September or October. The survival rate of liberated birds has nonetheless remained low.

Unable to accept the notion of a grassland without cattle, local ranchers have labeled the whole endeavor a failure and lobbied hard for the restoration of grazing privileges within the refuge. But time may yet prove them wrong. The current population of masked bobwhites at Buenos Aires is estimated at 300 to 500 birds, some of which are now breeding on their own, giving rise to a justifiable hope that after a century's absence, the masked bobwhite is back on the range.

Standing in the midst of the Buenos Aires grasslands, one is struck by how rare and special a place it is. A carpet of golden grass undulates with the breeze; in the distance, the purple-colored Baboquívaris rise up like a child's painting of a mountain range; meadowlarks sputter and chase one another across the plains. The visitor strains to hear beyond the wind, listening for a sharp, whistled "bob-white," a sound that is so familiar and yet so unexpected.

Another, less musical sound is unlikely ever to return to Arizona: the ear-splitting screeches of thick-billed parrots. Until the 1930s, flocks of these big emerald-green parrots would periodically head north from Mexico and settle in the mountains of Arizona and New Mexico. No one knows how often the birds crossed the border into the United States—in the twentieth century the principal incursions were in 1904 and 1917–1918, although some elderly Arizonans claim the parrots were present every year—nor is there any evidence the birds ever nested in this country. But the mountains of Arizona and New Mexico appear to contain suitable habitat, and thickbills still breed within 90 miles of the Arizona border.

A combination of hunting and cutting of the mountain pine forests quickly extirpated thickbills from the United States. Sightings after 1918 were few and far between, with the last confirmed records dating back to the mid-1930s. In its Mexican stronghold, the species is gravely threatened by shooting, illegal capture for the pet trade, and logging of the mature pine forests it requires for nesting and feeding. Once the pine forests close to the United States had been cut, the possibility of thickbills ever returning to this country on their own vanished. But that didn't preclude humans carrying them over the border.

In 1985 and 1986, enforcement agents of the U.S. Fish and Wildlife Service detected an enormous increase in the number of thick-billed parrots smuggled into the United States by bird sellers. Numerous birds were confiscated by U.S. officials. To one inspired officer, the sudden availability of a pool of confiscated parrots suggested the possibility of a reintroduction program. Remarkably, the idea cleared the usual bureaucratic hurdles in short order.

Over the next two years, approximately three dozen thickbills were released into the Chiricahua Mountains of southeastern Arizona. Most did not survive, a sad but not unanticipated outcome when birds are released into strange environments. Efforts to supplement the original cohort with young captive-bred thickbills also foundered when the youngsters showed little interest in flocking with the other parrots or in feeding on pine cones. Moreover, the released birds demonstrated an extraordinary wanderlust, at one point flying 250 miles northwest to the Mogollon Rim, reappearing in the Chiricahuas several months later, and then heading north again. By the spring of 1995, none of the released parrots was known to be alive, and the reintroduction program was suspended indefinitely.

The scientists involved in this effort have vowed to try again someday, but for the time being, and perhaps forever, the Chiricahua Mountains have lost a part of their wildness. In years gone past, the thickbills streamed across the border like drunken revelers, shouting at the top of their voices, aimlessly wandering from mountain to mountain, bringing mayhem to the stolid forests. Without them, it's too damn quiet.

known to be left. Barring the miraculous discovery of a new population elsewhere in Maui, the po'ouli seems destined to disappear forever within the lifetimes of its discoverers—a species whose scientific "birth" will have nearly coincided with its biological death.

In many respects, the story of the po'ouli stands for all that is wonderful and tragic about the flora and fauna of islands. Islands in general are filled with unusual species. Consequently, the study of island life has been crucial to the development of contemporary ecology and evolutionary biology, from the nineteenth-century explorations of Charles Darwin and Alfred Russel Wallace in the Galápagos and Malay archipelagoes to the contemporary studies of Edward O. Wilson, Jared Diamond, and John Terborgh in the Caribbean, the Bismarck Archipelago, and elsewhere. But islands have also been the scenes of our most vicious assaults on nature, providing biologists with all too many examples of extinction at the hands of humankind.

Few places have suffered more grievously than Hawaii, which has one of the highest proportions of extinct or endangered species of any comparably sized area on earth. This fact comes as a genuine surprise to most first-time visitors, who are invariably impressed with the islands' lush greenery and abundant birds and butterflies. But, as we shall see, most of the plants and animals that tourists see when they visit Hawaii are not native to the archipelago; they are interlopers, brought there by people. Hawaii's native flora and fauna has been in full retreat for centuries. To protect even a fraction of the native species now at risk will require a level of commitment from government institutions and private individuals that dwarfs anything we have seen elsewhere in the United States. There is something of a Shakespearean tragedy in the story of Hawaii's battered biota, for the very qualities that make its flora and fauna so unique and so fascinating make those same species extremely vulnerable to extinction. To explore this linkage between uniqueness and vulnerability, we first need to address a simple but important question: How do species end up on islands?

Ecologists divide islands into two groups: landbridge islands and oceanic islands. Landbridge islands arise when a piece of a continent or other large land mass is severed from the mainland by rising waters. The island of Trinidad, located off the coast of Venezuela, is a good example. Until the end of the Pleistocene epoch, approximately 10,000 years ago, it was connected to the South American mainland. The earth was significantly cooler then, and a tremendous volume of water was locked up in glaciers and snowpacks in the northern latitudes. As the climate warmed, these glaciers and snowpacks melted, raising the level of the world's oceans by more than 300 feet. This rise in sea level was enough to flood the lowland areas connecting Trinidad to the mainland, thereby creating the present-day island. The island of Trinidad, in other words, was "born" with an intact flora and fauna, consisting of those species that were living on the site prior to its isolation from the continent. Britain, too, is an example of a landbridge island; 10,000 years ago it was connected to the European mainland. Not surprisingly, virtually all of the native plants and animals in Britain also occur in Europe.

Oceanic islands, such as Hawaii, are an altogether different story. They arise de novo through the actions of undersea volcanoes, starting out as lifeless deposits of lava ejected from the earth's innards. The species inhabiting them—every microorganism, every plant, every animal—can be traced back to colonists originating somewhere else, typically the nearest mainland.

There are essentially four ways for a plant or animal to reach the Hawaiian Islands, which lie approximately 2,500 miles from the North American mainland and 2,100 miles from Asia. It can fly there, an option reserved for birds, bats, and the stronger insects. It can swim there, as did all marine fishes, sea turtles, and the ancestors of the unique Hawaiian monk seal. It can float there, on the surface of the ocean (the coconut being a prime example) or aboard rafts of flotsam set adrift from the mainland (a frequent mode of transport for insects and other small animals); it also can float in the wind, a method of dispersal widely used by spiders and plants. And finally, it can hitchhike to the island, as happens when burrs and other seeds attach themselves to the feathers of migratory birds.

Dispersal to an oceanic island is at best a lottery. The winds or currents must be just right, or the floating seed or insect will sail past the island. Similarly, the pioneering bird, bat, or butterfly must make it to shore before it exhausts itself and drops to its death in the sea below. Once the species in question reaches the island, it will not survive unless the plants or animals it depends upon for food and shelter have preceded it—the order in which species arrive is therefore critical. Finally, for the species as a whole to persist on the island, a pioneering individual must be fortunate enough to have a mate arrive on the scene more or less contemporaneously. For every plant or animal that succeeds in colonizing an island, uncountable others must perish unnoticed in the seas. We remember the Christopher Columbuses of this world, not the sailors who disappeared en route to uncharted lands.

Unlike a true lottery, however, not all of the players in the island colonization game have an equal chance of winning. Some groups—for example, birds and insects—are more capable of crossing water barriers than others. Freshwater fishes and amphibians, which cannot fly and generally cannot tolerate salt water, almost never succeed. Even within a group, there tend to be important differences in dispersal abilities. For reasons nobody understands, woodpeckers rarely appear on oceanic islands; rails do so with amazing frequency. Dragonflies, strong fliers that they are, make it to many isolated archipelagoes; ants do not. Behind every Hawaiian species is a tale of ancestral wandering and discovery, of fortuitous timing and intrinsic capabilities—a story of luck and pluck.

Once a species makes it to an island, however, it is likely to find itself in an environment with fewer competitors and predators than it faced on the mainland (because not all of its competitors and predators will have reached the island). Thus, islands provide species with an abundance of "vacant" niches and, consequently, tremendous opportunities for evolution and diversification. If the island is part of an archipelago, the species in question may even hopscotch from one island to another, establishing secondary populations that evolve over time into separate, distinct species. Evolutionary biologists refer to this process of colonization, expansion, and diversification as "adaptive radiation." In the Hawaiian archipelago, it has generated a stunning array of species from a handful of bedraggled colonists.

A single flock of finches, blown off course millions of years ago, evolved into the over forty-five species of birds called Hawaiian honeycreepers. Although the original colonists probably had stubby bills like most seed-eating birds, their descendants have diversified in extraordinary ways to include red birds with long sickle-shaped beaks for sipping nectar from flowers; little yellow birds with thin, pointed beaks for gleaning insects from leaves; and green birds with big parrotlike beaks ideal for snapping apart twigs to expose wood-boring insects. Even the vacant niche of the woodpecker was filled by a honeycreeper: The yellow 'akiapola'au sports a dual-purpose beak, with a long, decurved upper mandible for probing and picking and a straight, stout lower mandible that it uses to chisel wood.

Entomologists, who must tire of hearing ornithologists sing the praises of Hawaii's birds, point to its fruit flies as an even more spectacular (if underappreciated) example of adaptive radiation. Hawaii is the indisputable hub for drosophilid fruit flies, the little insects featured in college genetics labs the world over. Nearly five hundred species have been described to date from the archipelago. Another two hundred species have been collected but not yet described, while an unknown number await discovery in the remote rainforests of Maui, Kauai, Oahu, Molokai, Lanai, and the Big Island of Hawaii. All seven hundred or more species are derived from one or two founding species. Much as Hawaii's birds have radiated in diverse directions to fill different niches, so too have its fruit flies. For example, most fruit flies throughout the world lay their eggs in rotting fruit, but in Hawaii, various species have taken to laying their eggs in rotting leaves and bark, mushrooms, dead flowers, sap bleeding from trees, and even the eggs of spiders.

Hawaii's honeycreepers and fruit flies have gone where no finches or fruit flies have gone before—literally and metaphorically—and in the process they have evolved novel approaches to living on an isolated island. From its woodpecker-like finch with a Swiss Army knife for a beak to its fruit flies that prefer spider eggs to fruit, the Hawaiian fauna has been rightly called "one of the rarest and most improbable living assemblages on the earth." It's an Alice-in-Wonderland world that could exist nowhere else—and doesn't. The vast majority of native plants and animals living in the Hawaiian Islands occur nowhere else, including all of the honeycreepers, all of the fruit flies, 96 percent of the flowering plants, and 65 percent of the ferns. In the parlance of ecology, these species are endemic to Hawaii.

And there's the rub: Such high levels of endemicity make the Hawaiian fauna and flora exceptionally vulnerable to extinction because there are no populations of these species elsewhere to serve as conservation "backups." When gray wolves were extirpated from the western United States, there were healthy populations in Canada to sustain the species and to serve eventually as a source of colonists to repopulate Montana and Wyoming. Not so with the 'akiapola'au or the Hawaiian monk seal; if they disappear from Hawaii, they are gone forever.

Recall also that one characteristic of most oceanic islands is the presence of numerous vacant niches. Many of these are filled eventually as species colonize the archipelago and diversify, but others remain unfilled. In Hawaii, for example, there have never been any native browsing mammals akin to the elk and deer that occur on the North American continent. Nor are there any native predatory mammals such as weasels or cats. Over time, therefore, many Hawaiian species lost their physical and behavioral defenses against such threats. The native Hawaiian nettle, or mamaki, is virtually nettleless. The little rail that once occurred on Laysan Island, at the extreme western edge of the

Hawaiian archipelago, was flightless, as was another rail that in-habited the Big Island until the end of the nineteenth century. There was even a flightless fly living on the slopes of Diamond Head in Oahu. From an evolutionary perspective, this apparent "defenselessness" made sense: Why should a plant waste valu-able energy growing thorns if no big mammal was likely to eat its leaves or stems? Why should a rail grow strong wings if it had no reason to fly? It certainly had no need to migrate away from Hawaii's hospitable climate, nor was there any native mammal that could ambush it on the ground.

When humans arrived, they abruptly ended Hawaii's isola-tion by bringing with them an array of plants and animals that could never have gotten there on their own. These species were brought as food, as pets, as reminders of home; as something to hunt or simply to watch; as stowaways aboard ships and planes; or as means to control other species that had gotten out of con-trol. Suddenly, after millions of years without them, the Hawaiian Islands were filled with cattle, goats, pigs, sheep, cats, rats, mongooses, and thousands of other alien animals and plants. The consequences to the native flora and fauna were pre-dictably deadly.

The first alien species accompanied the first humans—the Polynesians—who arrived approximately 1,500 years ago and brought with them pigs, dogs, chickens, and Pacific rats. The pigs, dogs, and chickens were intentionally carried to Hawaii; the rats may have been stowaways aboard the big double-hulled canoes used by the Polynesians. But it was the arrival of British naval captain James Cook and his crew, who reached Hawaii in 1778, that marked the start of a massive (and ongoing) influx of alien species. Over the course of the next two centuries, thou-sands of plants and animals from other lands would be released in Hawaii.

Cook's contribution to the fauna was goats; he left two billy goats and a nanny on Niihau. His fellow British explorer George Vancouver added cattle and sheep in 1793. From that point on, things began to spin of control. Horses were brought over in 1803, domestic turkeys in 1815. Donkeys and cats followed shortly thereafter. Disappointed with the paucity of game birds they found in the Hawaiian Islands (no quail, no grouse, no pigeons, and few water birds), the settlers set about remedying the "problem." California quail and ring-necked pheasants had been added to the fauna by 1855 and 1865, respectively, followed by Japanese and Gambel's quails in the 1920s. Since then, game managers have manifested a flair for the exotic, liberating gray francolins and black francolins from India, Kalij pheasants from the Himalayas, Luzon bleeding-heart pigeons from the Philippines, bronze-winged doves from Australia, and even the rare masked bobwhite from the southwestern United States and Mexico. In all, about 78 species of game birds from around the world have been released in Hawaii. Most disappeared, but about a dozen species have established self-sustaining populations in the archipelago. Mammals were introduced deliberately as well. With no native mammals to hunt besides a small bat and a rare seal, the residents of Hawaii imported their own big game, releasing mouflon sheep, axis deer, mule deer, and even pronghorn.

As settlers cleared the forests for crops and pastures, and as settlements grew into cities, the native flora and fauna retreated, leaving behind a disturbingly quiet landscape. The response of the citizens was to bring in songbirds from elsewhere. "Owners of vessels leaving foreign ports for Honolulu will confer a great favor by sending out birds, when it can be done without great expense. We need more songsters here," pleaded one newspaper writer in 1860. There was even a club, the Hui Manu, formed in 1930 for the sole purpose of bringing more birds from other lands to Hawaii. Dozens and dozens of species were introduced, including northern cardinals and western meadowlarks from the United States, skylarks from England, white-rumped shamas from Malaysia, and white-eyes from Japan. Many failed to survive, but others established thriving populations on one or more islands. Between the game birds and the songbirds, Hawaiian ornithologist Andrew Berger has estimated that at least 170 alien species were released in the Hawaiian archipelago.

Hundreds, perhaps thousands, of additional species were brought to the Hawaiian Islands unintentionally, as stowaways aboard ships and planes. Among them were many of the creatures whose initial absence had made the Hawaiian Islands seem like a paradise to early visitors: ship rats, ants, cockroaches, mosquitoes, scorpions, and centipedes.

These invaders affected the native species in four ways: as herbivores, as predators, as disease vectors, and as competitors. Cattle, goats, pigs, and sheep, for example, found themselves in a "paradise of fodder without thorns, toxins, distasteful substances or other vegetative defenses." Nor did they have to contend with wolves, coyotes, grizzly bears, or other predators (except humans). Numbers of free-ranging cattle grew throughout the mid- to late nineteenth century, paralleling the contemporaneous overgrazing that was under way in the southwestern United States. In Hawaii, the beasts ate their way up the mountains, consuming the young trees and turning rich forests into pasturelands. Fearful that the deforestation, if left unchecked, would ruin the watersheds that supplied water for agriculture, the citizens of Hawaii began to take action. Greater use of fencing, coupled with organized hunts and cattle drives in the 1920s and 1930s, eventually brought the feral cattle under partial control, but not before they had destroyed literally thousands of acres of native forest.

During this same period, goats and pigs also established large feral populations. The heyday of the goats may have been the mid-1800s, when tens of thousands of goatskins were exported annually from Hawaii, but they remain a bane to Hawaiian conservationists to this day. So gravely were feral goats damaging the vegetation in Maui's Haleakala Crater—in particular, its population of endangered silversword plants— that the National Park Service constructed a 32-mile hog-wire fence around the entire rim of the crater in an effort to exclude the animals. Feral pigs are an even more widespread problem in Hawaii, digging and rooting up some of rarest plant communities on earth. Their complicity in the near-extinction of the po'ouli has already been described.

The most dramatic example of devastation by an introduced herbivore does not come from any of the main islands, however. That dubious distinction goes to tiny Laysan Island, a one-and-a-half-square-mile atoll lying at the extreme northwestern end of the Hawaiian archipelago, nearly a thousand miles from Honolulu. Among biologists, it came to be known for its unique flora and fauna. Laysan harbored a variety of plants and animals, including two honeycreepers, a flightless rail, a miller-bird, a duck, and numerous insects, that existed nowhere else. It also served as the breeding grounds for immense numbers of albatrosses, boobies, terns, and other seabirds.

The guano generated by those seabirds attracted the attention of the North Pacific Phosphate and Fertilizer Company, which set up a guano mining business on Laysan in 1890. After the guano deposits were depleted, Max Schlemmer, the driven superintendent of the mining operation, tried several other schemes to sustain a business on the atoll, including a coconut plantation and a feather harvesting operation, neither of which succeeded and both of which further damaged Laysan's fragile environment. His master stroke—and the deed for which he will forever be enshrined in the environmental despoilers' hall of fame—was the introduction of rabbits to Laysan.

He released the rabbits around 1903 with the intention of creating a commercial meat cannery. Finding themselves on an island with thornless, tasty plants and no predators, the rabbits lived up to their reputation for fertility. When a team of scientists sponsored by the Bureau of Biological Survey (progenitor of today's Fish and Wildlife Service), the Bernice P. Bishop Museum, and the U.S. Navy, dubbed the Tanager Expedition, visited Laysan in 1923, they were stunned to discover that the little island had become a virtual desert. Almost all of the vegetation was gone, stripped clean by the rabbits. The only plants left untouched were a couple of coconut palms, some ironwood trees, and a few patches of tobacco that had been planted by the guano miners and disdained by the rabbits.

The scientists set about exterminating the remaining rabbits (starvation having already taken care of most of them), but they were too late to save some of the native species. The Laysan millerbird was gone; the flightless rail population was reduced to two individuals, which perished shortly after the scientists left; and the Laysan duck numbered no more than seven. The Laysan finch, one of the two honeycreepers endemic to the island, was down to a few dozen individuals. Its resourceful behavior, which included eating the eggs of other birds, had enabled it to hold on despite the desertification of the island. The other honeycreeper, the Laysan 'apapane, was less fortunate. Despite much searching, the scientists could find only three. They filmed one of them, a bright red male, as it perched atop a piece of dead coral and sang. A few days later, a three-day gale enveloped the island in a cloud of blowing sand, and when the weather cleared, the 'apapanes were gone forever.

Ornithologists are not the only ones to mourn the destruction caused by Mr. Schlemmer's rabbits. Laysan at one time harbored at least fourteen species of arthropods (insects, spiders, crustaceans, and the like) that occurred nowhere else. Five of them are now extinct.

Beyond losing habitat bite by bite to alien herbivores, the Hawaiian fauna has had to contend with the introduction of large numbers of new predators. Ground-nesting birds such as the Hawaiian goose and dark-rumped petrel have been especially hard hit by rats, cats, dogs, and mongooses. Today, for example, the survival of both the goose and the petrel depends in part on ongoing efforts to control predatory mammals within their breeding ranges. Ironically, some of these alien predators were brought to Hawaii to control previously introduced species that had become pests. Indian mongooses, for example, were released in the sugar plantations in the 1880s to control rodents. It was a foolish idea from the start, inasmuch as mongooses are diurnal and rats are nocturnal. Instead of dining on rats, the mongooses developed a taste for birds, including the highly endangered dark-rumped petrel. The whole business is reminiscent of the children's song about the little old lady who swallows a fly and, in attempting to rid herself of the creature, ends up swallowing a veritable menagerie of other animals until she herself is killed.

Cats, mongooses, and other carnivorous mammals make their presence known in a variety of conspicuous ways—from the half-eaten corpse of an endangered petrel to unmistakable pawprints in the mud—but they are by no means the only alien predators in the archipelago. Among the 2,600 foreign insect species that have gained a foothold in Hawaii are hundreds of ants and parasitic wasps, and in their Lilliputian world, they are predators every bit as fearsome as the mammals are in theirs.

Parasitic wasps reproduce by immobilizing another insect and laying an egg within the host's body cavity. When the egg hatches, the larval wasp dines on the viscera of its host, literally consuming it from within. Hawaii has a variety of native parasitic wasps, against which the indigenous insects have developed an array of defensive behaviors. Such behaviors, however, are relatively ineffective against the introduced wasps, many of which were released intentionally by agricultural specialists, who looked upon them as "organic" controls for various crop pests (themselves introduced by earlier settlers). This is yet another example of the comparative defenselessness of island species, analogous to the flightlessness of Laysan's rails. One prominent victim of the introduced parasites is the koa bug, a spectacular green and pink bug that was once a common resident on all the major islands, even within the city of Honolulu. Because of its abundance, agricultural specialists used the koa bug as an alternative host for rearing alien parasites for use in the battle against agricultural pests. By using the hapless koa bug in this fashion, they essentially ensured that whatever parasites they released would victimize it in addition to the intended targets. Very few koa bugs have been seen since 1978, and the species may well become extinct unless special measures are taken to protect it against the very creatures it helped to nourish.

Other victims of the parasitic wasps include Hawaii's native moths, or more precisely, their caterpillars. How many of these moths are now extinct or endangered is an open question, as is the effect of their disappearance on the plants they pollinate or the native birds that eat them. As one group of scientists has noted, "The effect of invasive alien arthropods means that we could save the forest and still lose the bugs, but we would eventually lose the forest as well because of the loss of pollinators and other functional groups of insects."

Of the thousands of insects brought to Hawaii over the past two centuries, surely the least welcome (and perhaps the most harmful) have been the mosquitoes. As noted earlier, Hawaii has no native mosquitoes. Their arrival allegedly dates back to 1826, when sailors from the British ship *Wellington*, having traveled from Mexico to Maui, went ashore to replenish their supply of fresh water. They proceeded to dump the dregs from their water barrels, which contained mosquito larvae, into a nearby stream. From that inauspicious start, the mosquitoes spread rapidly, colonizing the other islands and moving from the lowlands up into the mountains. In the process, they became the vectors, or transmitters, of two diseases that devastated the native songbirds: avian pox and avian malaria.

By the late 1890s, naturalists on Oahu and the Big Island were reporting native forest birds with grotesque tumorlike swellings on their feet, legs, and faces, an indication of avian pox. Contemporaneously, forest bird populations on those islands declined precipitately. In 1902, one baffled naturalist wrote, "The author has lived in Hawaii only six years, but within this time large areas of forest, which are yet scarcely touched by the axe save on the edges and except for a few trails, have become almost absolute solitude. One may spend hours in them and not hear the note of a single native bird. Yet a few years ago these areas were abundantly supplied with native birds." Avian malaria was not detected in Hawaii until 1938, when it was found in feral pigeons in Honolulu. Because it does not disfigure birds the way pox does, its spread is tougher to document.

Much like the native Hawaiian people, who had little immunity to the measles and other diseases brought by the settlers, the native birds appear to have little resistance to either pox or malaria. This much can be deduced by capturing native birds in the high montane forests, where the mosquitoes have not yet settled, and bringing them to the lowlands, where mosquitoes are abundant. Birds placed in cages surrounded by mosquito-proof mesh survive reasonably well; those without the mesh quickly sicken and die. In one experiment, 90 percent of 'i'iwi (a bright red Hawaiian honeycreeper) given a dose of malaria equivalent to what they might receive from a single mosquito bite died.

How these two diseases (as opposed to the mosquitoes that transmit them) got to the Hawaiian Islands is something of a mystery. Today, the main reservoir of avian pox is barnyard fowl; that fact, coupled with its early appearance on the islands, suggests it may have arrived with a shipment of chickens, ducks, or other fowl from the mainland. Avian malaria could have been introduced to Hawaii via any one of the hundreds of species of exotic birds that have been released. Alternatively, it may have been present all along in some of the migratory waterfowl that periodically visit Hawaii; without the mosquitoes, however, it could not spread to the resident birds.

At higher elevations, densities of mosquitoes drop sharply, creating safe havens for the native birds. Most native songbirds now occur only in high-elevation forests, having disappeared from lowland and mid-elevation areas where they once were common. Unfortunately, the high-elevation forests may not contain particularly desirable habitat for some of these birds. It may be too cold or too wet for them, and food may be scarcer. Whatever the reason, there is some concern among scientists that we may be trying to preserve the last of Hawaii's songbirds in places that were never especially hospitable to them. To make matters worse, the mosquitoes appear to be adapting to colder temperatures and moving up the mountains, threatening birds in what were once mosquito-free zones.

Up until the late 1960s, Kauai was the only Hawaiian island where the full complement of birds present at the time of Captain Cook's arrival could still be found. Their mecca was the Alakai Swamp, a forested plateau in the center of the island. Here, a birdwatcher willing to face torrential downpours, waist-deep mud, and steep slopes could hope to see a half-dozen or more critically endangered birds, including Kauai 'akialoa, 'o'u, Kauai 'o'o, and kama'o. The 'akialoa disappeared in the late 1960s—a tragedy, certainly, but not an unexpected one, as it had long been the rarest bird—but biologists held out hope that the other species would persist. Then, suddenly, the avifauna collapsed. The population of kama'o (a type of thrush) went from "some hundreds, if not a few thousands" in the early 1960s, to approximately 24 in 1981, to none by 1990. The 'o'u, a pudgy green and yellow honeycreeper, declined from 60 birds in the early 1970s to fewer than 10 by 1981, and despite extensive searches, there have been no definite sightings in a decade, suggesting the species is now extinct.

The most poignant loss, however, may have been the Kauai 'o'o. A sleek chocolate-brown bird with bright yellow thighs, it was the last of a noble line of 'o'os that were celebrated in Hawaiian folklore for their beautiful feathers. The 'o'os that once lived on Oahu, the Big Island, and Molokai had been driven to extinction by the beginning of the twentieth century, leaving the Kauai species as the sole survivor. A small population held out in the heart of the Alakai wilderness, delighting the handful of intrepid ornithologists who sought them out. About 36 birds were thought to survive in the early 1970s. Within a decade, that number had dropped to only 2, a pair nesting in a big ohia tree. After a hurricane struck Kauai in 1982, only one individual, a male, could be located. He survived for 4 more years, vigilantly guarding his little territory, constantly singing for a mate that never appeared.

In the spring of 1996, a friend and I hiked into the Alakai, hoping against the odds that we might glimpse one of the lost birds—a kama'o or 'o'u, perhaps; maybe even an 'o'o. The forest was magnificent. Gnarled, ancient ohia trees festooned with bright red flowers still attracted the commoner birds, such as scarlet 'i'iwi, bright yellow 'anianiau, and green 'amakihi. Only a few decades ago, these very same trees had harbored 'o'o and 'o'u, kama'o and 'akialoa. But there was no sign of them now. We carried with us a little tape recorder on which we played old recorded songs of the missing birds. If any survived, we reasoned, they might answer our call. With the push of a button, the haunting whistles of the 'o'o rang out once again, and against the patter of incessant rain, we strained to hear a response. There was none.

Why the Alakai birds disappeared so rapidly will probably never be known with certainty, but a disease of some sort, presumably pox or malaria, is the likely suspect. That exotic diseases have contributed to the demise of Hawaii's native birds seems certain, but how significant diseases have been relative to other factors is a matter of debate among scientists. It is not clear, for example, why some birds should have been so much more susceptible to pox and malaria than other, closely related species, or why some honeycreepers vanished from areas that appeared to be above the elevational range of the mosquitoes.

An equally vexing question is the extent to which the multitude of alien birds released in Hawaii are competing with the native birds, perhaps usurping essential food or nesting sites. Even the wildest, most remote forests in the Hawaiian Islands have been invaded by non-native birds, such as the Japanese white-eye and northern cardinal. The white-eye, in fact, is now the most abundant land bird in the archipelago, eclipsing all of the native species. Statistical analyses of Hawaiian bird populations indicate a negative correlation between the abundance of white-eyes and the abundance of several native species, including the elepaio, 'i'iwi, 'amakihi, and 'akikiki: that is, the commoner the white-eye, the less common the other species. This finding suggests that white-eyes may be depressing populations of native birds, perhaps by competing with them for nectar and insects.

This question of whether introduced species are outcompeting native species is of more than academic interest, for it reflects a fundamental puzzle about island ecology in general: Are species on islands inherently weaker competitors than their counterparts on the mainland? Or put more crudely, does the isolation of an island result in a collection of wimps, a hodgepodge of peculiar species that cannot hold their own against street-smart invaders from the mainland? Ecologist Daniel Simberloff has cogently argued that there is, in fact, little evidence that island species are inherently poor competitors. Yes, alien species introduced by people appear to have an easier time establishing wild populations on islands than on mainlands. But their success on islands may have more to do with the existence of more "vacant" niches on islands than with any intrinsic competitive superiority over native island species.

Moreover, the spread of alien species is facilitated by the rampant destruction of natural habitats that has occurred in Hawaii and most other island ecosystems. From the ranching operations of the mid-1800s to the sugarcane plantations of the late 1800s to the explosion of pineapple fields at the beginning of the twentieth century, agriculture has caused the destruction of hundreds of thousands of acres of natural habitats in Hawaii. So too has the growth of the human population, which increased by more than 50 percent between 1970 and 1994 and is predicted to grow by another 32 percent by 2010. Many introduced plants and animals prosper in disturbed or artificial habitats, such as cattle pastures and residential neighborhoods. From there, they spread into the remaining patches of natural forest, where the native plants and animals live.

Yet, paradoxically, there are probably more species of birds, plants, and insects living in the Hawaiian Islands today than there were at the time of Captain Cook's arrival in 1778, despite the fact that no other part of the United States has suffered the loss of so many species. The increase is due entirely to the introduction of exotic plants and animals. On all of the main islands, one can drive for miles through lush forests filled with birds, where virtually every tree and every bird is a non-native species. In helter-skelter fashion, we have created artificial yet functioning ecosystems throughout Hawaii, mixing together plants and animals from all corners of the globe. Superficially, at least, it all seems rather pretty. But when one realizes that this menagerie has come at the expense of hundreds, perhaps thousands, of unique and irreplaceable Hawaiian species, these faux forests with their faux species lose much of their charm.

Until quite recently, most scientists assumed that the Hawaiian fauna was essentially intact until Captain Cook opened up the South Pacific to settlers from the West. We know, for example, that there were approximately fifty species of forest birds on the Hawaiian Islands at the time of Cook's arrival, and that nearly half of them have vanished subsequently as a result of habitat destruction, introduced species, and diseases. Similarly, 6 to 7 percent of the plants and 10 percent of the native land snails that have been found in Hawaii over the past two centuries are either extinct or "missing in action" and feared extinct. All of these losses can be attributed largely to the direct and indirect effects of foreign settlement.

In the early 1970s, however, Storrs Olson of the Smithsonian Institution and his co-workers began exploring sinkholes, caverns, sand dunes, and lava tubes in the Hawaiian Islands. They were searching for fossil bird bones, and what they found was nothing short of astounding. To date, they have unearthed the remains of sixty species of endemic birds that became extinct before any ornithologist could observe them. Among them are many types of birds that were thought never to have settled in Hawaii, including two species of flightless ibis, an eagle closely related to the bald eagle, four species of long-legged owls, and seven species of flightless geese, plus at least seventeen honeycreepers. With Olson's discoveries, it now appears that at least half (and perhaps more than two-thirds) of Hawaii's land birds vanished before Cook's arrival.

Deducing the reason for their extinction required some clever ornithological sleuthing. Could these birds have disappeared as a result of the warming of the earth's climate at the end of the Pleistocene epoch, some 10,000 years ago? Not likely. Radiocarbon dating of snail shells and crab claws found mixed with the fossil bird bones shows that all of these animals survived well beyond the Pleistocene. Some of these bones have even been found in Polynesian middens and hearths, suggesting that more than one flightless ibis or goose wound up in the stomachs of hungry Polynesians. In fact, all of these birds appear to have vanished after the arrival of the Polynesians and before Captain Cook's arrival. The circumstantial evidence strongly suggests these birds were exterminated by the Polynesians—but how?

Some of the larger flightless species, such as the ibises and geese, may have been hunted to extinction, and populations of others surely were harmed by the pigs, rats, and dogs brought by the Polynesians. But for the majority of birds, especially the small forest-dwelling species, the most probable cause of extinction was habitat loss. We know now, based on archaeological evidence and the writings of early explorers, that the Polynesians cleared most of the dry lowland forests of Hawaii for agriculture. By the time botanists reached the Hawaiian Islands at the beginning of the nineteenth century, only scattered, degraded remnants of these forests remained, yet they supported a distinctive assemblage of plants, including many highly localized species. It seems sensible to infer, therefore, that these forests were the primary habitats of many of the birds known only from fossil remains, and that the birds vanished when the forests were cleared.

Underscoring the importance of these now vanished forests is the discovery of fossil remains of extant Hawaiian birds in the places where these forests once grew. For example, the po'ouli, whose existence in the montane rain forests of Maui was not known until 1973, turns out to have lived in the lowland dry forests prior to the arrival of the Polynesians. The Laysan finch, historically known only from Laysan Island, once lived on the main islands as well, apparently inhabiting the lowland forests. The palila, a beautiful gray and yellow honeycreeper, today occurs only in mamane forests above 6,500 feet in elevation, but fossils have been found nearly at sea level. Discoveries such as these support the disturbing hypothesis that we are now trying to protect these birds in what has always been marginal habitat for them, a problem exacerbated by the introduction of mosquitoes, which has pushed some species even farther up the mountains.

The birds, of course, are only the tip of the iceberg. We may confidently assume that the lowland forests also harbored large numbers of endemic plants, insects, spiders, mites, and other small animals, many of which surely vanished when the forests were cleared. But since the soft, boneless bodies of plants and insects rarely become fossils, we will never know the full diversity of species that once inhabited the Hawaiian Islands.

As shocking as Olson's findings are, they fit into a general pattern for the tropical Pacific: Wherever "primitive" humans have occupied islands, they have left behind a legacy of extinction that, in the aggregate, is truly staggering. In New Zealand, Easter Island, the Marquesas Islands, Micronesia, the Society Islands, the Cook Islands, Samoa, Tonga, and Melanesia, paleontologists have uncovered fossils of previously unknown birds that vanished after the arrival of humans. Presumably, the same factors at play in Hawaii—overhunting, habitat destruction, and introduced predators, competitors, and diseases—are responsible for those losses, too. By one estimate, prehistoric humans may have eradicated over 2,000 species of birds in the tropical Pacific; this would represent a 20 percent worldwide reduction in the number of bird species. As one biologist dryly concluded, "We expect extinction after people arrive on an island. Survival is the exception."

Also destroyed by these findings is any notion that the Polynesians and other Pacific Islanders lived in "harmony" with nature. They, like the Westerners who displaced them, acted in their own self-interest, and in so doing, inflicted grave harm on island ecosystems that could not accommodate their demands. In this part of the world, as in so many other places, there was no amity between man and beast—just people scratching out a living at the expense of other species.

The situation in Hawaii today is as close to an ecological disaster as one is likely to find anywhere in the world: lots of very rare, poorly known species clinging to existence in marginal habitats; thriving populations of alien predators, competitors, and disease carriers; and more potentially harmful species arriving every year because of human foolishness or carelessness. Efforts to repair the damage are hampered by the extreme difficulty of controlling many of the exotic species plaguing Hawaii. There is, for example, no practical way to "recall" the multitude of wasps that parasitize the koa bug or the thousands of Japanese white-eyes that compete with native songbirds. Nor is it particularly easy to track down and kill feral pigs hiding out in some of the wettest, muddiest, most inaccessible forests on earth.

Further confounding efforts to restore native habitats in Hawaii is the remarkable ability of some exotic plants to alter fundamentally the very ecosystems they inhabit. "[T]hey don't merely compete with or consume native species, they change the rules of the game by altering environmental conditions or resource availability." Arguably the most dramatic example involves a half-dozen or so types of grass that were brought to Hawaii to provide forage for livestock. These grasses typically gain a beachhead in an area following some disturbance of the native vegetation, as might occur in the wake of a fire or logging operation. Adept at colonizing such disturbed sites and able to hog food, moisture, and sunlight, the alien grasses quickly crowd out the native plants attempting to grow there too. As the grass dies or becomes dormant, it leaves behind a large volume of standing dead blades, which are highly flammable. This fuel buildup leads to frequent fires, which tend to kill the native trees and shrubs while simultaneously creating ideal conditions for the spread of the grass. The process amounts to a positive feedback loop: grass begets fire, which begets more grass, which begets more fire, and so on until the forests are replaced by grasslands.

The future of conservation in Hawaii is likely to be one of ceaseless efforts to control non-native predators, competitors, and livestock in sensitive ecosystems, constant vigilance against accidental or unsupervised releases of new exotic species, and for a growing number of species, elaborate, expensive captive breeding programs. It is not a particularly rosy scenario, but remarkably, with enough effort and ingenuity, species and habitats can be saved, even in this battered and bruised corner of the world.

Consider Laysan Island, that flyspeck island overrun by rabbits at the beginning of the twentieth century. After the rabbits were eliminated, the vegetation began to recover. It wasn't a speedy process, and it required a head start in the form of seeds and rootstocks transplanted from other islands in the northwestern Hawaiian chain. But once the vegetation recovered, the birds did, too. The population of Laysan ducks, formerly down to as few as seven individuals, rose to as many as five hundred in the late 1980s (although it has recently declined for reasons as yet unknown). Laysan finches, reduced to a few dozen birds in 1923, now number in the thousands, and the albatrosses and other seabirds have returned en masse. There is, of course, the omnipresent risk that some destructive plant or animal will reach Laysan as a stowaway aboard a ship or encased in mud on some visitor's boots, but for the moment, at least, the island is once again an avian metropolis.

A small concrete building on a remote hillside on the Big Island offers a different kind of hope. Inside, a small team of biologists wearing sterile garb tend a row of incubators containing the eggs of Hawaiian crows and puaiohi (a type of thrush), two of Hawaii's rarest birds. Behind the incubators is a long corridor leading to a series of outdoor aviaries harboring the adult birds. Each aviary is covered by mosquito-proof mesh and monitored by a video camera. To an outside observer, the whole arrangement looks like a cross between a hospital nursery and a maximum-security prison, but, in fact, the life-affirming nursery is the more accurate image, because if either the crow or the thrush survives into the twenty-first century, it will probably be due to the offspring that are produced and released by this facility.

The only comparable facility that I know of is the one near San Diego used to breed California condors. Or perhaps the one in Maryland used to breed whooping cranes. Or maybe even the one in Wyoming used to raise black-footed ferrets. The sad truth is that there is no shortage of critically endangered species on the mainland, many of which require the same intensive care needed by so many Hawaiian species. So how truly different is Hawaii from the mainland?

This chapter began with the assertion that Hawaii was special, both in terms of the species that live there and the magnitude of the threats they face. But the threats themselves—habitat destruction, diseases, exotic species—are the same ones we have encountered time and time again elsewhere in the United States. True, the small ranges of most Hawaiian species make them especially sensitive to habitat destruction, but much the same can be said for the plants and animals of Lake Wales Ridge or the Florida Keys. The decimation of the Hawaiian avifauna due to exotic diseases is unmatched elsewhere in the United States, but individual species on the mainland, ranging from desert tortoises and bighorn sheep in the Mojave Desert to black-footed ferrets in Wyoming, have been grievously harmed by diseases spread by pets and livestock. Recall also the astounding assortment of alien fungi and insects that are picking off the trees of the eastern forests one by one.

Alien species, arguably the most intractable threat to the Hawaiian fauna, are a growing menace to wildlife throughout the mainland as well. Exotic fish species have been added to virtually every major lake and river in the United States, where they have become potent competitors and predators of native species. Much as Hawaii harbors more species of birds today than it did two centuries ago, so too does the Colorado River harbor more fishes. In both cases, the increases have come about because humans have destroyed much of the natural landscape and released alien species—much to the detriment of the native birds and fishes. The Colorado River, like Hawaii, represents an old and isolated environment, an "island" of water in a "sea" of arid land. It, too, spawned a collection of strange and wonderful species, some of which are unable to persist in the face of altered habitats and new competitors and predators.

Even the fire-inducing grasses that are supplanting Hawaii's native forests have their counterparts elsewhere in the United States. Throughout the Intermountain West, for example, millions of acres have been taken over by cheatgrass, which was brought accidentally to the United States from the Old World. Cheatgrass is a highly flammable plant that dies and dries out in the spring, creating ideal fuel for summer wildfires. The summer fires, in turn, sweep through the shrublands, killing or damaging the native plants. Because cheatgrass recovers rapidly after a fire, it is able to outgrow and outcompete the native species. In this way, it creates a positive feedback loop that facilitates its own spread.

Hawaii is special. And vulnerable. But so are many of the nooks and crannies of the American landscape. Perhaps the most frightening aspect of the Hawaiian story is not the immense numbers of imperiled species living there, but the possibility that it foreshadows what could happen elsewhere in the United States.

CHAPTER EIGHT

The Condor's Shadow

The last quarter of the nineteenth century and the beginning of the twentieth has been called the most destructive period in the history of American wildlife. The demise of the passenger pigeon and Carolina parakeet, the near-extinction of the sea otter and northern elephant seal, the slaughter of the bison, the rampant overgrazing of the arid grasslands of the Southwest, the clearing of the longleaf pine forests, the ruthless campaigns to eliminate wolves, grizzlies, and other large predators, and the commercial exploitation of shorebirds and waterfowl all reached a crescendo then. The modern environmental movement began in large part as a backlash against this destruction, and, thankfully, it succeeded in stopping some of the worst abuses. In subsequent decades, many of the most heavily persecuted species staged remarkable comebacks, demonstrating a degree of resilience that few observers at the time would have anticipated.

The sheer growth of both the human population and the economy of the United States over the past 50 years has brought us to a similarly momentous juncture. At stake this time is a far greater number of species, facing a more diverse and powerful set of threats. Overhunting, the bane of conservationists at the start of the twentieth century, is no longer a major threat to terrestrial animals, having long been supplanted by three far more ruthless and indiscriminate killers: habitat destruction, alien species, and pollution. Together, they have ensured that a larger proportion of the American fauna and flora is in danger of extinction than at any time since the Ice Age. Whereas most of the animals that were disappearing at the close of the nineteenth century were game species (pursued under a rather broad definition of "game"), most of the species now at risk are not. By and large, the current crop of imperiled species consists of obscure little creatures—Puritan tiger beetles, Cumberland monkeyface pearly mussels, po'ouli, and the like—that would not have tugged at the heartstrings of early conservationists the way passenger pigeons or bison did. Even today, most of these species fail to arouse much compassion in any but a small cadre of diehard wildlife aficionados. Yet little lives are significant lives nonetheless, and each is part of a distinctly American tapestry of wildlife and wilderness.

At the present time, the U.S. Fish and Wildlife Service has placed nearly 1,200 U.S. plants and animals on the official endangered list, thereby granting them protection under the Endangered Species Act. As the Service readily admits, however, the current list contains only a small proportion of the species at risk of extinction in the United States, partly because scientists know so little about most species, and partly because adding a species to the official list is a ponderous, politically charged process. Let us assume that approximately 16 percent of the U.S. fauna and flora is in immediate danger of extinction, a figure derived from data compiled by The Nature Conservancy (as discussed in the Introduction). With over 100,000 species described to date in the United States, it is possible that at least 16,000 species are in grave danger of extinction, more than thirteen times the number of species currently on the official list.

Such arithmetic immediately conjures up the image of an endangered species in every backyard and vacant lot in America and an entire nation chafing under land use restrictions occasioned by the need to protect this multitude of rare plants and animals. In fact, such a scenario has no basis in fact. One of the more remarkable aspects of our endangered species is the degree to which they are concentrated in a few key regions. Most places contain very few endangered species; a small number of places contain lots. Four regions in particular—Hawaii, southern California, the southeastern coastal states, and the southern Appalachian Mountains—contain the vast majority of endangered species in this country. What these areas have in common is that they are home to large numbers of species with small ranges (endemic species), as well as being places where development is proceeding at a rapid pace. It is an explosive combination, one certain to generate large numbers of endangered species now and in the future. A disproportionate share of the plants and animals added to the endangered species list over the next several decades are certain to come from these areas. Indeed, I suspect the current "hot spots" for endangered species will get significantly hotter long before other regions of the country feel much heat.

My prediction will bring little joy to the developers, loggers, ranchers, and other resource users who currently live in these crucial regions and feel unduly constrained by the dictates of various environmental laws. But it could be genuinely good news for the country in general, for it suggests that we can aspire to save most of our endangered species, now and in the future, without usurping immense swaths of land from Connecticut to California and from Alabama to Alaska. There are exceptions, to be sure: protecting grizzly bears in the northern Rockies or spotted owls in the Cascades will entail restrictions on certain activities, such as logging, over a vast area. We are fortunate that the majority of their current habitat lies in the public estate, in national forests and national parks where it should be incumbent upon the federal government to exercise restraint in the exploitation of natural resources.

Such musings about the theoretical feasibility of protecting the nation's vanishing wildlife bear little resemblance to the current situation, however. According to the most recent assessment by the U.S. Fish and Wildlife Service, fewer than 10 percent of the plants and animals protected by the Endangered Species Act are actually increasing in numbers and on the road to recovery. An additional 27 percent are judged to be stable, indicating that the decline in numbers or the loss of habitat that earned them a place on the endangered list has been halted at least temporarily; 33 percent are still declining, despite protection under the act; and for an additional 31 percent, the Fish and Wildlife Service lacks enough data to determine trends. One can quibble with the accuracy of some of these numbers, inasmuch as they are based on professional judgment rather than hard data and analysis, but the overall picture they provide is clear: Despite a number of heartening success stories, a distressingly large fraction of America's imperiled wildlife continues to slip closer to extinction.

There are almost as many explanations for this apparent lack of success as there are interest groups fighting over control of the nation's land and water. That said, four factors in particular strike me as especially significant contributors to the problem. First, across the nation, efforts to monitor trends in wildlife populations are woefully inadequate. Most of our game animals fall under the watchful eye of state and federal agencies, but game animals constitute only a tiny fraction of our total fauna. The nation's birdwatchers do a reasonably good job of tracking population trends among songbirds, adding a few

hundred more species to the watch list. But for the vast majority of species—from minnows to mice to mussels—monitoring
programs are fragmentary, inconsistent, and often nonexistent.
This ignorance is for the most part self-imposed: Proposals to
expand the monitoring capabilities of agencies like the Fish and
Wildlife Service inevitably draw fire from anti-environmental
ideologues and their allies in Congress, who would rather not
know about a problem affecting wildlife, lest it necessitate a
costly or controversial solution.

Second, by the time a trend becomes too obvious to ignore
and the institutions charged with safeguarding the nation's
wildlife are jostled awake, it is often too late to take effective
action. The plants and animals that end up on the federal
endangered species list typically are added to that list only after
their populations have dropped to critically low levels. A 1993
study found that the median population size of an animal
species when it is finally placed on the endangered species list is
approximately 1,000 individuals; the corresponding value for
plants is less than 120. Such small populations are easily erased
by random events, such as a hurricane (Schaus' swallowtail) or
industrial accident (Clinch River mussels), or even by random
fluctuations in birth and death rates. A number of plants have
been added to the endangered list when only one or two individuals were known to be left.

Third, when the relevant institutions and agencies finally
step forward to protect vanishing species, they usually do so
with inadequate resources. A strong case can be made that the
amount of money available for endangered species recovery
programs (which was never enough to begin with) has not kept
pace with the growing number of species now recognized as
imperiled. During the past two decades, for example, the
endangered species budget of the U.S. Fish and Wildlife
Service climbed from $16,534,000 in 1978 to $77,181,000 in
1998. Adjusted for inflation, this represents approximately an
87 percent increase in funding. During this same period, however, the number of species on the endangered list jumped by
over 450 percent, from 199 to 1,107. The inescapable result is

that each year the Fish and Wildlife Service finds itself with fewer dollars to spend per species. Further compounding this disparity is the fact that throughout the history of the Endangered Species Act, a disproportionately large share of the money has been spent on a handful of charismatic species. During a recent three-year period, for example, nearly half of all the dollars expended under the Endangered Species Act were spent on just a dozen species.

Finally, until recently, we have failed to give landowners any incentive to help endangered species. The Endangered Species Act relies on the threat of fines and jail sentences to discourage people from engaging in conduct harmful to vanishing wildlife. Such measures are an important and necessary step toward saving these species, but they do little to motivate people to go beyond the basic requirements of the law and actively assist endangered wildlife. Many landowners, for example, are capable of aiding in the recovery of endangered species by creating or restoring habitats on their land, but are unwilling to do so. Their unwillingness stems from a fear that if they take actions that attract endangered species to their property or increase the populations of endangered species that are already there, their "reward" for doing so will be more regulatory restrictions on the use of that property. In its most extreme manifestation, this fear has prompted some landowners to destroy unoccupied habitat before the endangered animals could find it. One man, noting the presence of red-cockaded woodpeckers on a small section of his property, announced his intention to clearcut the trees on the rest of it. "I cannot afford to let those woodpeckers take over the rest of the property," he declared, "I'm going to start massive clearcutting."

Stories such as these prompted the Fish and Wildlife Service to initiate a "safe harbor" policy in the spring of 1995. Under this policy, landowners who agree to restore or enhance the habitats of endangered species on their property—something they are not required to do by law—can receive permission from the Service to develop that land at a later date, even if it has become inhabited by an endangered species. One hopes,

of course, that landowners will choose not to exercise that right, but without such assurance, they will not agree to undertake the improvements. The safe harbor policy thus removes a long-standing disincentive many people felt about attracting endangered species to their property. To date, it has proved to be immensely popular in those states where it has been tried, with well over a million acres of land currently enrolled in the program. The next obvious step is to provide landowners with some sort of financial incentive to undertake the desired habitat restoration. Restoring a tallgrass prairie or a longleaf pine forest may require a considerable amount of money, and thus far landowners who want to do so have had to bear most of the cost themselves, even though everyone stands to benefit from their good deeds.

Given these obstacles to effective conservation—a lack of information, a tendency to ignore a problem until it becomes a crisis, a failure to commit adequate resources, and a failure to reward landowners who aid in the restoration of imperiled wildlife—and given the steadily increasing population and growing economy of the United States, the future seems clear: shrinking pieces of nature harboring a growing roster of endangered species and demanding ever more intensive and expensive management. The need for intensive management follows ineluctably from the reduction in the amount of habitat. Many of the small, isolated scraps of undeveloped land that are set aside as nature reserves eventually will be overrun by alien plants and animals unless some sort of control program is put in place. For species that live in habitats created by fire, such as the Kirtland's warbler and red-cockaded woodpecker, prescribed burns must replace the wildfires that are now routinely suppressed out of concern for human safety and property.

By one estimate, over 60 percent of the plants and animals on the endangered species list are vulnerable to either alien species or fire suppression. The uncomfortable implication of this finding is that many of these species could disappear even if every single acre of their habitat were protected from

development, unless that habitat was managed properly. Management takes money (someone must be paid to pull up the melaleuca, trap the feral pigs, or carefully burn the jack pines), and no federal or state agency has created a permanent endowment for this sort of stewardship. We are, in short, running up a hefty stewardship bill with little thought as to how we shall pay it. And pay it we must, for not to do so would defeat the purpose behind laws like the Endangered Species Act and our investment in our national wildlife refuges and national parks.

We are, for better or worse, the guardians of a significant share of the nation's flora and fauna. The extent of that responsibility grows with every species added to the endangered list and with every foreign plant or animal that gains a foothold in this country due to our negligence or stupidity. I know of only two ways to reduce the magnitude of that burden. One is to walk away from it — to decide that a nation without whooping cranes, red wolves, Colorado squawfish, and thousands of other rare plants and animals is no poorer for their absence. The other is to grow out of it — to increase the amount of habitat available to these species through the science and art of ecological restoration. Doing so will not only boost populations of many imperiled species, it will also provide them with larger blocks of habitat that may be better able to sustain fires and other natural disturbances or withstand the onslaught of alien species.

In the past, we have been the beneficiaries of nature's own remarkable recuperative abilities. The eastern forests (and the wildlife within them) returned to life with relatively little assistance from us after they were cleared in the eighteenth and nineteenth centuries. To an increasing degree, however, the restoration of degraded ecosystems and missing species will require our active involvement. Not all ecosystems can be restored, and not all species can be reintroduced to restored habitats, but enough can to prompt the question, will we rise to the challenge? To some extent we already have, as evidenced by the landowners eagerly enrolling in the Fish and Wildlife Service's safe harbor program, or the popular support

projects such as the restoration of the Everglades or the re-establishment of wolves within Yellowstone.

In the long run, however, even our best efforts at ecological restoration could be foiled by our failure to control a potentially sinister and pervasive threat to wildlife: global climate change. Atmospheric concentrations of greenhouse gases such as carbon dioxide and methane are increasing due to the burning of fossil fuels, the destruction of forests, the spread of intensive agriculture, and other changes in land use. Many scientists now predict that a continuation of these activities will result in a rise in average global temperatures of between 0.9 and 3.5 degrees Celsius over the course of the next century. That increase could trigger a significant rise in sea level as well as changes in weather patterns, including droughts and floods.

How all of this will affect wildlife is unknown, but the possible effects are enormous. The habitats of some species may simply disappear, as could happen if a rising ocean submerges the nesting beaches of sea turtles and other coastal species. In other cases, the changes are likely to be more subtle but no less disruptive. An increase or decrease in precipitation or the length of the growing season could be enough to alter the vegetation in a given region of the country, favoring the growth of certain types of trees, shrubs, or grasses over other types, thereby scrambling and rearranging the habitats of many animals. Of course, the American flora and fauna have been through this type of disruption before, most notably during the Pleistocene epoch, when the climate cooled and warmed for reasons unrelated to human activities. On those earlier occasions, the ranges of plants and animals contracted and expanded in response to the changing climate. Species sought refuge in southern latitudes and at low elevations during cold periods and then moved northward and upward as the climate warmed. Today, however, there is no longer a big, empty continent for them to move across. Cities, farms, highways, and a multitude of other artifacts have usurped much of the landscape. The escape routes for wildlife have disappeared.

As the causes of species endangerment have expanded, so too has the range of issues that must be addressed by conservationists. What we eat, how we farm, where we build houses and highways, the energy we use to fuel our economy, even the kinds of animals we allow to be sold as pets—all these factors and many more will determine the future of wildlife in America. The fact that we are increasingly aware of these linkages is a positive sign. So too are the growing numbers of people who have joined in efforts to restore degraded ecosystems and conserve imperiled species. But it remains to be seen whether enough people will speak out on behalf of wildlife to have an impact comparable to that of the men and women who first rose to defend our embattled fauna more than a century ago.

On a warm autumn day in 1984, a friend and I decided to say good-bye to the California condor. At that time, only fifteen condors remained in the wild, and the species' extinction seemed both imminent and inevitable. Leaving Los Angeles in the predawn darkness, we traveled north into the foothills bordering the San Joaquin Valley, to an overlook at the edge of the Los Padres National Forest. Ahead of us stretched the once extensive grasslands of the valley, now largely converted to agriculture; behind us lay the shrinking wilderness of the Sierra Madre, and behind the mountains, the ever-expanding Los Angeles megalopolis. As the sun burned away the morning fog, the birds of prey began to appear. A prairie falcon raced by, followed later by two red-tailed hawks and a golden eagle. We continued to watch and wait, as the sun climbed higher and higher.

The condor appeared without fanfare or warning. One moment, the sky ahead of us contained nothing; the next moment, an immense black bird materialized in the void—a raptor so large it made all of the previous falcons, hawks, and eagles seem small and insignificant. Hands trembling, I raised my binoculars to my eyes and watched slack-jawed as the condor passed alongside the foothills and out over the valley, until its image simply vanished in the shimmering heat waves. Gone forever, I thought.

During the Pleistocene, California condors ranged across most of the southern United States, from California to Florida, and south into northern Mexico. Then, 10,000 to 11,000 years ago, they vanished from most of that area, a disappearance that coincided with the demise of the mammoths, ground sloths, camels, and other large Ice Age mammals. It is not difficult to imagine a linkage between the two events. Condors are giant vultures—scavengers that depend upon an abundant supply of large, dead mammals. With the Ice Age mammals gone, the condors may have been starved out of much of their former range. If humans were responsible for the extinction of these mammals, as many anthropologists believe, then the beginning of the end for the condor can be traced back to the arrival of the first humans in the New World, making it our oldest endangered species.

By the time the first Spanish settlers reached the West Coast, condors were restricted to a narrow strip along the Pacific coast from British Columbia to Baja California. Here, the dead whales and seals that periodically washed ashore, plus the abundant herds of tule elk, mule deer, and pronghorn in the Central Valley of California, provided enough food to sustain them. But if there has been one constant throughout the long and storied history of the California condor, it is simply this: People and condors don't mix. People shoot condors, harass them, and, purposefully or not, drive them away. By the latter half of the nineteenth century, condors had vanished from the Pacific Northwest; by the 1930s, they were gone from Baja, too, leaving only a small area in the rugged mountains of southern California as their last refuge. The whales and seals were much reduced in numbers by then, and the herds of elk and pronghorn in the Central Valley and elsewhere had long since been supplanted by cattle and sheep. Fortunately, the livestock—or, more precisely, their carcasses—made up for the native mammals that humans had displaced or extirpated. The birds continued to eat the carcasses of wild animals when they found them, but by and large, most of their food now came from livestock. Thus the condors became indirectly dependent upon humans, even though humans were also their greatest enemy. That paradoxical relationship would grow even stronger in the coming decades.

Throughout the latter half of the twentieth century, California in general, and southern California in particular, grew by leaps and bounds, encroaching on the remaining wilderness and shrinking the condors' world. From a wild population of perhaps 100 to 200 individuals in the late 1930s, their numbers dropped to 50 or 60 individuals by the late 1960s, to 30 or fewer by the late 1970s, and to only 15 by the fall of 1984, when I went in search of them.

Faced with a small and rapidly declining condor population, state and federal officials began bringing a few young condors and even eggs into captivity in 1982 in the hope of breeding them in zoos. When 6 of the 15 birds left in the wild disappeared in the winter of 1984–1985, the Fish and Wildlife Service made the risky decision to capture all of the remaining individuals, a process that was completed on Easter Sunday in 1987. For the first time in hundreds of thousands, if not millions, of years, the skies of North America were devoid of free-flying condors. The fate of the species now rested with the curators and zookeepers charged with caring for the handful of captive individuals, a situation made all the more unnerving by the fact that no one had ever bred California condors in captivity.

To their credit, the zoos came through with flying colors. The captive population has grown with astonishing speed. By January of 1992, state and federal officials were ready to begin releasing young condors back into the wild. Those initial releases did not go well. Some of the young birds collided with power lines and were killed. Others showed a disturbing lack of fear of humans—they approached hikers, landed on rooftops, and swooped into buildings. The condor recovery team addressed these problems by moving the release sites farther back into the wilderness, by employing adverse conditioning techniques to teach the birds a healthy distrust for humans and power lines, and by providing the young condors with a steady supply of fresh carcasses to reduce their wanderlust. Thus far, the new techniques seem to be working. By the spring of 1998, nineteen condors were flying free in southern California, and deaths due to collisions with power lines and other mishaps had declined.

The condor recovery team is also attempting to create a second wild population by releasing birds in the Grand Canyon, where condors have been absent for over 10,000 years. To win the approval of people who live near the release site, the U.S. Fish and Wildlife Service has promised to impose no new restrictions on activities such as logging, mining, and grazing on behalf of the birds. The agency's eagerness to placate local residents has ruffled a few feathers within the environmental community, but it may be the case that no new restrictions on human activities are needed to make this experiment a success. With the right conditioning and a supply of fresh carcasses courtesy of the government, the birds may yet prosper in the Grand Canyon.

Time alone will tell whether these earnest efforts constitute the beginnings of a condor renaissance or merely a blip in the final phase of a 10,000-year slide to extinction. For the moment, however, a keen naturalist can hike to an overlook at the edge of the Grand Canyon or the San Joaquin Valley and still hope to see a grand and glorious sight, an Ice Age survivor, as it sails across a landscape that may seem timeless but is, in fact, constantly changing.

Notes

Introduction

2 the Ice Age: My main references for the discussion of the Ice Age extinctions are: B. Kurtén, *Before the Indians* (New York: Columbia University Press, 1988); E. C. Pielou, *After the Ice: The Return of Life to Glaciated North America* (Chicago: University of Chicago Press, 1991); F. H. West, ed., *American Beginnings: The Prehistory and Palaeoecology of Beringia* (Chicago: University of Chicago Press, 1996); E. J. Dixon, *Quest for the First Americans* (Albuquerque: University of New Mexico Press, 1993); P. S. Martin, "Refuting Late Pleistocene Extinction Models," in *Dynamics of Extinction*, edited by D. K. Elliott (New York: John Wiley & Sons, 1986); P. D. Ward, *The Call of Distant Mammoths: Why the Ice Age Mammals Disappeared* (New York: Copernicus, 1997); and Professor Carole Mandryk, Harvard University. I am grateful to Professor Mandryk for helping me to make sense of some of the recent discoveries in this confusing and fast-changing field.

2 the Laurentide ice field . . . and the Cordilleran ice field: Geologists continue to debate the precise boundaries of these ice fields. See Pielou, *After the Ice.*

5 the earliest Americans . . . began modifying the land: See S. J. Pyne, "Indian Fires," *Natural History*, February 1983.

5 humans have essentially reconfigured the American landscape: Statistics on habitat loss are from R. F. Noss, E. T. LaRoe III, and J. M. Scott, *Endangered Ecosystems of the United States: A Preliminary Assessment of Loss and Degradation*, National Biological Service, Biological Report 28 (February 1995).

7 100,000 native species: Figures for the total number of described species and the total number of described insects in the United States are taken from T. Eisner, J. Lubchenco, E. O. Wilson, D. S. Wilcove, and M. J. Bean, "Building a Scientifically Sound Policy for Protecting Endangered Species," *Science* 269 (1995): 1231–32; tallies for vascular plants and vertebrates are from B. A. Stein and S. R. Flack, *1997 Species Report Card: The State of U.S. Plants and Animals* (Arlington, Va.: The Nature Conservancy, 1997).

8 The Nature Conservancy estimates: Status information on species is from Stein and Flack, *1997 Species Report Card.* At least 110 species in the United States are known to be extinct and another 416 are currently missing and possibly extinct.

8 Edward O. Wilson: *The Diversity of Life* (Cambridge, Mass.: Belknap Press, 1992), 253.

8 Of the five: The data on the percentages of species threatened by various factors are taken from D. S. Wilcove, D. Rothstein, J. Dubow, A. Phillips, and E. Losos, "Quantifying Threats to Imperiled Species in the United States," *BioScience* 48 (1998): 607–15. The percentages do not add up to 100 because a given species may be harmed by more than one factor.

Chapter 1

18 The cutting began: M. Williams, *Americans and Their Forests* (Cambridge: Cambridge University Press, 1989); D. W. MacCleery, *American Forests: A History of Resiliency and Recovery*, Publication FS-540 (Washington, D.C.: U.S. Forest Service, 1992). The quotation is from Williams, 193.

18 less than 2 percent: Percentage of remaining old growth from R. F. Noss, E. T. LaRoe III, and J. M. Scott, *Endangered Ecosystems of the United States: A Preliminary Assessment of Loss and Degradation*, National Biological Service, Biological Report 28 (February 1995).

19 the precolonial landscape: My description of the Indian settlements, the population sizes, and their effect on the forests is taken from Williams, *Americans and Their Forests*.

19 many tribes burned the forests: See S. J. Pyne, "Indian Fires," *Natural History*, February 1983.

19 one colonist wrote: Quotation of the Reverend Francis Higginson from Williams, *Americans and Their Forests*, 41–42.

20 explorer James Rosier: Rosier's trip is described in W. Cronon, *Changes in the Land: Indians, Colonists, and the Ecology of New England* (New York: Hill and Wang, 1983), 27.

20 the precolonial forests: J. G. Dickson, "Birds and Mammals of Pre-Colonial Southern Old-Growth Forests," *Natural Areas Journal* 11 (1991): 26–33.

20 Colonist after colonist wrote home: Cronon, *Changes in the Land*, 24–25.

20 "Our whole concept of a healthy and mature forest": T. Horton and W. Eichbaum, *Turning the Tide: Saving the Chesapeake Bay* (Washington, D.C.: Island Press, 1991), 131.

20 north of Harrisburg, Pennsylvania: Details of the Pennsylvania hunt are taken from H. W. Shoemaker, *Extinct Pennsylvania Animals*, part I: *The Panther and the Wolf* (Altoona, Pa.: The Altoona Tribune Publishing Company, 1917). The quotations are from pages 29–30.

21 to get rid of them: The extirpation of the gray wolf is discussed in Cronon, *Changes in the Land*; P. Matthiessen, *Wildlife in America*, revised, updated edition (New York: Viking, 1987); and D. S. Lee, "Maryland's Vanished Birds and Mammals: Reflections of Ethics Past," in *Threatened and Endangered Plants and Animals of Maryland*, edited by A. W. Norden, D. C. Forester, and G. Fenwick, Natural Heritage Special Publication 84-1 (Annapolis: Maryland Department of Natural Resources, 1984).

21 red wolf: For information on the history of the red wolf and on-going efforts to restore it, see W. Booth, "Questioned Pedigree Clouds Wolf Program," *Washington Post*, 24 June 1991; C. Dold, "Six Year Effort to Return Red Wolves to Wild Is Making Headway," *New York Times*, 5 October 1993; J. DeBlieu, *Meant to Be Wild: The Struggle to Save Endangered Species Through Captive Breeding* (Golden, Colo.: Fulcrum Publishing, 1991). It should be noted that a genetic analysis of both living red wolves and century-old skins failed to find any features that could be considered unique to red wolves; the genes were identical to the genes of coyotes and gray wolves. This finding raises the possibility that the red wolf is not, and perhaps never was, a distinct species, but rather a naturally occurring hybrid between the gray wolf and coyote. As such, it would be ineligible for protection under the Endangered Species Act. Other scientists, pointing to skull and pelt features, hotly dispute the notion that the red wolf is anything other than a full species. Either way, it is a magnificent animal.

22 mountain lion: The extirpation of the mountain lion is discussed in Matthiessen, *Wildlife in America*.

23 In tropical forests: For a discussion of the importance of large predators in tropical forests, see J. Terborgh, "The Big Things that Run the World," *Conservation Biology* 2 (1988): 402–3; J. Terborgh, *Diversity and the Tropical Rain Forest* (New York: Scientific American Library, 1992), and B. Loiselle and W. Hoppes, "Nest Predation in Insular and Mainland Lowland Rainforest in Panama," *Condor* 85 (1983): 93–95.

23 bison were the first to go: The disappearance of the ungulates is detailed in Matthiessen, *Wildlife in America*; R. Mansueti, "Extinct and Vanishing Mammals of Maryland and District of Columbia," *Maryland Naturalist* 22 (Winter-Spring 1950): 3–48; and J. Madson, "Bringing the 'Bou Back to Its Old Stomping Grounds," *Smithsonian*, May 1991. Elk from the Rocky Mountains were reintroduced to Pennsylvania in 1913. In early 1998, that population totaled about 345 individuals (G. Ferrence, Indiana University at Pennsylvania, personal communication).

24 the white-tailed deer: The decline of the white-tailed deer is discussed in Cronon, *Changes in the Land*; Matthiessen, *Wildlife in America*; and Mansueti, "Extinct and Vanishing Mammals."

24 one Maryland naturalist would write: Mansueti, "Extinct and Vanishing Mammals," 14.

25 The Great North Woods: The quotation is from Matthiessen, *Wildlife in America*, 77. The details of the Hudson Bay sale are described in Matthiessen, *Wildlife in America*.

25 "keystone species": For more information on this concept, see L. Gilbert, "Food Web Organization and the Conservation of Neotropical Diversity," in *Conservation Biology: An Evolutionary-Ecological Perspective*, edited by M. Soulé and B. Wilcox (Sunderland, Mass.: Sinauer Associates, 1980) and R. Primack, *Essentials of Conservation Biology* (Sunderland, Mass.: Sinauer Associates, 1993).

26 "death of the beaver": Cronon, *Changes in the Land*, 107.

27 a native parrot: The extinction of the Carolina parakeet is discussed in J. C. Greenway Jr., *Extinct and Vanishing Birds of the World*, Special Publication no. 13 (New York: American Committee for International Wildlife Protection, 1958; reprint, New York: Dover, 1967); and J. M. Forshaw, *Parrots of the World*, 2d (rev.) ed. (Melbourne, Australia: Lansdowne Press, 1978).

27 Audubon: Quotation taken from Forshaw, *Parrots of the World*, 432.

27 the primary cause of its demise: Greenway develops this argument at length in his book, although I tend to believe he undervalues the significance of habitat destruction. Forshaw acknowledges the importance of both hunting and habitat destruction, but speculates there may have been other, unknown factors involved.

27 passenger pigeon: This discussion is adapted from Greenway, *Extinct and Vanishing Birds*; E. Fuller, *Extinct Birds* (New York: Facts on File Publications, 1987); and D. S. Wilcove, "In Memory of Martha and Her Kind," *Audubon*, September 1989.

29 natural historians . . . were remarking: Quotations about the passenger pigeon are taken from Matthiessen, *Wildlife in America*, 158.

30 a compelling explanation: D. E. Blockstein and H. B. Tordoff, "Gone Forever: A Contemporary Look at the Extinction of the Passenger Pigeon," *American Birds* 39 (1985): 845 – 51.

31 biologist James Tanner: *The Ivory-billed Woodpecker*, National Audubon Society Research Report no. 1 (New York: National Audubon Society, 1942; reprint, New York: Dover, 1966).

31 occurs in Cuba: N. J. Collar, L. P. Gonzaga, N. Krabbe, A. Madroño Nieto, L. G. Naranjo, T. A. Parker III, and D. C. Wege, *Threatened Birds of the Americas, The ICBP/IUCN Red Data Book* (Washington, D.C.: Smithsonian Institution Press, 1992).

32 Bachman's warbler: My discussion of the extinction of Bachman's warbler is taken from F. M. Chapman, *The Warblers of North America* (New York: D. Appleton & Company, 1907); J. Terborgh, *Where Have All the Birds Gone?* (Princeton, N.J.: Princeton University Press, 1989); and J. Dunn and K. Garrett, *A Field Guide to Warblers of North America* (Boston: Houghton Mifflin, 1997). The bamboo hypothesis is discussed in J. V. Remsen Jr., "Was Bachman's Warbler A Bamboo Specialist?" *Auk* 103 (1986): 216 – 19.

33 logged at least once: S. L. Pimm and R. A. Askins, "Forest Losses Predict Bird Extinctions in Eastern North America," *Proceedings of the National Academy of Sciences USA* 92 (1995): 9343 – 47; Terborgh, *Where Have All the Birds Gone?*, 159.

33 refuges for forest-dwelling species: Pimm and Askins, "Forest Losses"; Terborgh, *Where Have All the Birds Gone?*

33 six species of feather mites: The mites of the Carolina parakeet are described in E. O. Wilson, *The Diversity of Life* (Cambridge, Mass.: Belknap Press, 1992).

34 *Franklinia alatamaha:* The discovery and disappearance of *Franklinia* is discussed in K. S. Thomas, "Benjamin Franklin's Lost Tree," *American Scientist* 78 (1990): 203 – 6. The use of the name *alatamaha* in the scientific name for *Franklinia* apparently reflects a popular variant of "Altamaha."

34 marginal cropland . . . was abandoned: Even where farming continued to be practiced, it became a more intensive, mechanized mode of farming that provided fewer of the hedgerows and pastures that many open-country species require. Thus the amount of forest habitat grew as the amount of open habitat decreased.

35 Breeding Bird Survey: C. S. Robbins, D. Bystrak, and P. H. Geissler, *The Breeding Bird Survey: Its First Fifteen Years, 1965–1979* (Washington, D.C.: U.S. Fish and Wildlife Service, 1986); R. A. Askins, "Population Trends in Grassland, Shrubland, and Forest Birds in Eastern North America," *Current Ornithology* 11 (1993): 1–34.

35 early successional habitats: Although the loss of early successional habitats is undoubtedly the major factor behind the decline of these birds, one must not assume it is the only factor. Loggerhead shrikes, for example, are disappearing throughout the United States—not just in the East—and other species of shrikes are vanishing in other parts of the world. Changes in agricultural practices, climate, or prey populations may be important factors, too. See R. Yosef, "An Evaluation of the Global Decline in the True Shrikes (Family Laniidae)," *Auk* 111 (1994): 228–233; and C. K. Yoon, "Mystery Surrounds Global Decline of a Flying Robin-Size Predator," *New York Times*, 2 March 1993.

35 the regal fritillary: K. Terwilliger, ed., *Virginia's Endangered Species* (Blacksburg, Va.: McDonald and Woodward, 1991), 243–45.

35 spectacular comebacks: See R. DiSilvestro, ed., *The Endangered Kingdom: The Struggle to Save America's Wildlife* (New York: John Wiley & Sons, 1989) and J. Conaway, "Eastern Wildlife—Bittersweet Success," *National Geographic*, February 1992.

36 the longleaf pine ecosystem: My history of this ecosystem is largely derived from C. C. Frost, "Four Centuries of Changing Landscape Patterns in the Longleaf Pine Ecosystem," in *Proceedings of the Tall Timbers Fire Ecology Conference*, no. 18, edited by S. M. Hermann (Tallahassee, Fla.: Tall Timbers Research Station, 1993).

37 red-cockaded woodpecker: U.S. Fish and Wildlife Service, *Red-cockaded Woodpecker Recovery Plan* (Atlanta, Ga.: U.S. Fish and Wildlife Service, 1985); R. G. Hooper, "Longleaf Pines Used for Cavities by Red-cockaded Woodpeckers," *Journal of Wildlife Management* 52 (1988): 392–98.

38 had declined by over 20 percent: F. C. James, "The Status of the Red-cockaded Woodpecker in 1990 and the Prospect for Recovery," in *The Red-cockaded Woodpecker: Species Recovery, Ecology and Management*, edited by D. L. Kulhavy, R. Costa, and R. G. Hooper (Nacogdoches, Tex.: Stephen F. Austin State University, 1995).

38 twenty-seven other plants and animals: Noss, LaRoe, and Scott, "Endangered Ecosystems of the United States."

39 has begun to decline again: Maryland forest data were provided by Gene Piotrowski, chief of the Urban Forestry and Reforestation Section, Maryland Department of Natural Resources (1993), and taken from Maryland Office of Planning, "State of Maryland Land Use Projections, 1988–2020," an undated memorandum made available to the public by the state government. Pennsylvania data are from Horton and Eichbaum, *Turning the Tide.*

39 forest-dwelling songbirds are disappearing: The decline of forest-dwelling songbirds is discussed in Terborgh, *Where Have All the Birds Gone?*; D. Finch, *Population Ecology, Habitat Requirements, and Conservation of Neotropical Migratory Birds*, General Technical Report RM-205 (Ft. Collins, Colo.: U.S. Forest Service, 1991); J. M. Hagan and D. W. Johnston (eds.), *Ecology and Conservation of Neotropical Migrant Landbirds* (Washington, D.C.: Smithsonian Institution Press, 1992); D. S. Wilcove, "Nest Predation in Forest Tracts and the Decline of Migratory Songbirds," *Ecology* 66 (1985): 1211–14; D. S. Wilcove, "Changes in the Avifauna of the Great Smoky Mountains: 1947–1988," *Wilson Bulletin* 100 (1988): 256–71; and S. K. Robinson and D. S. Wilcove, "Forest Fragmentation in the Temperate Zone and Its Effects on Migratory Songbirds," *Bird Conservation International* 4 (1994): 233–49.

40 Neotropical migrants: These species (and others) continue to pass through Cabin John Island as migrants during the spring and fall, but no longer remain to breed.

40 declines in populations: See F. James, D. Widenfeld, and C. McCulloch, "Trends in Breeding Populations of Warblers," in *Ecology and Conservation of Neotropical Migrant Landbirds.*

41 Rates of nest predation: See Wilcove, "Nest Predation in Forest Tracts."

41 17,000 raccoons: "Raccoons: The District's Denizens of the Night," *Washington Post*, 3 August 1990.

43 Perhaps . . . sustained by emigrants: S. K. Robinson, F. R. Thompson III, T. M. Donovan, D. R. Whitehead, and J. Faaborg,

"Regional Forest Fragmentation and the Nesting Success of Migratory Birds," *Science* 267 (1995): 1987–1990.

44   safeguarding our forest songbirds: Another problem facing migratory birds—not discussed in this book—is the loss of their wintering habitat. Approximately 60 species of U.S. birds winter in mature tropical forests south of the border. Most winter in Mexico, northern Central America, and the Greater Antilles. Within this region, large amounts of forest are being converted to cattle pastures, sugarcane fields, coffee plantations, and other agricultural uses. This deforestation will surely have a major effect on songbird populations, if it hasn't already. For further details, see Terborgh, *Where Have All the Birds Gone?*

44   overabundance of white-tailed deer: The resurgence of deer is discussed in Conaway, "Eastern Wildlife"; T. Horton, "Deer on Your Doorstep," *New York Times Magazine*, 28 April 1991; P. Durkin, "Too Many Deer Pose a Dilemma for the Nation's Parks," *Bangor Daily News*, 5–6 January 1991; W. Alverson, D. Waller, and S. Solheim, "Forests Too Deer: Edge Effects in Northern Wisconsin," *Conservation Biology* 2 (1988): 348–58; S. G. Miller, S. P. Bratton, and J. Hadidian, "Impacts of White-tailed Deer on Endangered and Threatened Vascular Plants," *Natural Areas Journal* 12 (1992): 67–74; C. P. Balgooyen and D. M. Waller, "The Use of *Clintonia borealis* and Other Indicators to Gauge Impacts of White-tailed Deer on Plant Communities in Northern Wisconsin, USA," *Natural Areas Journal* 15 (1995): 308–18; and J. Diamond, "Must We Shoot Deer to Save Nature?" *Natural History*, August 1992. See also D. Mladenoff and F. Stearns, "Eastern Hemlock Regeneration and Deer Browsing in the Northern Great Lakes Region: A Re-examination and Model Simulation," *Conservation Biology* 7 (1993): 889–900; these two authors dispute the findings in Alverson et al., "Forests Too Deer."

46   oak and hickory seedlings grew: F. W. Woods and R. E. Shanks, "Natural Replacement of Chestnut by Other Species in the Great Smoky Mountains National Park," *Ecology* 40 (1959): 349–61; H. L. E. Mackey Jr. and N. Sivec, "The Present Composition of a Former Oak-Chestnut Forest in the Allegheny Mountains of Western Pennsylvania," *Ecology* 54 (1973): 915–19.

46   the same story is repeating itself: My discussion of the diseases and pests harming trees is based in large part on F. T. Campbell and S. E. Schlarbaum, *Fading Forests: North American Trees and the Threat of Exotic Pests* (New York: Natural Resources Defense Council, 1994). See also "A Disease of Dogwoods is Unmasked," *New York Times*, 14 May 1991; D. Cohn, "Shenandoah Hemlocks Under Siege," *Washington Post*, 4 September 1993. For information on changes in bird populations in Fraser fir forests, see K. N. Rabenold, P. T. Fauth, B. W. Goodner, J. A. Sadowski, and P. G. Parker, "Response of Avian Communities to Disturbance by an Exotic Insect in Spruce-Fir Dominated Forests of the Southern Appalachians," *Conservation Biology* 12 (1998): 177–89.

Chapter 2

51 the largest effort at fire control: Details of the firefighting effort can be found in C. Elfring, "Yellowstone: Fire Storm over Fire Management," *BioScience* 39 (1989): 667–72, and P. Schullery, "The Fires and Fire Policy," *BioScience* 39 (1989): 686–94.

52 a national effort to prevent and suppress wildfires: See M. Williams, *Americans and Their Forests* (Cambridge: Cambridge University Press, 1989).

52 a "let-burn" approach: See Schullery, "The Fires and Fire Policy."

53 historical precedent: My discussion of Yellowstone's fire history is taken from W. H. Romme and D. G. Despain, "Historical Perspective on the Yellowstone Fires of 1988," *BioScience* 39 (1989): 695–99.

53 effect of the fires on Yellowstone's wildlife: Data on losses of animals due to fires are from F. J. Singer, W. Schreier, J. Oppenheim, and E. O. Garton, "Drought, Fires, and Large Mammals," *BioScience* 39 (1989): 716–22.

54 presumably declined: Not surprisingly, the effects of the 1988 fires have been most intensively studied with respect to birds. See R. L. Hutto, "Composition of Bird Communities Following Stand-Replacement Fires in Northern Rocky Mountain (U.S.A.) Conifer Forests," *Conservation Biology* 9 (1995): 1041–58.

54 a panel of scientists: N. L. Christensen et al., "Interpreting the Yellowstone Fires of 1988," *BioScience* 39 (1989): 683.

55 the park's approach to managing its elk herds: The history of Yellowstone's elk is taken from D. B. Houston, *The Northern Yellowstone Elk: Ecology and Management* (New York: Macmillan, 1982); Yellowstone National Park, *Yellowstone's Northern Range: Complexity and Change in a Wildland Ecosystem* (Mammoth Hot Springs, Wyo.: Yellowstone National Park, 1997); D. Despain, D. Houston, M. Meagher, and P. Schullery, *Wildlife in Transition:*

Man and Nature on Yellowstone's Northern Range (Boulder, CO: Roberts Rinehart, 1986); and F. H. Wagner, "Scientist Says Yellowstone Park Is Being Destroyed," *High Country News*, 30 May 1994. Most of the elk population figures reported in this chapter were provided by Dr. F. Wagner, Utah State University. Those wanting more information about the strengths and weaknesses of the historical censuses of Yellowstone's elk should consult Houston's book.

55 wolves were completely eliminated: Information on the elimination of predators in Yellowstone is taken from P. Matthiessen, *Wildlife in America*, revised, updated edition (New York: Viking, 1987); A. Chase, *Playing God in Yellowstone* (Boston: Atlantic Monthly Press, 1986); Houston, *The Northern Yellowstone Elk*; and S. Begley, L. Wilson, M. Hager, and P. Annin, "Return of the Wolf," *Newsweek*, 12 August 1991.

56 Thousands were removed: See Chase, *Playing God in Yellowstone*.

56 a National Parks Advisory Committee: A. S. Leopold, S. A. Cain, C. M. Cottam, I. N. Gabrielson, and T. L. Kimball, *Wildlife Management in the National Parks*. Report of the Advisory Board on Wildlife Management appointed by Secretary of the Interior Udall, 4 March 1963, 4.

57 report has been wrongly interpreted: Leopold himself supported reduction of ungulate populations if other checks did not control their numbers, both in his testimony at a 1967 Senate hearing and in a 1983 letter to the Sequoia National Park superintendent (see Wagner, "Scientist Says Yellowstone Park Is Being Destroyed").

57 major changes in the vegetation: The changes in plant communities and the evidence pointing to elk as the cause are discussed in S. W. Chadde and C. E. Kay, "Tall-Willow Communities on Yellowstone's Northern Range: A Test of the 'Natural-Regulation' Paradigm," in *The Greater Yellowstone Ecosystem: Redefining America's Wilderness Heritage*, edited by R. B. Keiter and M. S. Boyce (New Haven: Yale University Press, 1991), 231–62; C. E. Kay, "The Impact of Native Ungulates and Beaver on Riparian Communities in the Intermountain West," *Natural Resources and Environmental Issues* 1 (1994): 25–44; C. E. Kay and F. H. Wagner, "Historical Condition of Woody Vegetation on Yellowstone's Northern Range: A Critical Evaluation of the 'Natural Regulation' Paradigm," paper presented at the First Biennial Scientific Conference on the Greater Yellowstone Ecosystem, Yellowstone National Park, Mammoth Hot Springs,

Wyo., 16–17 September 1991; and F. H. Wagner and C. E. Kay, "'Natural' or 'Healthy' Ecosystems: Are U.S. National Parks Providing Them?" in *Humans as Components of Ecosystems*, edited by M. J. McDonnelland S. T. A. Pickett (New York: Springer-Verlag, 1993), 257–70. The same arguments are presented in Chase, *Playing God in Yellowstone*, but these references provide better documentation and fewer polemics.

58 "absent from the northern range": Chadde and Kay, "Tall-Willow Communities," 255.

58 According to one study: Chadde and Kay, "Tall-Willow Communities," citing the work of G. L. Munther.

59 ecologist Charles Kay: C. E. Kay, "An Alternative Interpretation of the Historical Evidence Relating to the Abundance of Wolves in the Yellowstone Ecosystem," paper presented at the Second North American Symposium on Wolves: Their Status, Biology, and Management, University of Edmonton, Edmonton, Alberta, 25–27 August 1992.

59 an abundance of big game: See Yellowstone National Park, *Yellowstone's Northern Range*.

60 strong public support: Polling data from Begley et al., "Return of the Wolf." Gray wolves were listed as an endangered species in the coterminous United States in 1974; this designation does not apply to Alaskan wolves, which are still comparatively numerous.

60 significant changes in the ecosystem: J. Robbins, "In Two Years, Wolves Reshaped Yellowstone," *New York Times*, 30 December 1997.

61 could reduce populations: E. E. Bangs and S. H. Fritts, "Reintroduction of Gray Wolves to Yellowstone National Park and Central Idaho," *Endangered Species Technical Bulletin* 18 (3) (1993): 19; U.S. Fish and Wildlife Service, *The Reintroduction of Gray Wolves to Yellowstone National Park and Central Idaho: Draft Environmental Impact Statement* (Helena, Mont.: U.S. Fish and Wildlife Service, 1993).

61 One ecologist: Quotation from F. Wagner in "Scientist Says Yellowstone Park Is Being Destroyed," 15.

62 "Greater Yellowstone Ecosystem": See A. Harting and D. Glick, *Sustaining Greater Yellowstone: A Blueprint for the Future* (Bozeman, Mont.: Greater Yellowstone Coalition, 1994).

63 Annual harvest levels: Information on resource extraction in the Yellowstone region is taken from R. Rasker, N. Tirrell, and

D. Kloepfer, *The Wealth of Nature: New Economic Realities in the Yellowstone Region* (Washington, D.C.: The Wilderness Society, 1992).

63 no species has yet vanished: An excellent discussion of the effects of resource development on wildlife in the Yellowstone region can be found in Harting and Glick, *Sustaining Greater Yellowstone*.

64 snags: Hutto, "Composition of Bird Communities."

64 justified economically: Data on timber sales in the national forests surrounding Yellowstone are taken from The Wilderness Society, *Double Trouble: The Loss of Trees and Money in Our National Forests* (Washington, D.C.: The Wilderness Society, 1998). These data cover fiscal year 1996. It should be noted that the Forest Service disputes The Wilderness Society's calculation of a net loss of $2,200,000; the agency instead reports a net gain of $321,000. The difference stems from the fact that the Forest Service does not report all of its costs. It does not, for example, include the bulk of the costs associated with building logging roads, certain office expenses associated with running the timber program, and mandatory payments to the states in its calculations of the timber program's fiscal performance. I believe The Wilderness Society's calculations are a more accurate reflection of the true costs of the timber program.

64 75,000 cattle and 120,000 sheep: Numbers are from Harting and Glick, *Sustaining Greater Yellowstone*.

65 the source of this growth: My discussion of the changing economic profile of the Yellowstone region is largely taken from Rasker et al., *The Wealth of Nature*; Harting and Glick, *Sustaining Greater Yellowstone*; and R. Rasker and D. Glick, "Footloose Entrepreneurs: Pioneers of the New West?" *Illahee* 1 (1994): 34–43.

65 As one environmental organization noted: Rasker et al., *The Wealth of Nature*, 7–8.

65 the growing population: See W. K. Stevens, "Latest Threat to Yellowstone: Admirers Are Loving It to Death," *New York Times*, 13 September 1994.

66 prime wintering range . . . and habitat: Harting and Glick, *Sustaining Greater Yellowstone*.

66 a 1991 survey: Statistic and quotation from Harting and Glick, *Sustaining Greater Yellowstone*, 96; see also Rasker et al., *The Wealth of Nature*.

67 Lt. Edward Beale: Quotation taken from C. F. Cooper, "Changes in Vegetation, Structure, and Growth of Southwestern Pine Forests Since White Settlement," *Ecological Monographs* 30 (1960): 130.

67 transformation is so pervasive: My discussion of the effects of logging and grazing on ponderosa pine forests is based on Cooper, "Changes in Vegetation"; W. H. Moir, B. Geils, M. A. Benoit, and D. Scurlock, "Ecology of Southwestern Ponderosa Pine Forests," in *Songbird Ecology in Southwestern Ponderosa Pine Forests: A Literature Review*, edited by W. M. Block and D. M. Finch. General Technical Report RM-GTR-292 (Ft. Collins, Colo.: U.S. Forest Service, 1997); and D. Scurlock and D. M. Finch, "A Historical Overview," also in *Songbird Ecology*.

67 for over three hundred years: The land was not entirely uninhabited by white settlers, but they were few in number. Both they and the Indians maintained livestock, but the total numbers of cattle and sheep were a small fraction of the hordes to come when Anglo-Americans gained control of the land. See Scurlock and Finch, "A Historical Overview."

68 the territorial governor of Arizona: Quotation taken from Cooper, "Changes in Vegetation," 135.

68 The rate of cutting: Only within the past decade have logging levels in the national forests of Arizona and New Mexico dropped significantly, largely in response to pressure from environmentalists and diminishing timber supplies (Scurlock and Finch, "A Historical Overview").

68 one group of scientists: P. Z. Fule, W. W. Covington, and M. M. Moore, "Determining Reference Conditions for Ecosystem Management of Southwestern Ponderosa Pine Forests," *Ecological Applications* 7 (1997): 895–908. I have converted their density values from hectares to acres.

69 focus on birds: My account of the changes in the avifauna of ponderosa pine forests is taken from D. M. Finch, J. L. Ganey, W. Yong, R. T. Kimball, and R. Sallabanks, "Effects and Interactions of Fire, Logging, and Grazing" in *Songbird Ecology*; S. J. Hejl, "Human-Induced Changes in Bird Populations in Coniferous Forests in Western North America during the Past 100 Years," in *A Century of Avifaunal Change in Western North America*, edited by J. R. Jehl Jr. and N. K. Johnson, Studies in Avian Biology, no. 15 (San Diego, Calif.: Cooper Ornithological Society, 1994).

69 Mexican wolf: The U.S. Fish and Wildlife Service has recently begun to release captive-reared Mexican wolves in the wilds of eastern Arizona.

71 have been dramatically reshaped: A. J. Belsky and D. M. Blumenthal, "Effects of Livestock Grazing on Stand Dynamics and Soils in Upland Forests of the Interior West," *Conservation Biology* 11 (1997): 315–27.

71 In California's Sierra Nevada: The effects of logging, grazing, and fire suppression on the Sierra Nevada forests are discussed in detail in J. Verner, K. S. McKelvey, B. R. Noon, R. J. Gutiérrez, G. I. Gould, Jr., and T. W. Beck, The California Spotted Owl: A Technical Assessment of Its Current Status, Gen. Tech. Rep. PSW-GTR-133 (Albany, Calif.: Pacific Southwest Research Station, U.S. Forest Service, 1992).

72 they will crowd out the Douglas-firs: E. A. Norse, *Ancient Forests of the Pacific Northwest* (Washington, D.C.: Island Press, 1990).

72 Studies conducted by The Wilderness Society: P. H. Morrison, D. Kloepfer, D. A. Leversee, C. M. Socha, and D. L. Feber, *Ancient Forests of the Pacific Northwest: Analysis and Maps of Twelve National Forests* (Washington, D.C.: The Wilderness Society, 1991).

73 Studies initiated as far back as the 1960s: E. D. Forsman, "The Spotted Owl: Literature Review," in U.S. Forest Service, Final Supplement to the Environmental Impact Statement for an Amendment to the Pacific Northwest Regional Guide. Spotted Owl Guidelines (Portland, Oreg.: U.S. Forest Service, 1988).

73 600 to 2,500 acres of ancient forest: D. S. Wilcove, "Turning Conservation Goals into Tangible Results: The Case of the Spotted Owl and Old-Growth Forests," in *Large-Scale Ecology and Conservation Biology*, edited by P. J. Edwards, R. May, and N. R. Webb (Oxford: Blackwell Scientific Publications, 1994).

73 1,000–8,000 other species: J. W. Thomas, team leader, *Forest Ecosystem Management: An Ecological, Economic, and Social Assessment*, Report of the Forest Ecosystem Management Assessment Team (U.S. Forest Service, National Marine Fisheries Service, Bureau of Land Management, U.S. Fish and Wildlife Service, National Park Service, Environmental Protection Agency), 1993.

74 young forests assume . . . characteristics of old-growth stands: J. W. Thomas, E. D. Forsman, J. B. Lint, E. C. Meslow, B. R. Noon, and J. Verner, *A Conservation Strategy for the Northern Spotted Owl* (Portland, Oreg.: U.S. Forest Service, Bureau of Land Management, U.S. Fish and Wildlife Service, and National Park Service, 1990).

74 The decision to spare these forests: U.S. Forest Service and Bureau of Land Management, *Final Supplemental Environmental Impact Statement on Management of Habitat for Late-Successional and Old-Growth Forest Related Species within the Range of the Northern Spotted Owl,* vol. 1 (Portland, Oreg.: U.S. Forest Service and Bureau of Land Management, 1994).

Chapter 3

79 about 25 percent is still intact: Readers desiring more information on the amount of surviving prairie may wish to consult the following sources: E. M. Steinauer and S. L. Collins, "Prairie Ecology — The Tallgrass Prairie," in *Prairie Conservation: Preserving North America's Most Endangered Ecosystem,* edited by F. B. Samson and F. L. Knopf (Washington, D.C.: Island Press, 1996); T. B. Bragg and A. A. Steuter, "Prairie Ecology—The Mixed Prairie," in *Prairie Conservation;* T. Weaver, E. M. Payson, and D. L. Gustafson, "Prairie Ecology—The Shortgrass Prairie," in *Prairie Conservation;* F. Samson and F. Knopf, "Prairie Conservation in North America," *BioScience* 44 (1994): 418–21; and T. Ricketts, E. Dinerstein, D. M. Olson, C. Loucks, P. Hedao, P. Hurley, R. Abell, S. Walters, and K. Carney, *A Conservation Assessment of the Terrestrial Ecoregions of North America* (Washington, D.C.: World Wildlife Fund, 1997). The reader will quickly discover, as I have, that it is very difficult to find solid estimates of the original and current acreages of the tallgrass, mixed, and shortgrass prairies. There are significant gaps in the data and no small amount of disagreement as to where to draw the boundaries between the different types. My data on tallgrass are taken from Steinauer and Collins. To obtain an estimate for the combined shortgrass and mixed-grass prairies, I used Ricketts et al., combining their prairie types 56, 58, 62, 63, and 64. The 60 percent figure for shortgrass is taken from Weaver et al.

81 the baseline conditions: My discussion of the difficulties in establishing a baseline for prairies is taken from an excellent paper by Kenneth Higgins. See K. F. Higgins, *Interpretation and Compendium of Historical Fire Accounts in the Northern Great Plains,* Resource Publication no. 161 (Washington, D.C.: U.S. Fish and Wildlife Service, 1986).

81 attributed the majority of fires . . . to Indians: See Higgins, *Interpretation and Compendium of Historical Fire Accounts*. Other authors have estimated that half of the fires in the tallgrass prairie were set by Indians; see Steinauer and Collins, "Prairie Ecology—The Tallgrass Prairie."

81 lightning-sparked fires: See Steinauer and Collins, "Prairie Ecology—The Tallgrass Prairie."

82 Early writers . . . describe the desolation: Quotation from J. T. Irving Jr., *Indian Sketches Taken During an Expedition to the Pawnee Tribes* [1833], edited by J. F. McDermott (Norman: University of Oklahoma Press, 1955), as cited in Higgins, *Interpretation and Compendium of Historical Fire Accounts*.

82 grazers of all different shapes and sizes: R. E. England and A. DeVos, "Influence of Animals on Pristine Conditions on the Canadian Grasslands," *Journal of Range Management* 22 (1969): 87–94.

82 between 4 and 22 black-tails per acre: The average density of prairie dogs is taken from A. D. Whicker and J. K. Detling, "Ecological Consequences of Prairie Dog Disturbances," *BioScience* 38 (1988): 778–85. This figure was originally presented as dogs per hectare, which I converted to dogs per acre. The range of the black-tail and the size of the Texas town are from B. Holmes, "The Big Importance of Little Towns on the Prairie," *National Wildlife*, June–July 1996. The "conversion rate" of dogs to cows is from L. Line, "Phantom of the Plains," *Wildlife Conservation*, August 1997.

83 plant under extreme grazing pressure: See A. Y. Cooperrider and D. S. Wilcove, *Defending the Desert: Conserving Biodiversity on BLM Lands in the Southwest* (Washington, D.C.: Environmental Defense Fund, 1995).

83 a recent study in Yellowstone: D. A. Frank and S. J. McNaughton, "Evidence for the Promotion of Aboveground Grassland Production by Native Large Herbivores in Yellowstone National Park," *Oecologia* 96 (1993): 157–61.

83 ecologist Sam J. McNaughton: My discussion of the Serengeti is based largely on McNaughton's "Ecology of a Grazing Ecosystem: The Serengeti," *Ecological Monographs* 55 (1985): 259–94.

84 anything but disconnected: Whicker and Detling, "Ecological Consequences of Prairie Dog Disturbances"; K. Krueger, "Feeding

Relationships among Bison, Pronghorn, and Prairie Dogs: An Experimental Analysis," *Ecology* 67 (1986): 760–70; D. L. Coppock, J. K. Detling, J. E. Ellis, and M. I. Dyer, "Plant-Herbivore Interactions in a North American Mixed-Grass Prairie," *Oecologia* 56 (1983): 1–9.

85 to detect predators: Krueger, "Feeding Relationships."

85 study in South Dakota: Whicker and Detling, "Ecological Consequences of Prairie Dog Disturbances."

85 biologists surveyed prairie dog colonies: T. W. Clark, T. M. Campbell III, D. G. Socha, and D. E. Casey, "Prairie Dog Colony Attributes and Associated Vertebrate Species," *Great Basin Naturalist* 42 (1982): 572–82.

86 a grazing association, not a succession: The distinction is spelled out in Krueger, "Feeding Relationships."

86 grassland birds in Illinois: J. R. Herkert, R. E. Szafoni, V. M. Kleen, and J. E. Schwegman, *Habitat Establishment, Enhancement, and Management for Forest and Grassland Birds in Illinois*, Natural Heritage Technical Publication no. 1 (Springfield: Division of Natural Heritage, Illinois Department of Conservation, 1993).

87 the Indians: The hunting of bison by Indians is discussed in P. Matthiessen, *Wildlife in America*, revised, updated edition (New York: Viking, 1987).

88 W. T. Hornaday: Quotation from *The Extermination of the American Bison*, Report of the U.S. National Museum, 1886–1887 (Washington, D.C.: U.S. National Museum, 1889), 388.

88 naturalist Ernest Thompson Seton: *Life-Histories of Northern Animals. An Account of the Mammals of Manitoba*, vol. I (New York: Charles Scribner's Sons, 1909).

89 the accuracy of Seton's estimate: J. H. Shaw, "How Many Bison Originally Populated Western Rangelands?" *Rangelands* 17 (1995): 148–50.

89 John James Audubon: Quotation from Matthiessen, *Wildlife in America*, 147.

89 The numerically minded Hornaday: see *Extermination of the American Bison*.

89 the cattlemen moved in: My account of the rise and fall of the cattle barons in the shortgrass prairie is taken from D. Worster, *Dust*

Bowl: The Southern Plains in the 1930s (New York: Oxford University Press, 1979). My description of the effort to eliminate predators is from Matthiessen, *Wildlife in America.*

90   the black-footed ferret: The demise and resurrection of the black-footed ferret is described in Holmes, "The Big Importance of Little Towns on the Prairie"; Line, "Phantom of the Plains"; and U.S. Fish and Wildlife Service, *Black-footed Ferret Recovery Plan* (Denver, Colo.: U.S. Fish and Wildlife Service, 1988).

91   a problem of the ranchers' own making: Line, "Phantom of the Plains."

92   the amount of forage available: M. E. O'Meilia, F. L. Knopf, and J. C. Lewis, "Some Consequences of Competition between Prairie Dogs and Beef Cattle," *Journal of Range Management* 35 (1982): 580–85.

92   the quality of the grass and forbs: Holmes, "The Big Importance of Little Towns on the Prairie."

93   historian Donald Worster: My account of the Dust Bowl, its origins, and its consequences is taken almost entirely from Worster, *Dust Bowl.* The quotation is from page 34.

94   the amount of prairie in Illinois: Estimates for 1800 and 1900 are from R. R. Graber and J. W. Graber, "A Comparative Study of Bird Populations in Illinois, 1906–1909 and 1956–1958," *Illinois Natural History Survey Bulletin* 28, no. 3 (1963): 383–528. Current estimate is from J. R. Herkert, "The Effects of Habitat Fragmentation on Midwestern Grassland Bird Communities," *Ecological Applications* 4 (1994): 461–71.

94   data compiled by the Department of the Interior: Quotation from F. L. Knopf, "Declining Grassland Birds," in *Our Living Resources: A Report to the Nation on the Distribution, Abundance, and Health of U.S. Plants, Animals, and Ecosystems,* edited by E. T. LaRoe (Washington, D.C.: National Biological Service, 1995), 296.

95   the mountain plover: Knopf, "Declining Grassland Birds."

95   one ornithologist has speculated: F. L. Knopf, "A Closer Look: Mountain Plover," *Birding* 29, no. 1 (1997): 39–44.

95   cattle are not bison: My discussion of the differences between bison and cattle is taken largely from D. C. Hartnett, A. A. Steuter, and K. R. Hickman, "Comparative Ecology of Native and Introduced

Ungulates," *Ecological Studies* 125 (1997): 72–101, and Cooperrider and Wilcove, *Defending the Desert.*

97 These two studies: Data from the two studies are presented and analyzed in Graber and Graber, "A Comparative Study of Bird Populations."

98 The Grabers estimated: Graber and Graber, "A Comparative Study of Bird Populations," 496–97.

98 bobolink populations in Illinois: J. R. Herkert, "Bobolink *Dolichonyx oryzivorus* Population Decline in Agricultural Landscapes in the Midwestern USA," *Biological Conservation* 80 (1977): 107–12; E. K. Bollinger, P. B. Bollinger, and T. A. Gavin, "Effects of Hay-Cropping on Eastern Populations of the Bobolink," *Wildlife Society Bulletin* 18 (1990): 142–50.

99 mice, voles, and shrews: E. M. Kirsch, "Small Mammal Community Composition in Cornfields, Roadside Ditches, and Prairies in Eastern Nebraska," *Natural Areas Journal* 17 (1997): 204–11.

100 of 1,100 species of insects: R. Panzer, D. Stillwaugh, R. Gnaedinger, and G. Derkovitz, "Prevalence of Remnant Dependence among the Prairie- and Savanna-Inhabiting Insects of the Chicago Region," *Natural Areas Journal* 15 (1995): 101–16.

100 smaller prairie fragments: Herkert, "The Effects of Habitat Fragmentation"; F. B. Samson, "Island Biogeography and the Conservation of Prairie Birds," *Proceedings of the North American Prairie Conference* 7 (1980): 293–305.

100 In Illinois: Herkert, "The Effects of Habitat Fragmentation."

100 Henslow's sparrow: S. K. Robinson, Illinois Natural History Survey, personal communication.

100 nest-plundering birds and mammals: R. G. Johnson and S. A. Temple, "Nest Predation and Brood Parasitism of Tallgrass Prairie Birds," *Journal of Wildlife Management* 54 (1990): 106–11.

100 Tallgrass insects: R. Panzer, "Managing Prairie Remnants for Insect Conservation," *Natural Areas Journal* 8 (1988): 83–90; Panzer et al., "Prevalence of Remnant Dependence."

102 Conservation Reserve Program: The history of the CRP is discussed in U.S. Department of Agriculture, *The Conservation Reserve Program*, Farm Service Agency Publication PA-1603 (Washington, D.C.: U.S. Department of Agriculture, 1997).

103 new nesting habitats: See D. H. Johnson and R. K. Koford, "Conservation Reserve Program and Migratory Birds in the Northern Great Plains," in *Our Living Resources*.

Chapter 4

106 The Nature Conservancy: The 1990 paper describing the status of aquatic species is L. Master, "The Imperiled Status of North American Aquatic Animals," *Biodiversity Network News* 3 (1990): 1–8; see also J. Brody, "Water-Based Animals Are Becoming Extinct Faster than Others," *New York Times*, 23 April 1991. The percentages that I give in this chapter are based on 1997 and 1998 updates of Master's paper, undertaken by The Nature Conservancy. See B. A. Stein and S. R. Flack, *1997 Species Report Card: The Status of U.S. Plants and Animals* (Arlington, Va.: The Nature Conservancy, 1997) and L. L. Master, S. R. Flack, and B. A. Stein, *Rivers of Life: Critical Watersheds for Protecting Freshwater Biodiversity* (Arlington, Va.: The Nature Conservancy, 1998).

106 rate of extinction has doubled: R. R. Miller, J. D. Williams, and J. E. Williams, "Extinctions of North American Fishes during the Past Century," *Fisheries* 14, no. 6 (1989): 22–38.

107 an extraordinarily diverse assortment: Data on species diversity in aquatic ecosystems are from J. D. Allan and A. S. Flecker, "Biodiversity Conservation in Running Waters," *BioScience* 43 (1993): 32–43; S. Palmer, "Some Extinct Molluscs of the U.S.A.," *Atala* 13, no. 1 (1985): 1–7; and Master, Flack, and Stein, *Rivers of Life*.

108 National Rivers Inventory: Information on the National Rivers Inventory is taken from A. C. Benke, "A Perspective on America's Vanishing Streams," *Journal of the North American Benthological Society* 9 (1990): 77–88. Regrettably, the survey has not been updated since 1982.

108 The number of dams: National Research Council, *Restoration of Aquatic Ecosystems: Science, Technology, and Public Policy* (Washington, D.C.: National Academy Press, 1992).

108 A recent study: M. Dynesius and C. Nilsson, "Fragmentation and Flow Regulation of River Systems in the Northern Third of the World,"

Science 266 (1994): 753–62. The authors define a large river system as one with an average annual flow equal to or exceeding 350 cubic meters per second (approximately equal to 460 cubic yards per second).

108 Muscle Shoals: The description of Muscle Shoals and the quotation by Ortmann are from W. Stolzenburg, "The Mussels' Message," *Nature Conservancy* 42, no. 6 (1992): 16–23.

109 their peculiar reproductive behavior: Mussel life history from R. Neves, "Mollusks," in *Virginia's Endangered Species*, edited by K. Terwilliger (Blacksburg, Va.: McDonald and Woodward, 1991), 251–63.

110 Carbo, Virginia: The Carbo spill is discussed in D. Bailey, "Protecting Aquatic Diversity from Toxic Effluents: The Clinch River Experience," in *The Big Kill: Declining Biodiversity in America's Lakes and Rivers*, edited by D. S. Wilcove and M. J. Bean (Washington, D.C.: Environmental Defense Fund, 1994), 101–9. The slow return of mussels to the 12-mile stretch of the Clinch River below the Carbo spill may have been due in part to water quality problems unrelated to the spill itself (R. Neves, Virginia Polytechnic Institute and State University, personal communication).

110 the first to go and the last to return: R. J. Neves, "A State-of-the-Unionids Address," in *Conservation and Management of Freshwater Mussels*, edited by K. S. Cummings, A. C. Buchanan, and L. M. Koch (Rock Island, Ill.: Upper Mississippi River Conservation Committee, 1993).

110 Pendleton Island: For additional information on Pendleton Island, see W. Stolzenburg, "The Mussels' Message"; The Nature Conservancy, *Clinch Valley Bioreserve Strategic Plan* (Charlottesville, Va.: The Nature Conservancy, Virginia Field Office, 1992).

110 worked closely with farmers: B. Kittrell and M. Lipford, The Nature Conservancy, personal communication.

111 stricter standard for copper: Bailey, "Protecting Aquatic Diversity."

112 in a 1994 assessment: U.S. Fish and Wildlife Service, *Report to Congress: Recovery Program, Endangered and Threatened Species* (Washington, D.C.: U.S. Government Printing Office, 1994).

113 sedimentation: T. F. Waters, *Sediments in Streams: Sources, Biological Effects, and Control.* American Fisheries Society Monograph 7 (Bethesda, Md.: American Fisheries Society, 1995); J. R. Karr, J. D. Allan, and A. C. Benke, "River Conservation in North America:

Science, Policy, and Practice," in *Global Perspectives on River Conservation*, edited by P. J. Boon, B. R. Davies, and G. E. Petts (West Sussex, England: John Wiley & Sons, in press).

114 breed . . . in captivity: R. Neves, Virginia Polytechnic Institute and State University, personal communication.

114 Duck River: The story of the Duck River mussels is elegantly told in M. Bean, "Conserving Endangered Species by Accident: The Duck River Experience," in *The Big Kill*, 111–22.

115 rare mussels are still there: Current status of the Duck River mussels provided by D. Biggins, U.S. Fish and Wildlife Service.

116 John Wesley Powell: For a masterful account of Powell's exploits and insights, see W. Stegner, *Beyond the Hundredth Meridian: John Wesley Powell and the Second Opening of the West* (1954; reprint, New York: Penguin Books, 1992).

117 evolved in relative isolation: See W. L. Minckley and M. E. Douglas, "Discovery and Extinction of Western Fishes: A Blink of the Eye in Geologic Time," in *Battle Against Extinction: Native Fish Management in the American West*, edited by W. L. Minckley and J. E. Deacon (Tucson: University of Arizona Press, 1991), 7–17.

117 provides water: P. Gray, "A Fight over Liquid Gold," *Time*, 22 July 1991; D. Pontius, *Colorado River Basin Study: Report to the Western Water Policy Review Advisory Commission* (Springfield, Va.: U.S. Department of Commerce National Technical Information Service, 1997).

119 of seventy razorback suckers: W. L. Minckley, P. C. Marsh, J. E. Brooks, J. E. Johnson, and B. L. Jensen, "Management toward Recovery of the Razorback Sucker" in *Battle Against Extinction*, 303–57; J. A. Stanford, *Instream Flows to Assist the Recovery of Endangered Fishes of the Upper Colorado River Basin*. National Biological Service, Biological Report 24 (July 1994).

120 a committee of the American Fisheries Society: Miller, Williams, and Williams, "Extinctions of North American Fishes."

120 half of the endangered fishes: D. S. Wilcove, D. Rothstein, J. Dubow, A. Phillips, and E. Losos, "Quantifying Threats to Imperiled Species in the United States," *BioScience* 48 (1998): 607–15.

121 In Arizona and New Mexico: D. S. Wilcove, M. Bean, and P. C. Lee, "Fisheries Management and Biological Diversity," in *Transactions* *of the 57th North American Wildlife and Natural Resources Conference* (Washington, D.C.: Wildlife Management Institute, 1992).

121 Green River: Details of the Green River poisoning can be found in P. Holden, "Ghosts of the Green River: Impacts of Green River Poisoning on Management of Native Fishes," in *Battle Against Extinction.*

122 Secretary of the Interior Stewart Udall: Quotation from Holden, "Ghosts of the Green River," 51.

122 Federal Aid in Sportfish Restoration Act: See D. S. Wilcove and R. Fujita, "Enlightened Fisheries Management: Solving Problems Instead of Creating Them," in *The Big Kill*, and T. Williams, "So Where Are All the Restored Sport Fish?" *Fly Rod & Reel*, November–December 1992.

124 Commercial fishing in the Great Lakes: Data on commercial fish catches are taken from U.S. Environmental Protection Agency and Government of Canada, *The Great Lakes: An Environmental Atlas and Resource Book*, 3d ed. (Chicago: U.S. Environmental Protection Agency, 1995).

125 Lake Michigan: My account of Lake Michigan's fishery is taken largely from L. Wells and A. L. McLain, *Lake Michigan: Man's Effects on Native Fish Stocks and Other Biota*, Technical Report no. 20 (Ann Arbor, Mich.: Great Lakes Fishery Commission, 1973). Additional information can be found in R. D. Ono, J. D. Williams, and A. Wagner, *Vanishing Fishes of North America* (Washington, D.C.: Stone Wall Press, 1983); E. L. Mills, J. H. Leach, J. T. Carlton, and C. L. Secor, "Exotic Species and the Integrity of the Great Lakes: Lessons from the Past," *BioScience 44* (1994): 666–76; and T. H. Whillans and F. Berkes, "Use and Abuse, Conflict and Harmony: The Great Lakes Fishery in Transition," *Alternatives* 13, no. 3 (1986): 10–18.

125 sea lamprey: Some ichthyologists maintain that the sea lamprey was, in fact, native to Lake Ontario, where the earliest records were obtained. Under this scenario, it spread to Lake Erie upon completion of the Welland Canal and then colonized the other Great Lakes.

126 U.S. Fish and Wildlife Service: Quotation taken from Ono, Williams, and Wagner, *Vanishing Fishes*, 33.

127 Lake Erie: My account of Lake Erie's fishery is taken largely from W. L. Hartman, *Effects of Exploitation, Environmental Changes,* *and New Species on the Fish Habitats and Resources of Lake Erie*, Technical Report no. 22 (Ann Arbor, Mich.: Great Lakes Fishery Commission, 1973).

129   a turning back of the clock: J. C. Makarewicz and P. Bertram, "Evidence for the Restoration of the Lake Erie Ecosystem," *BioScience* 41 (1991): 216–23; J. R. Luoma, "Biography of a Lake," *Audubon*, September–October 1996.

129   blue pike: The extinction of the blue pike is discussed in Ono, Williams, and Wagner, *Vanishing Fishes*; Hartman, *Effects of Exploitation.*

129   Lake trout were subsequently reintroduced: M. J. Hansen and J. W. Peck, "Lake Trout in the Great Lakes," in *Our Living Resources: A Report to the Nation on the Distribution, Abundance, and Health of U.S. Plants, Animals, and Ecosystems*, edited by E. T. LaRoe (Washington, D.C.: National Biological Service, 1995).

130   rate of one per year: Mills et al., "Exotic Species."

130   zebra mussel: History of the invasion is from A. J. Benson and C. P. Boydstun, "Invasion of the Zebra Mussel in the United States," in *Our Living Resources;* P. D. Hebert, C. C. Wilson, M. H. Murdoch, and R. Lazar, "Demography and Ecological Impacts of the Invading Mollusc *Dreissena polymorpha,*" *Canadian Journal of Zoology* 69 (1991): 405–9; Luoma, "Biography of a Lake"; T. Wilkinson, "Zebras Musseling In," *Washington Post*, 14 May 1997. Density of zebra mussels is from T. Keniry and J. E. Marsden, "Zebra Mussels in Southwestern Lake Michigan," in *Our Living Resources.*

130   Water clarity has increased: Keniry and Marsden, "Zebra mussels in Southwestern Lake Michigan."

131   7,000 zebra mussels attached to their shells: D. Schloesser and T. F. Nalepa, "Freshwater Mussels in the Lake Huron-Lake Erie Corridor," in *Our Living Resources.*

132   Estimates of the number of salmon: See M. Reisner, *Cadillac Desert: The American West and Its Disappearing Water* (New York: Penguin Books, 1993); National Research Council, *Upstream: Salmon and Society in the Pacific Northwest* (Washington, D.C.: National Academy Press, 1996); R. White, *The Organic Machine: The Remaking of the Columbia River* (New York: Hill and Wang, 1995), and J. M. Volkman, *A River in Common: The Columbia River, the Salmon Ecosystem, and Water Policy.* Report to the Western Water Policy Review Advisory Commission (Springfield, Va.: U.S. Department of Commerce National Technical Information Service, 1997). The quotation by Lewis and Clark is taken from Volkman, *A River in Common*, 18.

132 A recent study: National Research Council, *Upstream*.

132 Snake River sockeye: Information on the last of the Snake River sockeyes is from R. Jones, National Marine Fisheries Service, B. Iwamoto, Northwest Fisheries Science Center, T. Flagg, Manchester Laboratory, and D. Carter, National Marine Fisheries Service (all personal communications); see also T. Egan, "Fight to Save Salmon Starts Fight over Water," *New York Times*, 1 April 1991; T. Kenworthy, "Last Ditch Effort to Preserve Sockeye," *Washington Post*, 14 January 1993; and J. Balzar, "Columbia River Sockeye Salmon Ruled Imperiled," *Los Angeles Times*, 3 April 1991.

134 American Fisheries Society: W. Nehlsen, J. E. Williams, and J. A. Lichatowich, "Pacific Salmon at the Crossroads: Stocks at Risk from California, Oregon, Idaho, and Washington," *Fisheries* 16 (1991): 4–21.

134 annual sport catch of salmon: L. Swope-Lysistrata, M. Alexandersdottir, L. Tsunoda, and P. Hahn, *Washington State Sport Catch Fish Report 1994* (Olympia, Wash.: Department of Fish and Wildlife, Resource Assessment Division, 1997), 2.

135 a committee of the American Fisheries Society: See M. J. James, "Report of the Division of Commercial Fishing Presented at the 67th Annual Meting of the American Fisheries Society (1937)," as cited in Nehlsen, Williams, and Lichatowich, "Pacific Salmon at the Crossroads." The estimate of over 1,000 dams and diversions of all types in the Columbia River basin was kindly provided by S. Bellcoff, Pacific Northwest Hydrosite Database, personal communication.

135 "This fundamental engineering error": Quotation from P. Ford, "How the Basin's Salmon-Killing System Works," *High Country News*, 22 April 1991. "Anadromous fish" are fish that move from the sea to fresh water to spawn.

136 the efficacy of these efforts: National Research Council, *Upstream*.

136 hatchery-reared: National Research Council, *Upstream*; P. Koberstein, "Are Hatcheries Producing Salmon 'Wimps'?" *High Country News*, 22 April 1991.

136   genetic differences between stocks: C. C. Krueger and B. May, "Ecological and Genetic Effects of Salmonid Introductions in North America," *Canadian Journal of Fisheries and Aquatic Sciences* 48 (1991), suppl. 1: 66–77; National Research Council, *Upstream.*

137   the ultimate problem with hatcheries: For more information on hatcheries, see R. Hilborn, "Hatcheries and the Future of Salmon in the Northwest," *Fisheries* 17, no. 1 (1992): 5–8; B. Goodman, "Keeping Anglers Happy Has a Price," *BioScience* 41 (1991): 294–99; and Koberstein, "Are Hatcheries Producing Salmon 'Wimps'?" The quotation is by Bill Bakke, Oregon Trout, and is taken from Koberstein, "Are Hatcheries Producing Salmon 'Wimps'?" 27.

Chapter 5

140   42 percent of the U.S. population: Bureau of the Census, *Statistical Abstract of the United States* (Washington, D.C.: U.S. Government Printing Office, 1995), table 39. Includes counties bordering the Atlantic seaboard, Gulf of Mexico, and Pacific Ocean.

142   great auk: The history of the great auk is taken from J. C. Greenway Jr., *Extinct and Vanishing Birds of the World*, Special Publication no. 13 of the American Committee for International Wild Life Protection (New York: American Committee for International Wild Life Protection, 1958; reprint, New York: Dover, 1967); E. Fuller, *The Great Auk* (Southborough, England: Errol Fuller, 1998).

142   the Bering Sea: The history of Steller's sea cow is taken from P. Matthiessen, *Wildlife in America*, revised, updated edition (New York: Viking, 1987); the history of spectacled cormorant is from Greenway, *Extinct and Vanishing Birds*, and E. Fuller, *Extinct Birds* (New York: Facts on File Publications, 1987).

143   One such hunt . . . was graphically described: Captain Scammon, as quoted in J. A. Allen, *History of North American Pinnipeds. A Monograph of the Walruses, Sea-Lions, Sea-Bears, and Seals of North America*. U.S. Geological and Geographical Survey of the Territories, Miscellaneous Publications no. 12 (Washington, D.C.: U.S. Department of the Interior, 1880).

144   sea otters: Historical information on sea otters is taken from M. A. Riedman and J. A. Estes, *The Sea Otter* (Enhydra lutris): *Behavior, Ecology, and Natural History*, Biological Report 90 (14) (Washington, D.C.: U.S. Fish and Wildlife Service, 1990); A. A. Schoenherr,

A Natural History of California (Berkeley: University of California Press, 1992); and Matthiessen, *Wildlife in America*.

144 the Atlantic coast: Although the Atlantic coast never experienced a fur trade comparable to that of the Pacific coast, at least one Atlantic coast mammal was driven to extinction for its pelt. A large brown weasel called the sea mink, probably a subspecies of the common mink, lived along the coastline of New England, where it was hunted for its fine pelage. It vanished sometime around 1860–1880, almost certainly as a result of overexploitation. Bones recovered from Indian middens are all that remain of this little-known animal. See R. H. Manville, "The Extinct Sea Mink, With Taxonomic Notes," *Proceedings of the United States National Museum* 122, no. 3584 (1966): 1–12.

146 All were fair game: The effect of market hunting on shorebirds is well described in A. C. Bent, *Life Histories of North American Shore Birds* (1927; reprint, New York: Dover, 1962).

146 Wrote one observer: M. H. Swenk, 1915, as quoted in Bent, *Life Histories of North American Shore Birds*, 133.

147 a single bird seen along the Texas coast in the spring of 1963: K. Kaufman, *Lives of North American Birds* (Boston: Houghton Mifflin, 1996).

147 the nation's ducks: See A. C. Bent, *Life Histories of North American Wild Fowl*, United States National Museum Bulletin no. 126 (Washington, D.C.: Smithsonian Institution, 1923); R. L. DiSilvestro, *The Endangered Kingdom: The Struggle to Save America's Wildlife* (New York: John Wiley & Sons, 1989).

147 Labrador duck: The history of the Labrador duck is taken from Greenway, *Extinct and Vanishing Birds*; Fuller, *Extinct Birds*; and T. Halliday, *Vanishing Birds: Their Natural History and Conservation* (New York: Holt, Rinehart, and Winston, 1978).

148 The growing popularity of feathers: My description of the plume trade is from Matthiessen, *Wildlife in America*; Bent, *Life Histories of North American Shore Birds*; and A. C. Bent, *Life Histories of North American Gulls and Terns* (1921; reprint, New York: Dover, 1963).

148 Even gulls were not immune: Bent, *Life Histories of North American Gulls and Terns*; B. G. Blodget, "The East Coast Gull Explosion," *Massachusetts Wildlife* 38, no. 1 (1988): 12–19.

148 Along the West Coast: J. Grinnell, H. C. Bryant, and T. I. Storer, *The Game Birds of California* (Berkeley: University of California

Press, 1918). With the notable exception of this work, it has proved more difficult to find information on the feather and flesh trade along the West Coast than it has for the East Coast. Veteran California ornithologist Howard Cogswell reports that a now deceased friend of his, Max de Laubenfels, began watching birds in southern California in the early years of the twentieth century and then temporarily abandoned the hobby in the 1920s. When he resumed birdwatching in the 1940s, he was quite impressed by the greater numbers of egrets, terns, and shorebirds he saw then compared with the 1920s, an increase he attributed to recovery from market hunting (H. Cogswell, personal communication).

149   ornithologist Joseph Grinnell: Grinnell, Bryant, and Storer, *Game Birds*, 11.

149   spokesmen in their defense: Matthiessen, *Wildlife in America*, 165.

149   State and federal laws: Matthiessen, *Wildlife in America*; M. J. Bean and M. J. Rowland, *The Evolution of National Wildlife Law*, 3d ed. (Westport, Conn.: Praeger, 1997).

149   relief came at about the same time: Matthiessen, *Wildlife in America*; Bean and Rowland, *Evolution of National Wildlife Law*.

150   a remarkable transformation: My discussion of the return of the sea otter and its effect on marine ecosystems is taken largely from: Riedman and Estes, *The Sea Otter*; J. A. Estes, D. O. Duggins, and G. B. Rathbun, "The Ecology of Extinctions in Kelp Forest Communities," *Conservation Biology* 3 (1989): 252–64; U.S. Fish and Wildlife Service, *Draft Southern Sea Otter Recovery Plan* (Ventura, Calif.: U.S. Fish and Wildlife Service, 1995). It should be noted that translocation efforts in Oregon and off San Nicolas Island, California, have been unsuccessful; see Riedman and Estes, *The Sea Otter*.

151   keystone species: The role of otters as a keystone species is explored in Riedman and Estes, *The Sea Otter*; Estes, Duggins, and Rathbun, "The Ecology of Extinctions"; and D. O. Duggins, C. A. Simenstad, and J. A. Estes, "Magnification of Secondary Production by Kelp Detritus in Coastal Marine Ecosystems," *Science* 245 (1989): 170–73.

151   hundreds of millions of pounds of marine life annually: Finding out just how much an elephant seal eats in the wild is no easy task, given that they forage in the deep ocean. The figures I have used are based on data provided by B. LeBoeuf, University of California at

Santa Cruz (personal communication). Dr. LeBoeuf estimates that an adult female elephant seal ingests 4,800 kilograms per year of marine life and an adult male ingests approximately 19,170 (assuming they are eating something like squid). I converted his numbers to pounds and rounded them off to two significant figures.

152 white abalone: The story of the white abalone is recounted in D. Malakoff, "Extinction on the High Seas," *Science* 277 (1997): 486–88.

153 spiny lobsters: See Estes, Duggins, and Rathbun, "The Ecology of Extinctions." There is also considerable uncertainty as to the relationship between spiny lobsters and sea otters. Otters eat lobsters. Whether, in an undisturbed environment, they do so to such an extent as to make the lobsters minor players in the ecosystem is an open question.

153 Aleutian Islands: The decline of sea otters in the Aleutians is discussed in J. A. Estes, M. T. Tinker, T. M. Williams, and D. F. Doak, "Killer Whale Predation on Sea Otters Linking Oceanic and Nearshore Ecosystems," *Science* 282 (1998): 473–76. See also J. Kaiser, "Sea Otter Declines Blamed on Hungry Killers," *Science* 282 (1998): 390–91.

154 Ecologist Jerome B. C. Jackson: "Reefs since Columbus," *Coral Reefs* 16 (Supplement) (1997): S23–S32.

154 General William T. Sherman: Quotation from C. K. Dodd Jr., "Nesting of the Green Turtle, *Chelonia mydas* (L.), in Florida: Historic Review and Present Trends," *Brimleyana* 7 (1981): 39–54.

155 The cause was quickly identified: My account of the sea turtles and shrimp fishing is based on M. Weber, D. Crouse, R. Irvin, and S. Iudicello, *Delay and Denial: A Political History of Sea Turtles and Shrimp Fishing* (Washington, D.C.: Center for Marine Conservation, 1995); National Research Council, *Decline of the Sea Turtles: Causes and Prevention* (Washington, D.C.: National Academy Press, 1990).

155 extraordinarily wasteful: See C. Safina, *Song for the Blue Ocean: Encounters along the World's Coasts and Beneath the Seas* (New York: Henry Holt, 1997); C. Safina, "The Audubon Guide to Seafood," *Audubon*, May–June 1998.

155 a boxlike structure: The original TEDs were boxlike. They now come in a variety of sizes, shapes, and materials.

156 habitat destruction: My discussion of beach development, sand replenishment, and artificial lighting and their effects on sea turtles is taken from National Research Council, *Decline of the Sea Turtles;* National Marine Fisheries Service, *Recovery Plan for U.S. Population of Atlantic Green Turtle* (St. Petersburg, Fla.: National Marine Fisheries Service, 1990); National Marine Fisheries Service, *Recovery Plan for U.S. Population of Loggerhead Turtle* (St. Petersburg, Fla.: National Marine Fisheries Service, 1990).

157   nesting beaches: J. R. Luoma, "Oceanfront Battlefront," *Audubon,* July–August 1998.

158   plastic in their stomachs: National Marine Fisheries Service, *Recovery Plan for U.S. Population of Leatherback Turtle* (St. Petersburg, Fla.: National Marine Fisheries Service, 1990).

158   major population declines: Population trends for shorebirds are discussed in M. A. Howe, P. H. Geissler, and B. A. Harrington, "Population Trends of North American Shorebirds Based on the International Shorebird Survey," *Biological Conservation* 49 (1989): 185–99; B. A. Harrington, J. P. Myers, and J. S. Grear, "Coastal Refueling Sites for Global Bird Migrants," in *Coastal Zone '89: Proceedings of the Sixth Symposium on Coastal and Ocean Management* (New York: American Society of Civil Engineers, 1989), 4293–4307; J. P. Myers, "The Sanderling," in *Audubon Wildlife Report 1988/1989*, edited by W. J. Chandler (New York: Academic Press, 1988).

159   problems posed by gulls: The population explosion of gulls and its effect on other species is discussed in Blodget, "The East Coast Gull Explosion"; U.S. Fish and Wildlife Service, *Piping Plover* (Charadrius melodus), *Atlantic Coast Population, Revised Recovery Plan* (Hadley, Mass.: U.S. Fish and Wildlife Service, 1996); U.S. Fish and Wildlife Service, *Roseate Tern Recovery Plan — Northeastern Population, First Update* (Hadley, Mass.: U.S. Fish and Wildlife Service, 1998).

159   millions of tons of by-catch: According to one estimate, the world's fishing fleets generate 27 million metric tons of by-catch each year — approximately a quarter of the total global catch. See Safina, *Song for the Blue Ocean.*

160   Efforts to control expanding gull populations in New England: The history of these efforts is described in B. G. Blodget, "The Half-Century Battle for Gull Control," *Massachusetts Wildlife* 38, no. 2 (1988): 4–10.

160   gull control programs have come under attack: S. Rimer, "Gulls Are Cast as Threat to Avian Neighbors; Agency Is Cast in a Bad Light," *New York Times,* 27 May 1996.

160 753 condominiums: L. C. Hood, *Frayed Safety Nets: Conservation Planning Under the Endangered Species Act* (Washington, D.C.: Defenders of Wildlife, 1998).

161 The San Francisco Estuary: Information on alteration of the San Francisco Bay ecosystem comes from A. N. Cohen, *An Introduction to the Ecology of the San Francisco Estuary* (Oakland, Calif.: San Francisco Estuary Project, 1991); J. Krautkraemer, "Using Market Forces to Protect Biodiversity: The Central Valley Project Improvement Act," in *The Big Kill: Declining Biodiversity in America's Lakes and Rivers*, edited by D. S. Wilcove and M. J. Bean (Washington, D.C.: Environmental Defense Fund, 1994); U.S. Fish and Wildlife Service, *Salt Marsh Harvest Mouse and California Clapper Rail Recovery Plan* (Portland, Oreg.: U.S. Fish and Wildlife Service, 1984).

162 "like Labrador retrievers": Jean Takekawa, San Francisco Bay National Wildlife Refuge, as quoted in L. Line, "Endangered Clapper Rails Making a Recovery," *New York Times*, 22 August 1995.

162 the most extensively invaded estuary in the world: As more data are gathered, other industrial bays, such as the waters around Hong Kong, may prove to be as infested with non-native species as San Francisco Bay (J. Burger, Rutgers University, personal communication).

163 234 non-native species: My discussion of alien species in San Francisco Bay is based largely on A. N. Cohen and J. T. Carlton, "Accelerating Invasion Rate in a Highly Invaded Estuary," *Science* 279 (1998): 555–58; and A. N. Cohen and J. T. Carlton, *Nonindigenous Aquatic Species in a United States Estuary: A Case Study of the Biological Invasion of the San Francisco Bay and Delta*, report for the U.S. Fish and Wildlife Service and the National Sea Grant College Program (Washington, D.C.: U.S. Fish and Wildlife Service, 1995).

165 Arthur Kill spill: My primary sources for the history of the spill are J. Burger, *Oil Spills* (New Brunswick, N.J.: Rutgers University Press, 1997); D. Martin, "Helping Nature Restore Life to a Waterway Left for Dead," *New York Times*, 30 September 1994.

166 *Exxon Valdez:* Information on the spill is taken primarily from J. A. Wiens, "Oil, Seabirds, and Science," *BioScience* 46 (1996): 587–97; R. B. Spies, S. D. Rice, D. A. Wolfe, and B. A. Wright, "The Effects of the *Exxon Valdez* Oil Spill on the Alaskan Coastal Environment," in *Proceedings of the* Exxon Valdez *Oil Spill Symposium*, American Fisheries Society Symposium 18 (1996): 1–16; P. G. Wells, J. N. Butler, and J. S. Hughes, "Introduction, Overview, Issues," in Exxon Valdez *Oil Spill:*

Fate and Effects in Alaskan Waters, edited by P. G. Wells, J. N. Butler, and J. S. Hughes, ASTM STP 1219 (Philadelphia, Pa.: American Society for Testing and Materials, 1995); S. E. Senner, "Book Review of Exxon Valdez *Oil Spill: Fate and Effects in Alaskan Waters*," *Wilson Bulletin* 109 (1997): 549–59; D. Postman, "The Spill and Its Spoils," *Sports Illustrated*, 25 September 1996; and Burger, *Oil Spills*. Rebuttals to portions of the Wiens article were published in D. E. Atkinson, "Science versus Environmental Advocacy," *BioScience* 46 (1996): 794, and M. McCammon, "See No Evil?" *BioScience* 47 (1997): 66–67.

167 some . . . have recovered, but others have not: *Exxon Valdez* Oil Spill Trustee Council, Exxon Valdez *Oil Spill Restoration Plan: Update on Injured Resources and Services, September 1996* (Anchorage, Alaska: *Exxon Valdez* Oil Spill Trustee Council, 1996).

167 sea otters . . . Harbor seals: Information is taken from *Exxon Valdez* Oil Spill Trustee Council, Exxon Valdez *Oil Spill Restoration Plan*; S. Senner, Exxon Valdez Oil Spill Trustee Council, personal communication.

167 in an ecosystem that is already stressed: In the South Farallon Islands off central California, a colony of common murres that numbered over 102,000 birds in 1982 fell to fewer than 50,000 by 1990, a result of several factors, including an El Niño event in 1982 that reduced the amount of food available to them, the drowning of thousands of murres in fishing nets, and two major and several minor oil spills. The population might have been able to weather any one of these factors, but the combination of all of them proved devastating. See J. F. Piatt, H. R. Carter, and D. N. Nettleship, "Effects of Oil Pollution on Marine Bird Populations," in *The Effects of Oil on Wildlife: Research, Rehabilitation, and General Concerns*, edited by J. White (Hanover, Pa.: Sheridan Press, 1991).

168 effects of chronic oil pollution: Burger, *Oil Spills*; W. N. Holmes and J. Cronshaw, "Biological Effects of Petroleum on Marine Birds," in *Effects of Petroleum on Arctic and Subarctic Marine Environments and Organisms*, vol. 2, *Biological Effects*, edited by D. C. Mains (New York: Academic Press, 1977).

168 The Environmental Protection Agency estimates: Burger, *Oil Spills*.

168 diminished reproductive rates: R. G. Butler, A. Harfenist, F. A. Leighton, and D. B. Peakall, "Impact of Sublethal Oil and Emulsion Exposure on the Reproductive Success of Leach's Storm-petrels: Short and Long-Term Effects," *Journal of Applied Ecology* 25 (1988): 125–43.

168 loss of vegetation: C. Hershner and J. Lake, "Effects of Chronic Oil Pollution on a Salt-Marsh Grass Community," *Marine Biology* 56 (1980): 163–73.

Chapter 6

171 The two seminal events: The third great colonization event, which is discussed in Chapter 7, is unique to our fiftieth state: the arrival of Polynesians in Hawaii some 1,500 years ago.

174 the Everglades functioned: See M. S. Douglas, *The Everglades: River of Grass* (New York: Rinehart, 1947). The "grass," in fact, is a sedge.

174 "the most glorious assemblage": Descriptions of the pristine Everglades and subsequent development programs are taken from S. M. Davis and J. C. Ogden (eds.), *Everglades: The Ecosystem and Its Restoration* (Delray Beach, Fla.: St. Lucie Press, 1994); G. H. Orians, M. J. Bean, R. Lande, K. Loftin, S. Pimm, R. E. Turner, and M. Weller, *Report of the Advisory Panel on the Everglades and Endangered Species,* Audubon Conservation Report no. 8 (New York: National Audubon Society, 1992); K. Schneider, "Returning Part of Everglades to Nature for $700 Million," *New York Times,* 11 March 1991; V. Monks, "Engineering the Everglades," *National Parks,* September–October 1990; W. K. Stevens, "Everglades: Paradise Not Quite Lost," *New York Times,* 22 March 1994; M. Derr, "Redeeming the Everglades," *Audubon,* September–October 1993; A. Mairson, "The Everglades: Dying for Help," *National Geographic,* April 1994. The quotation is from F. Graham, "Kite vs. Stork," *Audubon,* March 1990.

175 sugar price support program: B. Gifford, "The Government's Too-Sweet Deal," *Washington Post,* 9 January 1994; U.S. General Accounting Office, *Sugar Program: Impact on Sweetner Users and Producers,* GAO/T-RCED-95-204 (Washington, D.C.: U.S. General Accounting Office, 1995).

176 great white herons: The great white heron is a white color variety of the great blue heron. Great white herons are restricted to southern Florida and portions of Mexico and the Caribbean. The panhandling herons are discussed in G. V. N. Powell, A. H. Powell, and N. K. Paul, "Brother, Can You Spare a Fish?" *Natural History,* February 1988.

176 a challenge to the wading birds: My discussion of how the wading birds have responded to the hydrological changes in the Everglades is taken largely from J. C. Ogden, "A Comparison of Wading Bird Nesting Colony Dynamics (1931–1946 and 1974–1989) as an Indication of Ecosystem Conditions in the Southern Everglades," in Davis and Ogden, *Everglades;* S. M. Davis and J. C. Ogden, "Toward Ecosystem Restoration," in Davis and Ogden, *Everglades.*

177 "a series of pools": Quotation from Orians et al., *Report of the Advisory Panel on the Everglades,* 9.

177 wood stork population: Data on the wood stork from U.S. Fish and Wildlife Service, *Recovery Plan for the U.S. Breeding Population of the Wood Stork* (Atlanta, Ga.: U.S. Fish and Wildlife Service, 1986); Ogden, "A Comparison of Wading Bird Nesting Colony Dynamics"; "Wood Storks Flying High in Southeast," *Miami Herald,* 18 April 1996. There is apparently some disagreement among scientists as to the number of storks in the United States in the 1930s; the figure I have used is the high estimate.

179 the rescue plan: S. Davis, senior ecologist, South Florida Water Management Agency, as interviewed in *Environmental Review,* March 1995.

179 It seems unlikely: Davis and Ogden, "Toward Ecosystem Restoration."

179 Florida governor Lawton Chiles: Quotation from Schneider, "Returning Part of Everglades to Nature."

179 "the only West Indies one can drive to": J. D. Lazell Jr., *Wildlife of the Florida Keys: A Natural History* (Washington, D.C.: Island Press, 1989), 1.

180 they began as mounds of limestone: The formation of the Keys is described in Lazell, *Wildlife of the Florida Keys,* and J. Terborgh and B. Winter, "Some Causes of Extinction," in *Conservation Biology: An Evolutionary-Ecological Perspective,* edited by M. Soulé and B. Wilcox (Sunderland, Mass.: Sinauer Associates, 1980).

180 some of the earliest disappearances: Audubon's account of the quail-doves and zenaida doves is taken from A. C. Bent, *Life Histories of North American Gallinaceous Birds* (1932; reprint, New York: Dover, 1963) and H. W. Kale, ed., *Rare and Endangered Biota of Florida,* vol. 2, *Birds* (Gainesville: University of Florida Press, 1978). My discussion of the ecology and conservation of these birds is taken from these sources and G. Laycock, "Good Times are Killing the Keys," *Audubon,* September–October 1991.

181   The ensuing frenzy of development: The development of the Keys is described in Lazell, *Wildlife of the Florida Keys*, and M. Derr, *Some Kind of Paradise: A Chronicle of Man and Land in Florida* (New York: William Morrow, 1989).

182   the white-crowned pigeon: The life history of the white-crowned pigeon is taken largely from A. M. Strong and G. T. Bancroft, "Post-fledging Dispersal of White-crowned Pigeons: Implications for Conservation of Deciduous Seasonal Forests in the Florida Keys," *Conservation Biology* 8 (1994): 770–79; K. Kaufman, *Lives of North American Birds* (Boston: Houghton Mifflin, 1996). The percentage of hardwood forest that has been destroyed is from G. T. Bancroft, A. M. Strong, and M. Carrington, "Deforestation and Its Effects on Forest-Nesting Birds in the Florida Keys," *Conservation Biology* 9 (1995): 835–44.

183   the rarest mammals: An obvious exception to this pattern is the highly endangered West Indian manatee. It is a Caribbean mammal that has a small population in the extreme southeastern United States.

183   The Key deer: Data are taken from J. W. Hardin, W. D. Klimstra, and N. J. Silvy, "Florida Keys," in *White-tailed Deer: Ecology and Management*, edited by L. K. Halls (Harrisburg, Pa.: Stackpole Books, 1984) and S. R. Humphrey and B. Bell, "The Key Deer Population Is Declining," *Wildlife Society Bulletin* 14 (1986): 261–65.

184   its future remains in doubt: Humphrey and Bell, "The Key Deer Population Is Declining."

184   A 1988 study: S. R. Humphrey, "Density Estimates of the Endangered Key Largo Woodrat and Cotton Mouse (*Neotoma floridana smalli* and *Peromyscus gossypinus allapaticola*) Using the Nested-Grid Approach," *Journal of Mammalogy* 69 (1988): 524–31.

184   the Schaus' swallowtail: Information is based on T. C. Emmel and J. C. Daniels, "Is Schaus' Swallowtail Finally Licked?" *American Butterflies* 5, no. 2 (1997): 20–26; M. Yanno, "New Hope for the Schaus Swallowtail," *Endangered Species Bulletin* 21, no. 4 (1996): 22–23; and T. C. Emmel, University of Florida, personal communication.

186   "dry sandy flats": Quotation from W. Leary, "First U.S. Refuge for Plants Sought in Florida," *New York Times*, 18 June 1991. Additional information on the scrub is taken from U.S. Fish and Wildlife Service, *Recovery Plan for Nineteen Florida Scrub and High Pineland Plant Species* (Atlanta, Ga.: U.S. Fish and Wildlife Service, 1996); J. W.

Fitzpatrick, "Florida's Vanishing Scrubland," *In The Field* (Bulletin of the Field Museum of Natural History), January–February 1991; P. Morgan, "Cultivating Care for the Future," *Tampa Tribune-Times*, 24 February 1991; J. Klinkenberg, "Vanishing Habitat," *St. Petersburg Times*, 20 May 1990; D. K. Rogers, "Beginning of the End," *St. Petersburg Times*, 27 May 1989; J. Bourne, "Treasures in the Scrub," *Defenders*, November–December 1991; and C. Fergus, "Scrub: Learning to Love It," *Audubon*, May–June 1993.

187 A now-outdated estimate: Leary, "First U.S. Refuge for Plants."

187 they are poorly served: Under the federal Endangered Species Act, for example, citizens may not harm listed animals on private lands, with harm broadly defined to include killing, harassing, or the destruction of essential habitat. No such strictures apply to listed plants. Private citizens are free to destroy listed plants on private lands, provided they (1) do not require a federal permit in connection with whatever activity is resulting in the destruction of the plant, (2) are not knowingly violating any state law or regulation, and (3) are not violating a state criminal trespass law. See M. J. Bean and M. J. Rowland, *The Evolution of National Wildlife Law*, 3d ed. (Westport, Conn.: Praeger, 1997).

187 Florida scrub-jay: The behavior and ecology of this bird are described in G. E. Woolfenden and J. W. Fitzpatrick, *The Florida Scrub Jay: Demography of a Cooperative-Breeding Bird* (Princeton, N.J.: Princeton University Press, 1984); J. W. Fitzpatrick and G. E. Woolfenden, "The Helpful Shall Inherit the Scrub," *Natural History*, May 1984; G. E. Woolfenden and J. W. Fitzpatrick, "Florida's Scrub-jays: A Synopsis after Eighteen Years of Study," in *Cooperative Breeding in Birds*, edited by P. B. Stacey and W. D. Koenig (Cambridge: Cambridge University Press, 1990).

187 Recent biochemical studies: These studies are mentioned in Fitzpatrick, "Florida's Vanishing Scrubland." Older bird books treat the Florida jay as a subspecies or race of a predominately western species called the "scrub jay." However, now that it is considered a separate species, it has been given its own English name and scientific name (Florida scrub-jay, *Aphelocoma coerulescens*). The western birds are now classified as two separate species, the western scrub-jay (*Aphelocoma californica*) and the island scrub-jay (*Aphelocoma insularis*). If all of this sounds confusing, it is. Geography is the easiest way to sort the birds out: The Florida scrub-jay is found only on Lake Wales

Ridge and in portions of the coastal scrub in Florida, about a thousand miles to the east of the nearest western scrub-jay population.

189 500 species of vertebrates and 1,200 plants: The figure for vertebrates covers regularly occurring terrestrial and freshwater species and is taken from S. E. Jahrsdoerfer and D. M. Leslie Jr., *Tamaulipan Brushland of the Lower Rio Grande Valley of South Texas: Description, Human Impacts, and Management Options*, Biological Report 88 (36) (Washington, D.C.: U.S. Fish and Wildlife Service, 1988). The number of plants is from C. Douglis, "A Corridor in Peril," *Wilderness*, Winter 1989.

189 the valley has always been poor: The history of the Lower Rio Grande Valley is recounted in R. L. Maril, *The Poorest of Americans: The Mexican Americans of the Lower Rio Grande Valley of Texas* (Notre Dame, Ind.: University of Notre Dame Press, 1989).

190 more than 95 percent . . . has been destroyed: Jahrsdoerfer and Leslie, *Tamaulipan Brushland*; G. Harwell and D. P. Siminski, *Listed Cats of Texas and Arizona Recovery Plan (with Emphasis on the Ocelot)* (Albuquerque, N.M.: U.S. Fish and Wildlife Service, 1990).

191 86 vertebrates: The number of imperiled vertebrates is from Jahrsdoerfer and Leslie, *Tamaulipan Brushland*.

191 the jaguar: Information on the jaguar is taken from R. Perry, *The World of the Jaguar* (New York: Taplinger, 1970); Matthiessen, *Wildlife in America*, revised, updated edition (New York: Viking, 1987); C. A. W. Guggisberg, *Wild Cats of the World* (New York: Taplinger, 1975); and Harwell and Siminski, *Listed Cats*. Information on the ocelot, margay, and jaguarundi is from Matthiessen, *Wildlife in America*, and D. W. Lowe, J. R. Matthews, and C. J. Mosley (eds.), *The Official World Wildlife Fund Guide to Endangered Species of North America* (Washington, D.C.: Beacham Publishing, 1990); Harwell and Siminski, *Listed Cats*, and L. H. Emmons and F. Feer, *Neotropical Rainforest Mammals: A Field Guide*, 2d ed. (Chicago: University of Chicago Press, 1997). Less convincing accounts place the jaguar as far east as the Appalachian Mountains at the beginning of the colonial era (see Matthiessen, *Wildlife in America*).

191 re-establishing a viable population . . . is unthinkable: A. Rabinowitz, *The Status of Jaguars* (Panthera onca) *in the United States: Trip Report* (Bronx, N.Y.: Wildlife Conservation Society, undated).

193 A recent study: C. E. Rupert, "Breeding Densities and Habitat of Riparian Birds along the Lower Rio Grande, Texas" (master's thesis, University of Texas-Pan American, 1997). Although the conclusions of this study are consistent with those of studies conducted elsewhere in the United States, the sample sizes were low, so the results should be considered preliminary.

194   the mix of species: T. Brush and A. Cantu, "Changes in the Breeding Bird Community of Subtropical Evergreen Forest in the Lower Rio Grande Valley of Texas, 1970s–1990s," *Texas Journal of Science* 50 (1998): 123–32.

194   several . . . seem to be much rarer: Among the species that have declined are the red-billed pigeon, tropical parula warbler, hooded oriole, rose-throated becard, orchard oriole, summer tanager, orchard oriole, and gray hawk. See Brush and Cantu, "Changes in the Breeding Bird Community," and C. D. Castillo, Effects of Artificial Flooding on the Vegetation and Avifauna of Riparian Woodlands at Santa Ana National Wildlife Refuge, Hidalgo County, Texas" (master's thesis, University of Texas-Pan American, 1997).

194   a bold plan: U.S. Fish and Wildlife Service, "Land Protection Plan for the Lower Rio Grande Valley National Wildlife Refuge in Cameron, Hidalgo, Starr, and Willacy Counties," as reprinted in Harwell and Siminski, *Listed Cats;* Jahrsdoerfer and Leslie, *Tamaulipan Brushland;* N. C. Brown, "Lower Rio Grande Valley National Wildlife Refuge," *Endangered Species Bulletin* 23, no. 4 (1998): 36–39.

195   wrote one witness: H. Brown, "The Conditions Governing Bird Life in Arizona," *Auk* 17 (1900): 31–34.

196   masked bobwhite: The masked bobwhite is discussed in A. Phillips, J. Marshall, and G. Monson, *The Birds of Arizona* (Tucson: University of Arizona Press, 1964); J. Alcock, *The Masked Bobwhite Rides Again* (Tucson: University of Arizona Press, 1993); H. Brown, "Masked Bob-white *(Colinus ridgwayi)*," *Auk* 21 (1904): 209–13.

196   naturalist Herbert Brown: "Masked Bob-white," 210–11.

197   Worthen's sparrow: Information on Worthen's sparrow is from D. C. Wege, S. N. G. Howell, and A. Sada, "The Distribution and Status of Worthen's Sparrow, *Spizella wortheni:* A Review," *Bird Conservation International* 3 (1993): 211–20.

197   a variety of other grassland birds: See Phillips, Marshall, and Monson, *Birds of Arizona;* G. Monson, "Botteri's Sparrow in Arizona," *Auk* 64 (1947): 139–40.

197 comparatively little effect: For a more detailed comparison of grazing in the arid Southwest and the Great Plains, see A. Y. Cooperrider and D. S. Wilcove, *Defending the Desert: Conserving Biodiversity on BLM Lands in the Southwest* (Washington, D.C.: Environmental Defense Fund, 1995).

198 effort to restore the species: The bobwhite reintroduction program is described in Alcock, *Masked Bobwhite Rides Again;* C. Cadieux, *These Are the Endangered* (Washington, D.C.: Stone Wall Press, 1981); and Lowe, Matthews, and Mosley, *The Official World Wildlife Fund Guide.* The current release protocol and the current population estimate for the Buenos Aires National Wildlife Refuge were provided by S. Gall, Buenos Aires National Wildlife Refuge, personal communication.

199 local ranchers: K. Bagwell, "Cattlemen Want to Tame Quail Preserve," *Arizona Daily Star,* 10 December 1995.

199 thick-billed parrots: The disappearance and subsequent reintroduction of the thick-billed parrot is described in T. B. Johnson, N. F. R. Snyder, and H. A. Snyder, "The Return of Thick-billed Parrots to Arizona," *Endangered Species Technical Bulletin* 14 (1989): 1–5.

200 the possibility . . . vanished: Phillips, Marshall, and Monson, *Birds of Arizona.*

201 the reintroduction program was suspended: See "Effort to Reintroduce Thick-billed Parrots in Arizona is Dropped," *New York Times,* 30 May 1995.

Chapter 7

204 ornithological exploration . . . was complete: The Cape Sable sparrow was described from the marshes of South Florida as late as 1918, but most ornithologists now feel it is merely an isolated race of the seaside sparrow, a more widespread species that was described at the beginning of the nineteenth century.

204 *Melamprosops phaeosoma:* The discovery of the po'ouli is detailed in T. L. C. Casey and J. D. Jacobi, "A New Genus and Species of Bird from the Island of Maui, Hawaii (Passeriformes: Drepanididae), *Occasional Papers of the Bernice P. Bishop Museum, Honolulu, Hawaii* 24 (1974): 215–26. Its current status is briefly described in N. J. Collar, M. J. Crosby, and A. J. Stattersfield, *Birds to Watch 2: The World List of Threatened Birds* (Cambridge: BirdLife International, 1994).

204 Hawaiian honeycreepers: Some ornithologists question whether the po'ouli rightfully belongs in the Drepanididae group, or belongs with another family of birds.

204 the po'ouli population has crashed: S. Mountainspring, T. L. C. Casey, C. B. Kepler, and J. M. Scott, "Ecology, Behavior, and Conservation of the Poo-uli *(Melamprosops phaeosoma),*" *Wilson Bulletin* 102 (1990): 109–22.

205 the study of island life: The importance of islands to contemporary biology is well described in D. Quammen, *The Song of the Dodo: Island Biogeography in an Age of Extinctions* (New York: Scribner, 1996).

205 one of the highest proportions of extinct or endangered species: S. L. Pimm, G. J. Russell, J. L. Gittleman, and T. M. Brooks, "The Future of Biodiversity," *Science* 269 (1995): 347–50.

208 its fruit flies: My discussion of Hawaiian fruit flies is taken from J. L. Culliney, *Islands in a Far Sea: Nature and Man in Hawaii* (San Francisco: Sierra Club Books, 1988); D. Foote and H. L Carson, "*Drosophila* as Monitors of Change in Hawaiian Ecosystems," in *Our Living Resources: A Report to the Nation on the Distribution, Abundance, and Health of U.S. Plants, Animals, and Ecosystems*, edited by E. T. LaRoe (Washington, D.C.: National Biological Service, 1995).

208 drosophilid fruit flies: Fly aficionados distinguish between the drosophilid fruit flies (family Drosophilidae) and the "true" fruit flies (family Tephritidae), which will lay their eggs on fruit that is still attached to the plant. Several species of tephritid fruit flies have been brought by humans to Hawaii, where they are considered agricultural pests.

209 "one of the rarest": Culliney, *Islands in a Far Sea*, 56.

209 The vast majority . . . occur nowhere else: Percentages of endemic species in various groups are taken from Culliney, *Islands in a Far Sea*. By "native" species, I mean species that have arrived on the Hawaiian Islands without assistance from humans.

210 The first alien species: The species introduced by the Polynesians are taken from Culliney, *Islands in a Far Sea;* the European introductions are from R. Wallace, *Hawaii* (New York: Time-Life Books, 1973) and Culliney, *Islands in a Far Sea*.

211 remedying the "problem": Information about introduced birds is taken from A. J. Berger, *Hawaiian Birdlife*, 2d ed. (Honolulu: University of Hawaii Press, 1981); R. J. Shallenberger, ed., *Hawaii's Birds* (Honolulu: Hawaii Audubon Society, 1986); and Culliney, *Islands in a Far Sea.*

211 "We need more songsters here": Quotation from Berger, *Hawaiian Birdlife*, 171.

212 a "paradise of fodder": Culliney, *Islands in a Far Sea*, 336.

212 a 32-mile hog-wire fence: The fencing took 10 years to complete at a cost of $1.5 million.

213 Laysan Island: The sad history of Laysan Island is discussed in Culliney, *Islands in a Far Sea.* See also Berger, *Hawaiian Birdlife*, and J. C. Greenway, *Extinct and Vanishing Birds of the World*, Special Publication no. 13 (New York: American Committee for International Wildlife Protection, 1958; reprint, New York: Dover, 1967).

214 the flightless rail population: The demise of the Laysan rail is unique in the history of ornithology. Toward the end of the nineteenth century, some Laysan rails had been transplanted to Midway Island, where they did quite well. When the species disappeared from Laysan, it might have endured on Midway, had World War II and the resulting human traffic not led to the introduction of rats on Midway. By 1945, the rail was extinct on Midway and gone forever. Prior to its disappearance from Midway, some scientists had proposed reintroducing it to Laysan, but they were unable to secure a boat to carry out the project. Had they succeeded, the rail would probably be alive today on Laysan.

214 The other honeycreeper: The Laysan 'apapane *(Himantione sanguinea freethi)* was a distinctive subspecies or race of the common 'apapane. The common 'apapane still occurs on all the main Hawaiian Islands.

214 fourteen species of arthropods: F. G. Howarth, G. Nishida, and A. Asquith, "Insects of Hawaii," in *Our Living Resources.*

214 Indian mongooses: Information on mongooses is taken from Culliney, *Islands in a Far Sea*, and Berger, *Hawaiian Birdlife.*

215 2,600 foreign insect species: My discussion of introduced insects is based largely on Howarth, Nishida, and Asquith, "Insects of Hawaii."

216 "The effect of invasive alien arthropods": Quotation from Howarth, Nishida, and Asquith, "Insects of Hawaii," 367.

216 mosquitoes: The story of the introduction of mosquitoes to Hawaii is taken from Culliney, *Islands in a Far Sea*. For information on the effects of avian pox and malaria on Hawaiian birds, see Culliney, *Islands in a Far Sea*; Berger, *Hawaiian Birdlife*; R. E. Warner, "The Role of Introduced Diseases in the Extinction of the Endemic Hawaiian Avifauna," *Condor* 70 (1968): 101–20; C. van Riper III, S. G. van Riper, M. L. Goff, and M. Laird, "The Epizootiology and Ecological Significance of Malaria in Hawaiian Land Birds," *Ecological Monographs* 56 (1986): 327–44.

216 one baffled naturalist: Quotation by W. H. Henshaw, reprinted in Wallace, *Hawaii*, 92.

217 In one experiment: See J. D. Jacobi and C. T. Atkinson, "Hawaii's Endemic Birds," in *Our Living Resources*.

217 moving up the mountains: C. E. Herrmann and T. R. Snetsinger, "Pox-like Lesions on Endangered Puaiohi *(Myadestes palmeri)* and Occurrence of Mosquito *(Culex quinquefasciatus)* Populations Near Koaie Stream." *Elepaio* 57 (1997): 73–75.

217 Alakai Swamp: My account of the disappearance of birds from the Alakai Swamp is taken largely from J. M. Scott, S. Mountainspring, F. L. Ramsey, and C. B. Kepler, *Forest Bird Communities of the Hawaiian Islands: Their Dynamics, Ecology, and Conservation*, Studies in Avian Biology no. 9, a publication of the Cooper Ornithological Society (Lawrence, Kans.: Allen Press, 1986).

219 It is not clear: Berger, *Hawaiian Birdlife*.

219 a negative correlation: See Scott et al., *Forest Bird Communities*; S. Mountainspring and J. M. Scott, "Interspecific Competition among Hawaiian Forest Birds," *Ecological Monographs* 55 (1985): 219–39.

220 Ecologist Daniel Simberloff: "Why Do Introduced Species Appear to Devastate Islands More than Mainland Areas?" *Pacific Science* 49 (1995): 87–97.

220 agriculture has caused the destruction: See Culliney, *Islands in a Far Sea*.

220 the human population: Population trends are from Bureau of the Census, *Statistical Abstract of the United States* (Washington, D.C.: U.S. Government Printing Office, 1995).

220 more species of birds . . . today: By my calculations, there were approximately eighty species of nesting birds in the Hawaiian Islands at the time of Cook's arrival. This includes all nesting seabirds, water birds, upland birds, and forest birds. Today, there are over a hundred species nesting in the Hawaiian Islands, of which nearly half were introduced by people.

221 extinct or . . . feared extinct: Data on percentages of extinct species obtained from The Nature Conservancy, February 1997, and the Hawaii Biological Survey, Bishop Museum, November 1998.

221 Olson's discoveries: For information on the fossil avifauna of Hawaii, see S. L. Olson and H. F. James, "Fossil Birds from the Hawaiian Islands: Evidence for Wholesale Extinction by Man before Western Contact," *Science* 217 (1982): 633–35; D. W. Steadman, "Prehistoric Extinctions of Pacific Island Birds: Biodiversity Meets Zooarchaeology," *Science* 267 (1995): 1123–31; L. A. Freed, S. Conant, and R. C. Fleischer, "Evolutionary Ecology and Radiation of Hawaiian Passerine Birds," *Trends in Ecology and Evolution* 2 (1987): 196–203.

223 "We expect extinction": Quotation from Steadman, "Prehistoric Extinctions," 1130.

224 exotic plants: For more information on exotic grasses and fires, see C. M. D'Antonio and P. M. Vitousek, "Biological Invasions by Exotic Grasses, the Grass/Fire Cycle, and Global Change," *Annual Review of Ecology and Systematics* 23 (1992): 63–87; F. Hughes, P. M. Vitousek, and T. Tunison, "Alien Grass Invasion and Fire in the Seasonal Submontane Zone of Hawaii," *Ecology* 72 (1991): 743–46; P. M. Vitousek, C. M. D'Antonio, L. L. Loope, and R. Westbrooks, "Biological Invasions as Global Environmental Change," *American Scientist* 84 (1996): 468–78.

224 "[T]hey don't merely compete": D'Antonio and Vitousek, "Biological Invasions by Exotic Grasses," 64.

225 Laysan Island . . . began to recover: The recovery of Laysan is described in Culliney, *Islands in a Far Sea;* current bird populations are from Jacobi and Atkinson, "Hawaii's Endemic Birds" and Collar, Crosby, and Stattersfield, *Birds to Watch 2*.

227 cheatgrass: See G. W. Ferry, R. G. Clark, R. E. Montgomery, R. W. Mutch, W. P. Leenhouts, and G. T. Zimmerman, "Altered

Fire Regimes within Fire-Adapted Ecosystems," in *Our Living Resources;* D'Antonio and Vitousek, "Biological Invasions by Exotic Grasses."

Chapter 8

231   a few key regions: My discussion of the geography of endangered species is based largely on A. P. Dobson, J. P. Rodriguez, W. M. Roberts, and D. S. Wilcove, "Geographic Distribution of Endangered Species in the United States," *Science* 275 (1997): 550–53.

232   most recent assessment by the U.S. Fish and Wildlife Service: *Report to Congress: Recovery Program, Endangered and Threatened Species* (Washington, D.C.: U.S. Fish and Wildlife Service, 1994).

233   A 1993 study: D. S. Wilcove, M. McMillan, and K. C. Winston, "What Exactly Is an Endangered Species? An Analysis of the U.S. Endangered Species List: 1985–1991," *Conservation Biology* 7 (1993): 87–93.

233   the endangered species budget: The budget figures for the U.S. Fish and Wildlife Service are based on fiscal years, not calendar years. They were taken from F. Campbell, "The Appropriations History," in *Balancing on the Brink of Extinction,* edited by K. A. Kohm (Washington, D.C.: Island Press, 1991) for 1978 and from the U.S. Department of the Interior for 1998. To account for inflation, I adjusted the 1998 figure downward using the "All Urban Consumers" Consumer Price Index from the Bureau of Labor Statistics, U.S. Department of Labor (<http://stats.bls.gov/news.release/cpi>). A CPI for 1998 was obtained by averaging the first six months of the year. The number of endangered species was calculated as of the start of each fiscal year (September 30, 1977 and September 30, 1997). To be completely accurate, one should delete from the endangered species totals those species under the jurisdiction of the National Marine Fisheries Service, which has jurisdiction over certain endangered marine animals. If one does so, then the numbers of endangered species under the care of the Fish and Wildlife Service are 190 in 1978 and 1,090 in 1998. This minor correction does not change the conclusion that the Fish and Wildlife Service is being asked to do more with less.

234   nearly half of all the dollars expended: U.S. General Accounting Office, *Endangered Species: Management Improvements Could Enhance Recovery Program,* GAO/RCED-89-5 (Washington, D.C.: U.S. General Accounting Office, 1988).

234 "I'm going to start massive clearcutting": I. C. Sugg, "Ecosystem Babbitt-Babble," *Wall Street Journal*, 2 April 1993.

234 "safe harbor" policy: The originator of the safe harbor concept, I am proud to say, is my colleague Michael Bean at the Environmental Defense Fund. For more information about the safe harbor program, see R. Bonnie, "Safe Harbor for the Red-cockaded Woodpecker," *Journal of Forestry* 95 (4) (1997): 17–22; D. S. Wilcove, M. J. Bean, R. Bonnie, and M. McMillan, *Rebuilding the Ark: Toward a More Effective Endangered Species Act for Private Land* (Washington, D.C.: Environmental Defense Fund, 1996).

235 By one estimate: D. S. Wilcove and L. Y. Chen, "Management Costs for Endangered Species," *Conservation Biology* 12 (1998): 1405–07.

237 global climate change: For more information on the effects of global climate change, see J. T. Houghton, L. G. Meira Filho, B. A. Callander, N. Harris, A. Kattenberg, and K. Maskell (eds.), *Climate Change 1995: The Science of Climate Change*, part I of the Working Group Contribution to the Second Assessment Report of the Intergovernmental Panel on Climate Change (Cambridge: Cambridge University Press, 1995); R. L. Peters and T. E. Lovejoy (eds.), *Global Warming and Biological Diversity* (New Haven, Conn.: Yale University Press, 1992).

238 the California condor: My history of the California condor is taken largely from U.S. Fish and Wildlife Service, *California Condor Recovery Plan*, third revision (Portland, Oreg.: U.S. Fish and Wildlife Service, 1996) and from conversations with L. Kiff of The Peregrine Fund.

240 their numbers dropped: Two problems in particular seem to have driven the condor's decline in the 1970s and 1980s. First, condors continued to be shot by thugs, despite stringent protection under the Endangered Species Act and an extensive public education campaign. Second, a number of condors died from lead poisoning, apparently contracted when they fed on the carcasses of deer that had been shot with lead bullets.

241 nineteen condors: The number of condors in California is current as of March 20, 1998.

241 the Grand Canyon: S. D. Emslie, "Age and Diet of Fossil California Condors in Grand Canyon, Arizona," *Science* 237 (1987): 768–70.

Literature Cited

Alcock, J. *The Masked Bobwhite Rides Again.* Tucson: University of Arizona Press, 1993.

Alkire, C. *Wild Salmon as Natural Capital.* Washington, D.C.: The Wilderness Society, 1993.

Allan, J. D., and A. S. Flecker. "Biodiversity Conservation in Running Waters." *BioScience* 43 (1993): 32–43.

Allen, J. A. *History of North American Pinnipeds. A Monograph of the Walruses, Sea-Lions, Sea-Bears, and Seals of North America.* United States Geological and Geographical Survey of the Territories, Miscellaneous Publications no. 12. Washington, D.C.: U.S. Department of the Interior, 1880.

Alverson, W., D. Waller, and S. Solheim. "Forests Too Deer: Edge Effects in Northern Wisconsin." *Conservation Biology* 2 (1988): 348–58.

Askins, R. A. "Population Trends in Grassland, Shrubland, and Forest Birds in Eastern North America." *Current Ornithology* 11 (1993): 1–34.

Atkinson, D. E. "Science versus Environmental Advocacy." *BioScience* 46 (1996): 794.

Bagwell, K. "Cattlemen Want to Tame Quail Preserve." *Arizona Daily Star,* 10 December 1995.

Bailey, D. "Protecting Aquatic Diversity from Toxic Effluents: The Clinch River Experience." In *The Big Kill: Declining Biodiversity in America's Lakes and Rivers,* edited by D. S. Wilcove and M. J. Bean. Washington, D.C.: Environmental Defense Fund, 1994.

Balgooyen, C. P., and D. M. Waller. "The Use of *Clintonia borealis* and Other Indicators to Gauge Impacts of White-tailed Deer on Plant Communities in Northern Wisconsin, USA." *Natural Areas Journal* 15 (1995): 308–18.

Balzar, J. "Columbia River Sockeye Salmon Ruled Imperiled." *Los Angeles Times,* 3 April 1991.

Bancroft, G. T., A. M. Strong, and M. Carrington. "Deforestation and Its Effects on Forest-Nesting Birds in the Florida Keys." *Conservation Biology* 9 (1995): 835–44.

Bangs, E. E., and S. H. Fritts. "Reintroduction of Gray Wolves to Yellowstone National Park and Central Idaho." *Endangered Species Technical Bulletin* 18, no. 3 (1993): 19.

Bean, M. J. "Conserving Endangered Species by Accident: The Duck River Experience." In *The Big Kill: Declining Biodiversity in America's Lakes and Rivers*, edited by D. S. Wilcove and M. J. Bean. Washington, D.C.: Environmental Defense Fund, 1994.

Bean, M. J., and M. J. Rowland. *The Evolution of National Wildlife Law.* 3d ed. Westport, Conn.: Praeger, 1997.

Begley, S., L. Wilson, M. Hager, and P. Annin. "Return of the Wolf." *Newsweek*, 12 August 1991.

Belsky, A. J., and D. M. Blumenthal. "Effects of Livestock Grazing on Stand Dynamics and Soils in Upland Forests of the Interior West." *Conservation Biology* 11 (1997): 315–27.

Benke, A. C. "A Perspective on America's Vanishing Streams." *Journal of the North American Benthological Society* 9 (1990): 77–88.

Benson, A. J., and C. P. Boydstun. "Invasion of the Zebra Mussel in the United States." In *Our Living Resources: A Report to the Nation on the Distribution, Abundance, and Health of U.S. Plants, Animals, and Ecosystems*, edited by E. T. LaRoe. Washington, D.C.: National Biological Service, 1995.

Bent, A. C. *Life Histories of North American Gallinaceous Birds.* 1932. Reprint, New York: Dover, 1963.

Bent, A. C. *Life Histories of North American Gulls and Terns.* 1921. Reprint, New York: Dover, 1963.

Bent, A. C. *Life Histories of North American Shore Birds.* 2 vols. 1927. Reprint, New York: Dover, 1962.

Bent, A. C. *Life Histories of North American Wild Fowl.* United States National Museum Bulletin no. 126. Washington, D.C.: Smithsonian Institution, 1923.

Berger, A. J. *Hawaiian Birdlife.* 2d ed. Honolulu: University of Hawaii Press, 1981.

Blockstein, D. E., and H. B. Tordoff. "Gone Forever: A Contemporary Look at the Extinction of the Passenger Pigeon." *American Birds* 39 (1985): 845–51.

Blodget, B. G. "The East Coast Gull Explosion." *Massachusetts Wildlife* 38, no. 1 (1988): 12–19.

Blodget, B. G. "The Half-Century Battle for Gull Control." *Massachusetts Wildlife* 38, no. 2 (1988): 4–10.

Bollinger, E. K., P. B. Bollinger, and T. A. Gavin. "Effects of Hay-Cropping on Eastern Populations of the Bobolink." *Wildlife Society Bulletin* 18 (1990): 142–50.

Bonnie, R. "Safe Harbor for the Red-cockaded Woodpecker." *Journal of Forestry* 95 (4) (1997): 17–22.

Booth, W. "Questioned Pedigree Clouds Wolf Program." *Washington Post*, 20 June 1991.

Bourne, J. "Treasures in the Scrub." *Defenders*, November–December 1991.

Bragg, T. B., and A. A. Steuter. "Prairie Ecology—The Mixed Prairie." In *Prairie Conservation: Preserving North America's Most Endangered Ecosystem*, edited by F. B. Samson and F. L. Knopf. Washington, D.C.: Island Press, 1996.

Brody, J. "Water-Based Animals Are Becoming Extinct Faster Than Others." *New York Times*, 23 April 1991.

Brown, H. "The Conditions Governing Bird Life in Arizona." *Auk* 17 (1900): 31–34.

Brown, H. "Masked Bobwhite *(Colinus ridgwayi)*." *Auk* 21 (1904): 209–13.

Brown, N. C. "Lower Rio Grande Valley National Wildlife Refuge," *Endangered Species Bulletin* 23, no. 4 (1998): 36–39.

Brush, T., and A. Cantu. "Changes in the Breeding Bird Community of Subtropical Evergreen Forest in the Lower Rio Grande Valley of Texas, 1970s–1990s." *Texas Journal of Science* 50 (1998): 123–32.

Bureau of the Census. *Statistical Abstract of the United States.* Washington, D.C.: U.S. Government Printing Office, 1995.

Burger, J. *Oil Spills.* New Brunswick, N.J.: Rutgers University Press, 1997.

Butler, R. G., A. Harfenist, F. A. Leighton, and D. B. Peakall. "Impact of Sublethal Oil and Emulsion Exposure on the Reproductive Success of Leach's Storm-petrels: Short and Long-Term Effects." *Journal of Applied Ecology* 25 (1988): 125–43.

Cadieux, C. *These Are the Endangered.* Washington, D.C.: Stone Wall Press, 1981.

Campbell, F. "The Appropriations History." In *Balancing on the Brink of Extinction*, edited by K. A. Kohm. Washington, D.C.: Island Press, 1991.

Campbell, F. T., and S. E. Schlarbaum. *Fading Forests: North American Trees and the Threats of Exotic Pests.* New York: Natural Resources Defense Council, 1994.

Casey, T. L. C., and J. D. Jacobi. "A New Genus and Species of Bird from the Island of Maui, Hawaii (Passeriformes: Drepanididae)." *Occasional Papers of the Bernice P. Bishop Museum, Honolulu, Hawaii* 24 (1974): 215–26.

Castillo, C. D. *Effects of Artificial Flooding on the Vegetation and Avifauna of Riparian Woodlands at Santa Ana National Wildlife Refuge, Hidalgo County, Texas.* Master's thesis, University of Texas, Pan-American, 1997.

Chadde, S. W., and C. E. Kay. "Tall-Willow Communities on Yellowstone's Northern Range: A Test of the 'Natural Regulation' Paradigm." In *The Greater Yellowstone Ecosystem: Redefining America's Wilderness Heritage*, edited by R. B. Keiter and M. S. Boyce. New Haven: Yale University Press, 1991.

Chapman, F. M. *The Warblers of North America.* New York: D. Appleton & Company, 1907.

Chase, A. *Playing God in Yellowstone.* Boston: Atlantic Monthly Press, 1986.

Christensen, N. L. et al. "Interpreting the Yellowstone Fires of 1988." *BioScience* 39 (1989): 678–85.

Clark, T. W., T. M. Campbell III, D. G. Socha, and D. E. Casey. "Prairie Dog Colony Attributes and Associated Vertebrate Species." *Great Basin Naturalist* 42 (1982): 572–82.

Cohen, A. N. *An Introduction to the Ecology of the San Francisco Estuary.* Oakland, Calif.: San Francisco Estuary Project, 1991.

Cohen, A. N., and J. T. Carlton. "Accelerating Invasion Rate in a Highly Invaded Estuary." *Science* 279 (1998): 555–58.

Cohen, A. N., and J. T. Carlton. *Non-indigenous Aquatic Species in a United States Estuary: A Case Study of the Biological Invasion of the San Francisco Bay and Delta.* A report for the U.S. Fish and Wildlife Service and the National Sea Grant College Program. Washington D.C.: U.S. Fish and Wildlife Service, 1995.

Cohn, D. "Shenandoah Hemlocks Under Siege." *Washington Post*, 4 September 1993.

Collar, N. J., M. J. Crosby, and A. J. Stattersfield. *Birds to Watch 2: The World List of Threatened Birds.* Cambridge: BirdLife International, 1994.

Collar, N. J., L. P. Gonzaga, N. Krabbe, A. Madroño Nieto, L. G. Naranjo, T. A. Parker III, and D. C. Wege. *Threatened Birds of the Americas. The ICBP/IUCN Red Data Book.* Washington, D.C.: Smithsonian Institution Press, 1992.

Conaway, J. "Eastern Wildlife—Bittersweet Success." *National Geographic*, February 1992.

Cooper, C. F. "Changes in Vegetation, Structure, and Growth of Southwestern Pine Forests Since White Settlement." *Ecological Monographs* 30 (1960): 129–64.

Cooperrider, A. Y., and D. S. Wilcove. *Defending the Desert: Conserving Biodiversity on BLM Lands in the Southwest.* Washington, D.C.: Environmental Defense Fund, 1995.

Coppock, D. L., J. K. Detling, J. E. Ellis, and M. I. Dyer. "Plant-Herbivore Interactions in a North-American Mixed-Grass Prairie." *Oecologia* 56 (1983): 1–9.

Cronon, W. *Changes in the Land: Indians, Colonists, and the Ecology of New England.* New York: Hill and Wang, 1983.

Culliney, J. L. *Islands in a Far Sea: Nature and Man in Hawaii.* San Francisco: Sierra Club Books, 1988.

D'Antonio, C. M., and P. M. Vitousek. "Biological Invasions by Exotic Grasses, the Grass/Fire Cycle, and Global Change." *Annual Review of Ecology and Systematics* 23 (1992): 63–87.

Davis, S. M., and J. C. Ogden, eds. *Everglades: The Ecosystem and Its Restoration.* Delray Beach, Fla.: St. Lucie Press, 1994.

Davis, S. M., and J. C. Ogden. "Toward Ecosystem Restoration." In

Everglades: The Ecosystem and Its Restoration, edited by S. M. Davis and J. C. Ogden. Delray Beach, Fla.: St. Lucie Press, 1994.

DeBlieu, J. *Meant to Be Wild: The Struggle to Save Endangered Species Through Captive Breeding.* Golden, Colo.: Fulcrum Publishing, 1991.

Derr, M. "Redeeming the Everglades." *Audubon,* September–October 1993.

Derr, M. *Some Kind of Paradise: A Chronicle of Man and Land in Florida.* New York: William Morrow, 1989.

Despain, D., D. Houston, M. Meagher, and P. Schullery. *Wildlife in Transition: Man and Nature on Yellowstone's Northern Range.* Boulder, Colo.: Roberts Rinehart, 1986.

Diamond, J. "Must We Shoot Deer to Save Nature?" *Natural History,* August 1992.

Dickson, J. G. "Birds and Mammals of Pre-Colonial Southern Old-Growth Forests." *Natural Areas Journal* 11 (1991): 26–33.

"A Disease of Dogwoods is Unmasked." *New York Times,* 14 May 1991.

DiSilvestro, R. *The Endangered Kingdom: The Struggle to Save America's Wildlife.* New York: John Wiley & Sons, 1989.

Dixon, E. J. *Quest for the First Americans.* Albuquerque: University of New Mexico Press, 1993.

Dobson, A. P., J. P. Rodriguez, W. M. Roberts, and D. S. Wilcove. "Geographic Distribution of Endangered Species in the United States." *Science* 275 (1997): 550–53.

Dodd, C. K. Jr. "Nesting of the Green Turtle, *Chelonia mydas* (L.) in Florida: Historic Review and Present Trends." *Brimleyana* 7 (1981): 39–54.

Dold, C. "Six Year Effort to Return Red Wolves to Wild is Making Headway." *New York Times,* 5 October 1993.

Douglas, M. S. *The Everglades: River of Grass.* New York: Rinehart, 1947.

Douglis, C. "A Corridor in Peril." *Wilderness,* Winter 1989.

Duggins, D. O., C. A. Simenstad, and J. A. Estes. "Magnification of Secondary Production by Kelp Detritus in Coastal Marine Ecosystems." *Science* 245 (1989): 170–73.

Dunn, J., and K. Garrett. *A Field Guide to the Warblers of North America*. Boston: Houghton Mifflin, 1997.

Durkin, P. "Too Many Deer Pose a Dilemma for the Nation's Parks." *Bangor Daily News*, 5–6 January 1991.

Dynesius, M., and C. Nilsson. "Fragmentation and Flow Regulation of River Systems in the Northern Third of the World." *Science* 266 (1994): 753–62.

"Effort to Reintroduce Thick-billed Parrots in Arizona is Dropped." *New York Times*, 30 May 1995.

Egan, T. "Fight to Save Salmon Starts Fight Over Water." *New York Times*, 1 April 1991.

Eisner, T., J. Lubchenco, E. O. Wilson, D. S. Wilcove, and M. J. Bean. "Building a Scientifically Sound Policy for Protecting Endangered Species." *Science* 269 (1995): 1231–32.

Elfring, C. "Yellowstone: Fire Storm Over Fire Management." *BioScience* 39 (1989): 667–72.

Emmel, T. C., and J. C. Daniels. "Is Schaus' Swallowtail Finally Licked?" *American Butterflies* 5, no. 2 (1997): 20–26.

Emmons, L. H., and F. Feer. *Neotropical Rainforest Mammals: A Field Guide*. 2d ed. Chicago: University of Chicago Press, 1997.

Emslie, S. D. "Age and Diet of Fossil California Condors in Grand Canyon, Arizona." *Science* 237 (1987): 768–70.

England, R. E., and A. DeVos. "Influence of Animals on Pristine Conditions on the Canadian Grasslands." *Journal of Range Management* 22 (1969): 87–94.

Estes, J. A., D. O. Duggins, and G. B. Rathbun. "The Ecology of Extinctions in Kelp Forest Communities." *Conservation Biology* 3 (1989): 252–64.

Estes, J. A., M. T. Tinker, T. M. Williams, and D. F. Doak. "Killer Whale Predation on Sea Otters Linking Oceanic and Nearshore Ecosystems." *Science* 282 (1998): 473–76.

Exxon Valdez Oil Spill Trustee Council. Exxon Valdez *Oil Spill Restoration Plan: Update on Injured Resources and Services, September 1996*. Anchorage, Alaska: *Exxon Valdez* Oil Spill Trustee Council, 1996.

Fergus, C. "Scrub: Learning to Love It." *Audubon*, May–June 1993.

Ferry, G. W, R. G. Clark, R. E. Montgomery, R. W. Mutch, W. P. Leenhouts, and G. T. Zimmerman. "Altered Fire Regimes within Fire-Adapted Ecosystems." In *Our Living Resources: A Report to the Nation on the Distribution, Abundance, and Health of U.S. Plants, Animals, and Ecosystems*, edited by E. T. LaRoe. Washington, D.C.: National Biological Service, 1995.

Finch, D. *Population Ecology, Habitat Requirements, and Conservation of Neotropical Migratory Birds*. General Technical Report RM-205. Ft. Collins, Colo.: U.S. Forest Service, 1991.

Finch, D. M., J. L. Ganey, W. Yong, R. T. Kimball, and R. Sallabanks. "Effects and Interactions of Fire, Logging, and Grazing." In *Songbird Ecology in Southwestern Ponderosa Pine Forests: A Literature Review*, edited by W. H. Block and D. M. Finch. General Technical Report RM-GTR-292. Ft. Collins, Colo.: U.S. Forest Service, 1997.

Fitzpatrick, J. W. "Florida's Vanishing Scrubland." *In the Field* (Bulletin of the Field Museum of Natural History), January–February 1991.

Fitzpatrick, J. W., and G. E. Woolfenden. "The Helpful Shall Inherit the Scrub." *Natural History*, May 1984.

Foote, D., and H. L. Carson. "*Drosophila* as Monitors of Change in Hawaiian Ecosystems." In *Our Living Resources: A Report to the Nation on the Distribution, Abundance, and Health of U.S. Plants, Animals, and Ecosystems*, edited by E. T. LaRoe. Washington, D.C.: National Biological Service, 1995.

Ford, P. "How the Basin's Salmon-Killing System Works." *High Country News*, 22 April 1991.

Forshaw, J. M. *Parrots of the World*. 2d (rev.) ed. Melbourne, Australia: Landsdowne Press, 1978.

Forsman, E. D. "The Spotted Owl: Literature Review." In *Final Supplement to the Environmental Impact Statement for an Amendment to the Pacific Northwest Regional Guide. Spotted Owl Guidelines*. Portland, Oreg.: U.S. Forest Service, 1988.

Frank, D. A., and S. J. McNaughton. "Evidence for the Promotion of Aboveground Grassland Production by Native Large Herbivores in Yellowstone National Park." *Oecologia* 96 (1993): 157–61.

Freed, L. A., S. Conant, and R. C. Fleischer. "Evolutionary Ecology and Radiation of Hawaiian Passerine Birds." *Trends in Ecology and Evolution* 2 (1987): 196–203.

Frost, C. C. "Four Centuries of Changing Landscape Patterns in the Longleaf Pine Ecosystem." In *Proceedings of the Tall Timbers Fire Ecology Conference*, no. 18, edited by S. M. Hermann. Tallahassee, Fla.: Tall Timbers Research Station, 1993.

Fule, P. Z., W. W. Covington, and M. M. Moore. "Determining Reference Conditions for Ecosystem Management of Southwestern Ponderosa Pine Forests." *Ecological Applications* 7 (1997): 895–908.

Fuller, E. *Extinct Birds*. New York: Facts on File Publications, 1987.

Fuller, E. *The Great Auk*. Southborough, England: Errol Fuller, 1998.

Gifford, B. "The Government's Too-Sweet Deal." *Washington Post*, 9 January 1994.

Gilbert, L. "Food Web Organization and the Conservation of Neotropical Diversity." In *Conservation Biology: An Evolutionary-Ecological Perspective*, edited by M. Soulé and B. Wilcox. Sunderland, Mass.: Sinauer Associates, 1980.

Goodman, B. "Keeping Anglers Happy Has a Price." *BioScience* 41 (1991): 294–99.

Graber, R. R., and J. W. Graber. "A Comparative Study of Bird Populations in Illinois, 1906–1909 and 1956–1958." *Illinois Natural History Survey Bulletin* 28, no. 3 (1963): 383–528.

Graham, F. "Kite vs. Stork." *Audubon*, March 1990.

Gray, P. "A Fight Over Liquid Gold." *Time*, 22 July 1991.

Greenway, J. C. Jr. *Extinct and Vanishing Birds of the World*. 1958. Reprint, New York: Dover, 1967.

Grinnell, J., H. C. Bryant, and T. I. Storer. *The Game Birds of California*. Berkeley: University of California Press, 1918.

Guggisberg, C. A. W. *Wild Cats of the World*. New York: Taplinger, 1975.

Hagan, J. M., and D. W. Johnston, eds. *Ecology and Conservation of Neotropical Migrant Landbirds*. Washington, D.C.: Smithsonian Institution Press, 1992.

Halliday, T. *Vanishing Birds: Their Natural History and Conservation.* New York: Holt, Rinehart, and Winston, 1978.

Hansen, M. J., and J. W. Peck. "Lake Trout in the Great Lakes." In *Our Living Resources: A Report to the Nation on the Distribution, Abundance, and Health of U.S. Plants, Animals, and Ecosystems,* edited by E. T. LaRoe. Washington, D.C.: National Biological Service, 1995.

Hardin, J. W., W. D. Klimstra, and N. J. Silvy. "Florida Keys." In *White-tailed Deer: Ecology and Management,* edited by L. K. Halls. Harrisburg, Pa.: Stackpole Books, 1984.

Harrington, B. A., J. P. Myers, and J. S. Grear. "Coastal Refueling Sites for Global Bird Migrants." In *Coastal Zone '89: Proceedings of the Sixth Symposium on Coastal and Ocean Management,* 4293–4307. New York: American Society of Civil Engineers, 1989.

Harting, A., and D. Glick. *Sustaining Greater Yellowstone: A Blueprint for the Future.* Bozeman, Mont.: Greater Yellowstone Coalition, 1994.

Hartman, W. L. *Effects of Exploitation, Environmental Changes, and New Species on the Fish Habitats and Resources of Lake Erie.* Technical Report no. 22. Ann Arbor, Mich.: Great Lakes Fishery Commission, 1973.

Hartnett, D. C., A. A. Steuter, and K. R. Hickman. "Comparative Ecology of Native and Introduced Ungulates." *Ecological Studies* 125 (1997): 72–101.

Harwell, G., and D. P. Siminski. *Listed Cats of Texas and Arizona Recovery Plan (with Emphasis on the Ocelot).* Albuquerque, N.Mex.: U.S. Fish and Wildlife Service, 1990.

Hebert, P. D., C. C. Wilson, M. H. Murdoch, and R. Lazar. "Demography and Ecological Impacts of the Invading Mollusc *Dreissena polymorpha." Canadian Journal of Zoology* 69 (1991): 405–9.

Hejl, S. J. "Human-Induced Changes in Bird Populations in Coniferous Forests in Western North America in the Past 100 Years." In *A Century of Avifaunal Change in Western North America,* edited by J. R. Jehl Jr. and N. K. Johnson. Studies in Avian Biology, no. 15. San Diego, Calif.: Cooper Ornithological Society, 1994.

Herkert, J. R. "Bobolink *Dolichonyx oryzivorus* Population Decline in Agricultural Landscapes in the Midwestern U.S.A." *Biological Conservation* 80 (1977): 107–12.

Herkert, J. R. "The Effects of Habitat Fragmentation on Midwestern

Grassland Bird Communities." *Ecological Applications* 4 (1994): 461–71.

Herkert, J. R., R. E. Szafoni, V. M. Kleen, and J. E. Schwegman. *Habitat Establishment, Enhancement, and Management for Forest and Grassland Birds in Illinois.* Natural Heritage Technical Publication no. 1. Springfield: Division of Natural Heritage, Illinois Department of Conservation, 1993.

Hershner, C., and J. Lake. "Effects of Chronic Oil Pollution on a Salt-Marsh Grass Community." *Marine Biology* 56 (1980): 163–73.

Higgins, K. F. *Interpretation and Compendium of Historical Fire Accounts in the Northern Great Plains.* Resource Publication no. 161. Washington, D.C.: U.S. Fish and Wildlife Service, 1986.

Hilborn, R. "Hatcheries and the Future of Salmon in the Northwest." *Fisheries* 17, no. 1 (1991): 5–8.

Holden, P. "Ghosts of the Green River: Impacts of the Green River Poisoning on Management of Native Fishes." In *Battle Against Extinction: Native Fish Management in the American West,* edited by W. L. Minckley and J. E. Deacon. Tucson: University of Arizona Press, 1991.

Holmes, B. "The Big Importance of Little Towns on the Prairie." *National Wildlife,* June–July 1996.

Holmes, W. N., and J. Cronshaw. "Biological Effects of Petroleum on Marine Birds." In *Effects of Petroleum on Arctic and Subarctic Marine Environments and Organisms,* vol. 2, *Biological Effects,* edited by D. C. Mains. New York: Academic Press, 1977.

Hood, L. C. *Frayed Safety Nets: Conservation Planning Under the Endangered Species Act.* Washington, D.C.: Defenders of Wildlife, 1998.

Hooper, R. G. "Longleaf Pines Used for Cavities By Red-cockaded Woodpeckers." *Journal of Wildlife Management* 52 (1988): 392–98.

Hornaday, W. T. *The Extermination of the American Bison.* Report of the U.S. National Museum, 1886–1887. Washington, D.C.: U.S. National Museum, 1889.

Horton, T. "Deer on Your Doorstep." *New York Times Magazine,* 28 April 1991.

Horton, T., and W. Eichbaum. *Turning the Tide: Saving the Chesapeake Bay.* Washington, D.C.: Island Press, 1991.

Houghton, J. T., L. G. Meira Filho, B. A. Callander, N. Harris, A. Kattenberg, and K. Maskell (eds.). *Climate Change 1995: The Science of Climate Change.* Part I of the Working Group Contribution to the Second Assessment Report of the Intergovernmental Panel on Climate Change. Cambridge: Cambridge University Press, 1995.

Houston, D. B. *The Northern Yellowstone Elk: Ecology and Management.* New York: Macmillan, 1982.

Howarth, F. G., G. Nishida, and A. Asquith. "Insects of Hawaii." In *Our Living Resources: A Report to the Nation on the Distribution, Abundance, and Health of U.S. Plants, Animals, and Ecosystems,* edited by E. T. LaRoe. Washington, D.C.: National Biological Service, 1995.

Howe, M. A., P. H. Geissler, and B. A. Harrington. "Population Trends of North American Shorebirds Based on the International Shorebird Survey." *Biological Conservation* 49 (1989): 185–99.

Hughes, F., P. M. Vitousek, and T. Tunison. "Alien Grass Invasion and Fire in the Seasonal Submontane Zone of Hawaii." *Ecology* 72 (1991): 743–46.

Humphrey, S. R. "Density Estimates of the Endangered Key Largo Woodrat and Cotton Mouse (*Neotoma floridana smalli* and *Peromyscus gossypinus allapaticola*) Using the Nested-Grid Approach." *Journal of Mammalogy* 69 (1988): 524–31.

Humphrey, S. R., and B. Bell. "The Key Deer Population Is Declining." *Wildlife Society Bulletin* 14 (1986): 262–65.

Hutto, R. L. "Composition of Bird Communities Following Stand-Replacement Fires in Northern Rocky Mountain (U.S.A.) Conifer Forests." *Conservation Biology* 9 (1995): 1041–58.

Jackson, J. B. C. "Reefs Since Columbus." *Coral Reefs* 16 (Supplement) (1997): S23–S32.

Jacobi, J. D., and C. T. Atkinson. "Hawaii's Endemic Birds." In *Our Living Resources: A Report to the Nation on the Distribution, Abundance, and Health of U.S. Plants, Animals, and Ecosystems,* edited by E. T. LaRoe. Washington, D.C.: National Biological Service, 1995.

Jahrsdoerfer, S. E., and D. M. Leslie Jr. *Tamaulipan Brushland of the Lower Rio Grande Valley of South Texas: Description, Human Impacts, and Management Options.* Biological Report 88 (36). Washington, D.C.: U.S. Fish and Wildlife Service, 1988.

James, F. C. "The Status of the Red-cockaded Woodpecker in 1990 and the Prospect for Recovery." In *The Red-cockaded Woodpecker: Species Recovery, Ecology, and Management*, edited by D. L. Kulhavy, R. Costa, and R. G. Hooper. Nacogdoches, Tex.: Stephen F. Austin State University, 1995.

James, F. C., D. Widenfield, and C. McCulloch. "Trends in Breeding Populations of Warblers." In *Ecology and Conservation of Neotropical Migrant Landbirds*, edited by J. M. Hagan and D. W. Johnston. Washington, D.C.: Smithsonian Institution Press, 1992.

Johnson, D. H., and R. K. Koford. "Conservation Reserve Program and Migratory Birds in the Northern Great Plains." In *Our Living Resources: A Report to the Nation on the Distribution, Abundance, and Health of U.S. Plants, Animals, and Ecosystems*, edited by E. T. LaRoe. Washington, D.C.: National Biological Service, 1995.

Johnson, R. G., and S. A. Temple. "Nest Predation and Brood Parasitism of Tallgrass Prairie Birds." *Journal of Wildlife Management* 54 (1990): 106–11.

Johnson, T. B., N. F. R. Snyder, and H. A. Snyder. "The Return of Thick-billed Parrots to Arizona." *Endangered Species Technical Bulletin* 14 (1989): 1–5.

Kaiser, J. "Sea Otter Declines Blamed on Hungry Killers." *Science* 282 (1998): 390–91.

Kale, H. W., ed. *Rare and Endangered Biota of Florida*. Vol. 2, *Birds*. Gainesville: University of Florida Press, 1978.

Karr, J. R., J. D. Allan, and A. C. Benke. "River Conservation in North America: Science, Policy, and Practice." In *Global Perspectives on River Conservation*, edited by P. J. Boon, B. R. Davies, and G. E. Petts. West Sussex, England: John Wiley & Sons, in press.

Kaufman, K. *Lives of North American Birds*. Boston: Houghton Mifflin, 1996.

Kay, C. E. "An Alternative Interpretation of the Historical Evidence Relating to the Abundance of Wolves in the Yellowstone Ecosystem." Paper presented at the Second North American Symposium on Wolves: Their Status, Biology, and Management, University of Edmonton, Edmonton, Alberta, 25–27 August 1992.

Kay, C. E. "The Impact of Native Ungulates and Beaver on Riparian

Communities in the Intermountain West." *Natural Resources and Environmental Issues* 1 (1994): 24–44.

Kay, C. E., and F. H. Wagner. "Historical Condition of Woody Vegetation on Yellowstone's Northern Range: A Critical Evaluation of the 'Natural Regulation' Paradigm." Paper presented at the First Biennial Scientific Conference on the Greater Yellowstone Ecosystem, Yellowstone National Park, Mammoth Hot Springs, Wyo., 16–17 September 1991.

Keniry, T., and J. E. Marsden. "Zebra Mussels in Southwestern Lake Michigan." In *Our Living Resources: A Report to the Nation on the Distribution, Abundance, and Health of U.S. Plants, Animals, and Ecosystems*, edited by E. T. LaRoe. Washington, D.C.: National Biological Service, 1995.

Kenworthy, T. "Last Ditch Effort to Preserve Sockeye." *Washington Post*, 14 January 1993.

Kirsch, E. M. "Small Mammal Community Composition in Cornfields, Roadside Ditches, and Prairies in Eastern Nebraska." *Natural Areas Journal* 17 (1997): 204–11.

Klinkenberg, J. "Vanishing Habitat." *St. Petersburg Times*, 20 May 1990.

Knopf, F. L. "A Closer Look: Mountain Plover." *Birding* 29, no. 1 (1997): 39–44.

Knopf, F. L. "Declining Grassland Birds." In *Our Living Resources: A Report to the Nation on the Distribution, Abundance, and Health of U.S. Plants, Animals, and Ecosystems*, edited by E. T. LaRoe. Washington, D.C.: National Biological Service, 1995.

Koberstein, P. "Are Hatcheries Producing Salmon 'Wimps'?" *High Country News*, 22 April 1991.

Krautkraemer, J. "Using Market Forces to Protect Biodiversity: The Central Valley Project Improvement Act." In *The Big Kill: Declining Biodiversity in America's Lakes and Rivers*, edited by D. S. Wilcove and M. J. Bean. Washington, D.C.: Environmental Defense Fund, 1994.

Krueger, C. C., and B. May. "Ecological and Genetic Effects of Salmonid Introductions in North America." *Canadian Journal of Fisheries and Aquatic Sciences* 48 (1991), suppl. 1: 66–77.

Krueger, K. "Feeding Relationships Among Bison, Pronghorn, and Prairie Dogs: An Experimental Analysis." *Ecology* 67 (1986): 760–70.

Kurtén, B. *Before the Indians.* New York: Columbia University Press, 1988.

Laycock, G. "Good Times Are Killing the Keys." *Audubon,* September–October 1991.

Lazell, J. D. Jr. *Wildlife of the Florida Keys: A Natural History.* Washington, D.C.: Island Press, 1989.

Leary, W. "First U.S. Refuge for Plants Sought in Florida." *New York Times,* 18 June 1991.

Lee, D. S. "Maryland's Vanishing Birds and Mammals: Reflections of Ethics Past." In *Threatened and Endangered Plants and Animals of Maryland,* edited by A. W. Norden, D. C. Forester, and G. Fenwick. Natural Heritage Special Publication 84-1. Annapolis. Maryland Department of Natural Resources, 1984.

Leopold, A. S., S. A. Cain, C. M. Cottam, I. N. Gabrielson, and T. L. Kimball. *Wildlife Management in the National Parks.* Report of the Advisory Board on Wildlife Management appointed by Secretary of the Interior Udall, 4 March 1963.

Line, L. "Endangered Clapper Rails Making a Recovery." *New York Times,* 22 August 1995.

Line, L. "Phantom of the Plains." *Wildlife Conservation,* August 1997.

Loiselle, B., and W. Hoppes. "Nest Predation in Insular and Lowland Rainforest in Panama." *Condor* 85 (1983): 93–95.

Lowe, D. W., J. R. Matthews, and C. J. Mosley (eds.). *The Official World Wildlife Fund Guide to Endangered Species of North America.* Washington, D.C.: Beacham Publishing, 1990.

Luoma, J. R. "Biography of a Lake." *Audubon,* September–October 1996.

Luoma, J. R. "Oceanfront Battlefront." *Audubon,* July–August 1998.

MacCleery, D. W. *American Forests: A History of Resiliency and Recovery.* Publication FS-540. Washington, D.C.: U.S. Forest Service, 1992.

Mackey, H. L. E. Jr., and N. Sivec. "The Present Composition of a Former Oak-Chestnut Forest in the Allegheny Mountains of Western Pennsylvania." *Ecology* 54 (1973): 915–19.

Madson, J. "Bringing the 'Bou Back to Its Old Stomping Grounds." *Smithsonian,* May 1991.

Mairson, A. "The Everglades: Dying for Help." *National Geographic*, April 1994.

Makarewicz, J. C., and P. Bertram. "Evidence for the Restoration of the Lake Erie Ecosystem." *BioScience* 41 (1991): 216–23.

Malakoff, D. "Extinction on the High Seas." *Science* 277 (1997): 486–88.

Mansueti, R. "Extinct and Vanishing Mammals of Maryland and District of Columbia." *Maryland Naturalist* 22 (Winter-Spring 1950): 3–48.

Manville, R. H. "The Extinct Sea Mink, with Taxonomic Notes." *Proceedings of the United States National Museum* 122, no. 3584 (1996): 1–12.

Maril, R. L. *The Poorest of Americans: The Mexican Americans of the Lower Rio Grande Valley of Texas*. Notre Dame, Ind.: University of Notre Dame Press, 1989.

Martin, D. "Helping Nature Restore Life to a Waterway Left for Dead." *New York Times*, 30 September 1994.

Martin, P. S. "Refuting Late Pleistocene Extinction Models." In *Dynamics of Extinction*, edited by D. K. Elliot. New York: John Wiley & Sons, 1986.

Maryland Office of Planning. *State of Maryland Land Use Projections, 1988–2020*. Undated memorandum.

Master, L. "The Imperiled Status of North American Aquatic Animals." *Biodiversity Network News* 3 (1990): 1–8.

Master, L. L., S. R. Flack, and B. A. Stein. *Rivers of Life: Critical Watersheds for Protecting Freshwater Biodiversity*. Arlington, Va.: The Nature Conservancy, 1998.

Matthiessen, P. *Wildlife in America*. Revised, updated edition. New York: Viking, 1987.

McCammon, M. "See No Evil?" *BioScience* 47 (1997): 66–67.

McNaughton, S. J. "Ecology of a Grazing System: The Serengeti." *Ecological Monographs* 55 (1985): 259–94.

Miller, R. R., J. D. Williams, and J. E. Williams. "Extinction of North American Fisheries During the Past Century." *Fisheries* 14, no. 6 (1989): 22–38.

Miller, S. G., S. P. Bratton, and J. Hadidian. "Impacts of White-tailed Deer on Endangered and Threatened Vascular Plants." *Natural Areas Journal* 12 (1992): 67–74.

Mills, E. L., J. H. Leach, J. T. Carlton, and C. L. Secor. "Exotic Species and the Integrity of the Great Lakes: Lessons from the Past." *BioScience* 44 (1994): 666–76.

Minckley, W. L., and M. E. Douglas. "Discovery and Extinction of Western Fishes: A Blink of the Eye in Geologic Time." In *Battle Against Extinction: Native Fish Management in the American West*, edited by W. L. Minckley and J. E. Deacon. Tucson: University of Arizona Press, 1991.

Minckley, W. L., P. C. Marsh, J. E. Brooks, J. E. Johnson, and B. L. Jensen. "Management Toward Recovery of the Razorback Sucker." In *Battle Against Extinction: Native Fish Management in the American West*, edited by W. L. Minckley and J. E. Deacon. Tucson: University of Arizona Press, 1991.

Mladenoff, D., and F. Stearns. "Eastern Hemlock Regeneration and Deer Browsing in the Northern Great Lakes Region: A Re-examination and Model Simulation." *Conservation Biology* 7 (1993): 889–90.

Moir, W. H., B. Geils, M. A. Benoit, and D. Scurlock. "Ecology of Southwestern Ponderosa Pine Forests." In *Songbird Ecology in Southwestern Ponderosa Pine Forests: A Literature Review*, edited by W. H. Block and D. M. Finch. General Technical Report RM-GTR-292. Ft. Collins, Colo.: U.S. Forest Service, 1997.

Monks, V. "Engineering the Everglades." *National Parks*, September–October 1993.

Monson, G. "Botteri's Sparrow in Arizona." *Auk* 64 (1947): 139–40.

Morgan, P. "Cultivating Care for the Future." *Tampa Tribune-Times*, 24 February 1991.

Morrison, P. H., D. Kloepfer, D. A. Leversee, C. M. Socha, and D. L. Feber. *Ancient Forests of the Pacific Northwest: Analysis and Maps of Twelve National Forests*. Washington, D.C.: The Wilderness Society, 1991.

Mountainspring, S., T. L. C. Casey, C. B. Kepler, and J. M. Scott. "Ecology, Behavior, and Conservation of the Poo-uli *(Melamprosops phaeosoma)*." *Wilson Bulletin* 102 (1990): 109–22.

Mountainspring, S., and J. M. Scott. "Interspecific Competition among Hawaiian Forest Birds." *Ecological Monographs* 55 (1985): 219–39.

Myers, J. P. "The Sanderling." In *Audubon Wildlife Report 1988/1989*, edited by W. J. Chandler. New York: Academic Press, 1988.

National Marine Fisheries Service. *Recovery Plan for U.S. Population of Atlantic Green Turtle*. St. Petersburg, Fla.: National Marine Fisheries Service, 1990.

National Marine Fisheries Service. *Recovery Plan for U.S. Population of Leatherback Turtle*. St. Petersburg, Fla.: National Marine Fisheries Service, 1990.

National Marine Fisheries Service. *Recovery Plan for U.S. Population of Loggerhead Turtle*. St. Petersburg, Fla.: National Marine Fisheries Service, 1990.

National Research Council. *Decline of the Sea Turtles: Causes and Prevention*. Washington, D.C.: National Academy Press, 1990.

National Research Council. *Restoration of Aquatic Ecosystems: Science, Technology, and Public Policy*. Washington, D.C.: National Academy Press, 1992.

National Research Council. *Upstream: Salmon and Society in the Pacific Northwest*. Washington, D.C.: National Academy Press, 1996.

The Nature Conservancy. *Clinch Valley Bioreserve Strategic Plan*. Charlottesville, Va.: The Nature Conservancy, Virginia Field Office, 1992.

Nehlsen, W., J. E. Williams, and J. A. Lichatowich. "Pacific Salmon at the Crossroads: Stocks at Risk from California, Oregon, Idaho, and Washington." *Fisheries* 16 (1991): 4–21.

Neves, R. J. "A State-of-the-Unionids Address." In *Conservation and Management of Freshwater Mussels*, edited by K. S. Cummings, A. C. Buchanan, and L. M. Koch. Rock Island, Ill.: Upper Mississippi River Conservation Committee, 1993.

Norse, E. A. *Ancient Forests of the Pacific Northwest*. Washington, D.C.: Island Press, 1990.

Noss, R. F., E. T. LaRoe III, and J. M. Scott. *Endangered Ecosystems of the United States: A Preliminary Assessment of Loss and Degradation*. National Biological Service, Biological Report 28 (February 1995).

Ogden, J. C. "A Comparison of Wading Bird Nesting Colony Dynamics (1931–1946 and 1974–1989) as an Indication of Ecosystem Conditions in the Southern Everglades." In *Everglades: The Ecosystem and Its Restoration*, edited by S. M. Davis and J. C. Ogden. Delray Beach, Fla.: St. Lucie Press, 1994.

Olson, S. L., and H. F. James. "Fossil Birds from the Hawaiian Islands: Evidence for Wholesale Extinction by Man before Western Contact." *Science* 217 (1982): 633–35.

O'Meilia, M. E., F. L. Knopf, and J. C. Lewis. "Some Consequences of Competition between Prairie Dogs and Beef Cattle." *Journal of Range Management* 35 (1982): 580–85.

Ono, R. D., J. D. Williams, and A. Wagner. *Vanishing Fishes of North America*. Washington, D.C.: Stone Wall Press, 1983.

Orians, G. H., M. J. Bean, R. Lande, K. Loftin, S. Pimm, R. E. Turner, and M. Weller. *Report of the Advisory Panel on the Everglades and Endangered Species*. Audubon Conservation Report no. 8. New York: National Audubon Society, 1992.

Palmer, S. "Some Extinct Molluscs of the U.S.A." *Atala* 13, no. 1 (1985): 1–7

Panzer, R. "Managing Prairie Remnants for Insect Conservation." *Natural Areas Journal* 8 (1988): 83–90.

Panzer, R., D. Stillwaugh, R. Gnaedinger, and G. Derkovitz. "Prevalence of Remnant Dependence Among the Prairie- and Savanna-Inhabiting Insects of the Chicago Region." *Natural Areas Journal* 15 (1995): 101–16.

Perry, R. *The World of the Jaguar*. New York: Taplinger, 1970.

Peters, R. L., and T. E. Lovejoy (eds.). *Global Warming and Biological Diversity*. New Haven, Conn.: Yale University Press, 1992.

Phillips, A., J. Marshall, and G. Monson. *The Birds of Arizona*. Tucson: University of Arizona Press, 1964.

Piatt, J. F., H. R. Carter, and D. N. Nettleship. "Effects of Oil Pollution on Marine Bird Populations." In *The Effects of Oil on Wildlife: Research, Rehabilitation, and General Concerns*, edited by J. White. Hanover, Pa.: Sheridan Press, 1991.

Pielou, E. C. *After the Ice: The Return of Life to Glaciated North America*. Chicago: University of Chicago Press, 1991.

Pimm, S. L., and R. A. Askins. "Forest Losses Predict Bird Extinctions in Eastern North America." *Proceedings of the National Academy of Sciences USA* 92 (1995): 9343–47.

Pimm, S. L., G. J. Russell, J. L. Gittleman, and T. M. Brooks. "The Future of Biodiversity." *Science* 269 (1995): 347–50.

Pontius, D. *Colorado River Basin Study: Report to the Western Water Policy Review Advisory Commission.* Springfield, Va.: U.S. Department of Commerce National Technical Information Service, 1997.

Postman, D. "The Spill and Its Spoils." *Sports Illustrated,* 25 September 1996.

Powell, G. V. N., A. H. Powell, and N. K. Paul. "Brother, Can You Spare a Fish?" *Natural History,* February 1988.

Primack, R. *Essentials of Conservation Biology.* Sunderland, Mass.: Sinauer Associates, 1993.

Pyne, S. J. "Indian Fires." *Natural History,* February 1983.

Quammen, D. *The Song of the Dodo: Island Biogeography in an Age of Extinctions.* New York: Scribner, 1996.

Rabenold, K. N., P. T. Fauth, B. W. Goodner, J. A. Sadowski, and P. G. Parker. "Response of Avian Communities to Disturbance by an Exotic Insect in Spruce-Fir Dominated Forests of the Southern Appalachians." *Conservation Biology* 12 (1998): 177–89.

Rabinowitz, A. *The Status of Jaguars* (Panthera onca) *in the United States: Trip Report.* Bronx, N.Y.: Wildlife Conservation Society, undated.

"Raccoons: The District's Denizens of the Night." *Washington Post,* 3 August 1990.

Rasker, R., and D. Glick. "Footloose Entrepreneurs: Pioneers of the New West?" *Illahee* 1 (1994): 34–43.

Rasker, R., N. Tirrell, and D. Kloepfer. *The Wealth of Nature: New Economic Realities in the Yellowstone Region.* Washington, D.C.: The Wilderness Society, 1992.

Reisner, M. *Cadillac Desert: The American West and Its Disappearing Water.* New York: Penguin Books, 1993.

Remsen, J. V. Jr. "Was Bachman's Warbler A Bamboo Specialist?" *Auk* 103 (1986): 216–19.

Ricketts, T., E. Dinerstein, D. M. Olson, C. Loucks, P. Hedao, P. Hurley, R. Abell, S. Walters, and K. Carney. *A Conservation Assessment of the Terrestrial Ecoregions of North America*. Washington, D.C.: World Wildlife Fund, 1997.

Riedman, M. A., and J. A. Estes. *The Sea Otter* (Enhydra lutris): *Behavior, Ecology, and Natural History*. Biological Report 90 (14). Washington, D.C.: U.S. Fish and Wildlife Service, 1990.

Rimer, S. "Gulls Are Cast as Threat to Avian Neighbors; Agency is Cast in a Bad Light." *New York Times*, 27 May 1996.

Robbins, C. S., D. Bystrak, and P. H. Geissler. *The Breeding Bird Survey: Its First Fifteen Years, 1965–1979*. Washington, D.C.: United States Department of the Interior Fish and Wildlife Service, 1986.

Robbins, J. "In Two Years, Wolves Reshaped Yellowstone." *New York Times*, 30 December 1997.

Robinson, S. K., F. R. Thompson III, T. M. Donovan, D. R. Whitehead, and J. Faaborg. "Regional Forest Fragmentation and the Nesting Success of Migratory Birds." *Science* 267 (1995): 1987–1990.

Robinson, S. K., and D. S. Wilcove. "Forest Fragmentation in the Temperate Zone and Its Effects on Migratory Songbirds." *Bird Conservation International* 4 (1994): 233–49.

Rogers, D. K. "Beginning of the End." *St. Petersburg Times*, 27 May 1989.

Romme, W. H., and D. G. Despain. "Historical Perspective on the Yellowstone Fires of 1988." *BioScience* 39 (1989): 695–99.

Rupert, C. E. *Breeding Densities and Habitat of Riparian Birds Along the Lower Rio Grande, Texas*. Master's thesis, University of Texas, Pan-American, 1997.

Safina, C. "The Audubon Guide to Seafood." *Audubon*, May–June 1998.

Safina, C. *Song for the Blue Ocean: Encounters along the World's Coasts and Beneath the Seas*. New York: Henry Holt, 1997.

Samson, F. B. "Island Biogeography and the Conservation of Prairie Birds." *Proceedings of the North American Prairie Conference* 7 (1980): 293–305.

Samson, F., and F. Knopf. "Prairie Conservation in North America." *BioScience* 44 (1994): 418–21.

Schloesser, D., and T. F. Nalepa. "Freshwater Mussels in the Lake Huron-Lake Erie Corridor." In *Our Living Resources: A Report to the Nation on the Distribution, Abundance, and Health of U.S. Plants, Animals, and Ecosystems,* edited by E. T. LaRoe. Washington, D.C.: National Biological Service, 1995.

Schneider, K. "Returning Part of Everglades to Nature for $700 Million." *New York Times,* 11 March 1991.

Schoenherr, A. A. *A Natural History of California.* Berkeley: University of California Press, 1992.

Schullery, P. "The Fires and Fire Policy." *BioScience* 39 (1989): 686–94.

Scott, J. M., S. Mountainspring, F. L. Ramsey, and C. B. Kepler. *Forest Bird Communities of the Hawaiian Islands: Their Dynamics, Ecology, and Conservation.* Studies in Avian Biology no. 9. A publication of the Cooper Ornithological Society. Lawrence, Kans.: Allen Press, 1986.

Scurlock, D., and D. M. Finch. "A Historical Overview." In *Songbird Ecology in Southwestern Ponderosa Pine Forests: A Literature Review,* edited by W. H. Block and D. M. Finch. General Technical Report RM-GTR-292. Ft. Collins, Colo.: U.S. Forest Service, 1997.

Senner, S. E. "Book Review of Exxon Valdez *Oil Spill: Fate and Effects in Alaskan Waters.*" *Wilson Bulletin* 109 (1997): 549–59.

Seton, E. T. *Life Histories of Northern Animals. An Account of the Mammals of Manitoba.* Volume 1. New York: Charles Scribner's Sons, 1909.

Shallenberger, R. J., ed. *Hawaii's Birds.* Honolulu: Hawaii Audubon Society, 1986.

Shaw, J. H. "How Many Bison Originally Populated Western Rangelands?" *Rangelands* 17 (1995): 148–50.

Shoemaker, H. W. *Extinct Pennsylvania Animals.* Part I: *The Panther and the Wolf.* Altoona, Pa.: The Altoona Tribune Publishing Company, 1917.

Simberloff, D. "Why Do Introduced Species Appear to Devastate Islands More than Mainland Areas?" *Pacific Science* 49 (1995): 85–97.

Singer, F. J., W. Schreier, J. Oppenheim, and E. O. Garton. "Drought, Fires, and Large Mammals." *BioScience* 39 (1989): 716–22.

Spies, R. B., S. D. Rice, D. A. Wolfe, and B. A. Wright. "The Effects of the *Exxon Valdez* Oil Spill on the Alaskan Coastal Environment." In *Proceedings of the* Exxon Valdez *Oil Spill Symposium.* American Fisheries Society Symposium 18 (1996): 1–16.

Stanford, J. A. *Instream Flows to Assist the Recovery of Endangered Fishes of the Upper Colorado River Basin.* National Biological Service, Biological Report 24 (July 1994).

Steadman, D. W. "Prehistoric Extinction of Pacific Island Birds: Biodiversity Meets Zooarchaeology." *Science* 267 (1995): 1123–31.

Stegner, W. *Beyond the Hundredth Meridian: John Wesley Powell and the Second Opening of the West.* 1954. Reprint, New York: Penguin Books, 1992.

Stein, B. A., and S. R. Flack. *1997 Species Report Card: The State of U.S. Plants and Animals.* Arlington, Va.: The Nature Conservancy, 1997.

Steinauer, E. M., and S. L. Collins. "Prairie Ecology—The Tallgrass Prairie." In *Prairie Conservation: Preserving North America's Most Endangered Ecosystem,* edited by F. B. Samson and F. L. Knopf. Washington, D.C.: Island Press, 1996.

Stevens, W. K. "Everglades: Paradise Not Quite Lost." *New York Times,* 22 March 1994.

Stevens, W. K. "Latest Threat to Yellowstone: Admirers Are Loving It to Death." *New York Times,* 13 September 1994.

Stolzenburg, W. "The Mussels' Message." *Nature Conservancy* 42, no. 6 (1992): 16–23.

Strong, A. M., and G. T. Bancroft. "Post-fledging Dispersal of White-crowned Pigeons: Implications for Conservation of Deciduous Seasonal Forests in the Florida Keys." *Conservation Biology* 8 (1994): 770–79.

Sugg, I. C. "Ecosystem Babbitt-Babble." *Wall Street Journal,* 2 April 1993.

Swope-Lysistrata, L., M. Alexandersdottir, L. Tsunoda, and P. Hahn. *Washington State Sport Catch Fish Report 1994.* Olympia, Wash.: Department of Fish and Wildlife, Resource Assessment Division, 1997.

Tanner, J. *The Ivory-billed Woodpecker.* National Audubon Society Research Report no. 1. New York: National Audubon Society, 1942. Reprint, New York: Dover, 1966.

Terborgh, J. "The Big Things that Run the World." *Conservation Biology* 2 (1988): 402–3.

Terborgh, J. *Diversity and the Tropical Rainforest.* New York: Scientific American Library, 1992.

Terborgh, J. *Where Have All the Birds Gone?* Princeton, N.J.: Princeton University Press, 1989.

Terborgh, J., and B. Winter. "Some Causes of Extinction." In *Conservation Biology: An Evolutionary-Ecological Perspective,* edited by M. Soulé and B. Wilcox. Sunderland, Mass.: Sinauer Associates, 1980.

Terwilliger, K., ed. *Virginia's Endangered Species.* Blacksburg, Va.: McDonald and Woodward, 1991.

Thomas, J. W., E. D. Forsman, J. B. Lint, E. C. Meslow, B. R. Noon, and J. Verner. *A Conservation Strategy for the Northern Spotted Owl.* Portland, Oreg.: U.S. Forest Service, Bureau of Land Management, U.S. Fish and Wildlife Service, and National Park Service, 1990.

Thomas, J. W., team leader. *Forest Ecosystem Management: An Ecological, Economic, and Social Assessment.* Report of the Forest Ecosystem Management Assessment Team (U.S. Forest Service, National Marine Fisheries Service, Bureau of Land Management, U.S. Fish and Wildlife Service, National Park Service, Environmental Protection Agency), 1993.

Thomas, K. S. "Benjamin Franklin's Lost Tree." *American Scientist* 78 (1990): 203–6.

U.S. Department of Agriculture. *The Conservation Reserve Program.* Farm Service Agency Publication PA-1603. Washington, D.C.: U.S. Department of Agriculture, 1997.

U.S. Department of Labor, Bureau of Labor Statistics. *Consumer Price Index.* <http://stats.bls.gov/news.release/cpi>

U.S. Environmental Protection Agency and Government of Canada. *The Great Lakes: An Environmental Atlas and Resource Book.* 3d ed. Chicago: U.S. Environmental Protection Agency, 1995.

U.S. Fish and Wildlife Service. *Black Footed Ferret Recovery Plan.* Denver, Colo.: U.S. Fish and Wildlife Service, 1988.

U.S. Fish and Wildlife Service. *California Condor Recovery Plan.* Third revision. Portland, Oreg.: U.S. Fish and Wildlife Service, 1996.

U.S. Fish and Wildlife Service. *Draft Southern Sea Otter Recovery Plan.* Ventura, Calif.: U.S. Fish and Wildlife Service, 1995.

U.S. Fish and Wildlife Service. *Piping Plover* (Charadrius melodus), *Atlantic Coast Population, Revised Recovery Plan.* Hadley, Mass.: U.S. Fish and Wildlife Service, 1996.

U.S. Fish and Wildlife Service. *Recovery Plan for Nineteen Florida Scrub and High Pineland Plant Species.* Atlanta, Ga.: U.S. Fish and Wildlife Service, 1996.

U.S. Fish and Wildlife Service. *Recovery Plan for the U.S. Breeding Population of the Wood Stork.* Atlanta, Ga.: U.S. Fish and Wildlife Service, 1986.

U.S. Fish and Wildlife Service. *Red-cockaded Woodpecker Recovery Plan.* Atlanta, Ga.: U.S. Fish and Wildlife Service, 1985.

U.S. Fish and Wildlife Service. *The Reintroduction of Gray Wolves to Yellowstone National Park and Central Idaho: Draft Environmental Impact Statement.* Helena, Mont.: U.S. Fish and Wildlife Service, 1993.

U.S. Fish and Wildlife Service. *Report to Congress: Recovery Program, Endangered and Threatened Species.* Washington, D.C.: U.S. Government Printing Office, 1994.

U.S. Fish and Wildlife Service. *Roseate Tern Recovery Plan— Northeastern Population, First Update.* Hadley, Mass.: U.S. Fish and Wildlife Service, 1998.

U.S. Fish and Wildlife Service. *Salt Marsh Harvest Mouse and California Clapper Rail Recovery Plan.* Portland, Oreg.: U.S. Fish and Wildlife Service, 1984.

U.S. Forest Service and Bureau of Land Management. *Final Supplemental Environmental Impact Statement on Management of Habitat for Late-Successional and Old-Growth Forest Related Species within the Range of the Northern Spotted Owl,* vol. 1. Portland, Oreg.: U.S. Forest Service and Bureau of Land Management, 1994.

U.S. General Accounting Office. *Endangered Species: Management Improvements Could Enhance Recovery Program.* GAO/RCED-89-5. Washington, D.C.: U.S. General Accounting Office, 1988.

U.S. General Accounting Office. *Sugar Program: Impact on Sweetner Users and Producers.* GAO/T-RCED-95-204. Washington, D.C.: U.S. General Accounting Office, 1995.

van Riper, C. III, S. G. van Riper, M. L. Goff, and M. Laird. "The Epizootiology and Ecological Significance of Malaria in Hawaiian Land Birds." *Ecological Monographs* 56 (1986): 327–44.

Verner, J., K. S. McKelvey, B. R. Noon, R. J. Gutiérrez, G. I. Gould, Jr., and T. W. Beck. *The California Spotted Owl: A Technical Assessment of Its Current Status.* General Technical Report PSW-GTR-133. Albany, Calif.: Pacific Southwest Research Station, U.S. Forest Service, 1992.

Vitousek, P. M., C. M. D'Antonio, L. L. Loope, and R. Westbrooks. "Biological Invasions as Global Environmental Change." *American Scientist* 84 (1996): 468–78.

Volkman, J. M. *A River in Common: The Columbia River, the Salmon Ecosystem, and Water Policy.* Report to the Western Water Policy Review Advisory Commission. Springfield, Va.: U.S. Department of Commerce National Technical Information Service, 1997.

Wagner, F. H. "Scientist Says Yellowstone Park Is Being Destroyed." *High Country News,* 30 May 1994.

Wagner, F. H., and C. E. Kay. "'Natural' or 'Healthy' Ecosystems: Are U.S. National Parks Providing Them?" In *Humans as Components of Ecosystems,* edited by M. J. McDonnell and S. T. A. Pickett. New York: Springer-Verlag, 1993.

Wallace, R. *Hawaii.* New York: Time-Life Books, 1973.

Ward, P. D. *The Call of Distant Mammoths: Why the Ice Age Mammals Disappeared.* New York: Copernicus, 1997.

Warner, R. E. "The Role of Introduced Diseases in the Extinction of the Endemic Hawaiian Avifauna." *Condor* 70 (1968): 101–20

Waters, T. F. *Sediments in Streams: Sources, Biological Effects, and Control.* Monograph 7. Bethesda, Md.: American Fisheries Society, 1995.

Weaver, T., E. M. Payson, and D. L. Gustafson. "Prairie Ecology— The Shortgrass Prairie." In *Prairie Conservation: Preserving North America's Most Endangered Ecosystem,* edited by F. B. Samson and F. L. Knopf. Washington, D.C.: Island Press, 1996.

Weber, M., D. Crouse, R. Irvin, and S. Iudicello. *Delay and Denial: A Political History of Sea Turtles and Shrimp Fishing.* Washington, D.C.: Center for Marine Conservation, 1995.

Wege, D. C., S. N. G. Howell, and A. Sada. "The Distribution and Status of Worthen's Sparrow, *Spizella wortheni:* A Review." *Bird Conservation International* 3 (1993): 211–20.

Wells, L., and A. L. McLain. *Lake Michigan: Man's Effects on Native Fish Stocks and Other Biota.* Technical Report no. 20. Ann Arbor, Mich.: Great Lakes Fishery Commission, 1973.

Wells, P. G., J. N. Butler, and J. S. Hughes. "Introduction, Overview, Issues." In Exxon Valdez *Oil Spill: Fate and Effects in Alaskan Waters,* edited by P. G. Wells, J. N. Butler, and J. S. Hughes. ASTM STP 1219. Philadelphia, Pa.: American Society for Testing and Materials, 1995.

West, F. H., ed. *American Beginnings: The Prehistory and Palaeoecology of Beringia.* Chicago: University of Chicago Press, 1996.

Whicker, A. D., and J. K. Detling. "Ecological Consequences of Prairie Dog Disturbances." *BioScience* 38 (1988): 778–85.

Whillans, T. H., and F. Berkes. "Use and Abuse, Conflict and Harmony: The Great Lakes Fishery in Transition." *Alternatives* 13, no. 3 (1986): 10–18.

White, R. *The Organic Machine: The Remaking of the Columbia River.* New York: Hill and Wang, 1995.

Wiens, J. A. "Oil, Seabirds, and Science." *BioScience* 46 (1996): 587–97.

Wilcove, D. S. "Changes in the Avifauna of the Great Smoky Mountains: 1947–1988." *Wilson Bulletin* 100 (1988): 256–71.

Wilcove, D. S. "In Memory of Martha and Her Kind." *Audubon,* September 1989.

Wilcove, D. S. "Nest Predation in Forest Tracts and the Decline of Migratory Songbirds." *Ecology* 66 (1985): 1211–14.

Wilcove, D. S. "Turning Conservation Goals into Tangible Results: The Case of the Spotted Owl and Old-Growth Forests." In *Large-Scale Ecology and Conservation Biology,* edited by P. J. Edwards, R. May, and N. R. Webb. Oxford: Blackwell Scientific Publications, 1994.

Wilcove, D. S., M. J. Bean, R. Bonnie, and M. McMillan. *Rebuilding the Ark: Toward a More Effective Endangered Species Act for Private Land.* Washington, D.C.: Environmental Defense Fund, 1996.

Wilcove, D. S., M. J. Bean, and P. C. Lee. "Fisheries Management and Biological Diversity." In *Transactions of the 57th North American Wildlife and Natural Resources Conference.* Washington, D.C.: Wildlife Management Institute, 1992.

Wilcove, D. S., and L. Y. Chen. "Management Costs for Endangered Species." *Conservation Biology* 12 (1998): 1405–07.

Wilcove, D. S., and R. Fujita. "Enlightened Fisheries Management: Solving Problems Instead of Creating Them." In *The Big Kill: Declining Biodiversity in America's Lakes and Rivers,* edited by D. S. Wilcove and M. J. Bean. Washington, D.C.: Environmental Defense Fund, 1994.

Wilcove, D. S., M. McMillan, and K. C. Winston. "What Exactly Is an Endangered Species? An Analysis of the U.S. Endangered Species List: 1985–1991." *Conservation Biology* 7 (1993): 87–93.

Wilcove, D. S., D. Rothstein, J. Dubow, A. Phillips, and E. Losos. "Quantifying Threats to Imperiled Species in the United States." *BioScience* 48 (1998): 607–15.

The Wilderness Society. *Double Trouble: The Loss of Trees and Money in Our National Forests* Washington, D.C.: The Wilderness Society, 1998.

Wilkinson, T. "Zebras Musseling In." *Washington Post,* 14 May 1997.

Williams, M. *Americans and Their Forests.* Cambridge: Cambridge University Press, 1989.

Williams, T. "So Where Are All the Restored Sport Fish?" *Fly Rod & Reel,* November–December 1992.

Wilson, E. O. *The Diversity of Life.* Cambridge, Mass.: Belknap Press, 1992.

"Wood Storks Flying High in the Southeast." *Miami Herald,* 8 April 1996.

Woods, F. W., and R. E. Shanks. "Natural Replacement of Chestnut by Other Species in the Great Smoky Mountains National Park." *Ecology* 40 (1959): 349–61.

Woolfenden, G. E., and J. W. Fitzpatrick. *The Florida Scrub Jay: Demography of a Cooperative-Breeding Bird.* Princeton, N.J.: Princeton University Press, 1984.

Woolfenden, G. E., and J. W. Fitzpatrick. "Florida's Scrub-jays: A Synopsis after Eighteen Years of Study." In *Cooperative Breeding in Birds,* edited by P. B. Stacey and W. D. Koenig. Cambridge: Cambridge University Press, 1990.

Worster, D. *Dust Bowl: The Southern Plains in the 1930s.* New York: Oxford University Press, 1979.

Yanno, M. "New Hope for the Schaus Swallowtail." *Endangered Species Bulletin* 21, no. 4 (1996): 22–23.

Yellowstone National Park. *Yellowstone's Northern Range: Complexity and Change in a Wildlands Ecosystem.* Mammoth Hot Springs, Wyo.: Yellowstone National Park, 1997.

Yoon, C. K. "Mystery Surrounds Global Decline of a Flying Robin-Size Predator." *New York Times,* 2 March 1993.

Yosef, R. "An Evaluation of the Global Decline in the True Shrikes (Family Laniidae)." *Auk* 111 (1994): 228–233.

Index